A Place to Play

GLORY DAYS OF BASEBALL IN ANGIER, NORTH CAROLINA

Webster Lupton

A Place to Play:

Glory days of baseball in Angier, North Carolina

Copyright © 2007 Webster Lupton

Published by Warren Publishing, Inc.
www.Warrenpublishing.net

ISBN 978-1-886057-07-4
Library of Congress Control Number 2007939071

Printed in the United States of America
First Edition
Cornelius, North Carolina 28031

Dedication

To the Adams boys, who once built a baseball diamond in the middle of nowhere and made it somewhere.

Foreword

There was the stand-up sign that was placed directly below the stoplight on Main Street. "BASEBALL TONIGHT!" was printed across the top. Next was the game time, usually seven or seven-thirty at night. Then came the billing. "Braves vs. Fuquay Springs" or "Braves vs. Dunn-Erwin" or "Braves vs. Smithfield."

That modest advertising display was enough to make it a special day in Angier during the 1950s and early '60s. Barring the worst of droughts, no one wanted rain when the sign was out. The sign meant that Angier's version of the world's craftiest left-hander, Bob Cruze, would be on the pitching mound and that Jimmie Odell Matthews would be slamming line drives into the gaps. It was semipro baseball on its last legs, but it was the greatest show on dirt in and around Angier. At a time when gasoline went for pennies a gallon and fifteen cents could get you into the Saturday afternoon double feature, plus a ten-minute installment of the latest Flash Gordon serial, the Braves were a steal at fifty cents per ticket and half that for kids.

"Air conditioning" came in the form of window fans the size of airplane propellers. Families prosperous enough to own a television set were limited to one or two channels, weather permitting. If there was a golf course in Harnett County, it was well hidden and obviously constructed on land too rocky to grow a decent crop of tobacco. Football and basketball were just beginning to emerge as popular team sports. There was family. There was work. There was church. There was school. And there was semipro baseball.

Most of the "stars" were our friends, neighbors, and colleagues. By day, they farmed, sold groceries, wired houses, drove trucks, cut hair, fixed engines, and did all the things that marked the emergence of mainstream America in the years shortly after World War II. By night, they were our athletic warriors, our pride, joy, and enthusiastic entertainers. Their reward basically was the fun of playing the sport they loved and a sense of accomplishment for the community in which they had spent their lives.

But a key home run or a strong pitching performance usually meant that someone in the stands behind home plate would remove his straw hat, turn it upside down, place a dollar bill inside, and pass it down the line. When the hat made its way back, there would be a collection of perhaps ten or twenty bucks, much of it in pocket change, that would be presented to the hitter or pitcher at game's end.

With uncommon diligence, Webster Lupton has captured the essence of that priceless era in this treasure of a book. His accounts of the baseball root system in Angier, Pea Ridge, Fuquay, and beyond reflect a tireless piece of research on a topic that had to be very difficult to document. For those of us old enough to remember those wonderful town teams, "A Place to Play" could just as well be titled "A Time to Cherish."

Caulton Tudor

Table of Contents

Beginnings

The Pea Ridge Miracle

Going the Cycle

North Carolina Baseball Regions

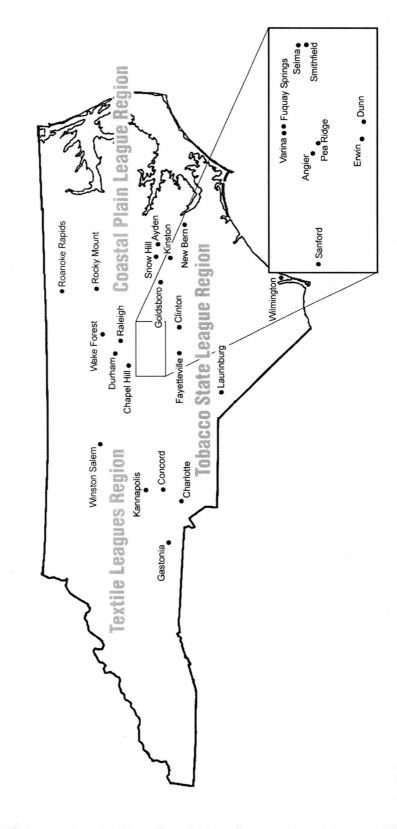

Introduction

This story is nearly forgotten. The memories of the few people alive who witnessed it are fading. And the tales they relayed to their children and grandchildren are quickly being lost in a hectic age. But it is a story of the lives and times of small-town America, where families knew each other and time passing was marked by special events like street dances and church picnics. This is a story of baseball in a small town from the 1930s to the early 1960s, years in which the game was important to towns and communities across America. They were the last years in which baseball could still be considered America's pastime; years when a lot of people played baseball, and a lot of fans in tiny farming towns such as Angier, North Carolina, came out to watch. They were years punctuated by depression, war, and almost-constant social change, elements that dwarfed the town game in importance and always drove it either directly or indirectly.

And it is the story of a group of men who lived their baseball lives during these years, starting as tykes who learned from sandlots and from watching hometown heroes, and ending up as hometown heroes themselves. They were men of America's pastime, because baseball had a close relationship to the lives they led. Men like Harold Ellen, whose mother considered survival like a batter weighs a pitching count; or Frank Gardner, whose exploits at second base led him to the love of his life; or Marshall Price, who cracked two home runs the day his first son was born; or the Adams boys, who didn't think twice when given the opportunity to build their own baseball park in the middle of nowhere.

It was because baseball was a big part of their lives that they always found a place to play. It was any spare lot big enough for a diamond and an outfield. In Angier, baseball followed an evolution of sorts, maturing on a town lot, reinvigorating on a country field, and playing out its last days at a schoolhouse field. When the game of the 1930s and '40s ran out of steam at the town park, the baseball eyes of the community gradually turned to the homemade baseball park two miles out in the country, where the men of one extended family gathered to play on weekends. It was at this Pea Ridge field that a semipro team grew into a power much bigger than the little park itself could handle. And when Pea Ridge played out its potential, the town brought back semipro ball one more time, until one year in the 1960s arrived, and there was no town team at all.

It was these small, relatively insignificant baseball diamonds that were the training grounds for future professionals and stomping grounds for players who had already been professionals. And they were places to play for guys who would simply be heroes in their hometown. They were tiny, simple bleacher parks with infields of cleared ground or clay.

These parks, and the town fans, attracted not only the hometown boys, but men from out of town and out of state as well. They were college kids such as Tommy Byrne of Baltimore or Connie Ryan of New Orleans, who would go on to make their marks in the major leagues. And they were money players like James Stevens and Carlton Mangum, who might have gone down in major league record books themselves had they not disliked the minor leagues so.

That was the nature of the sporting event that helped make a game a pastime: semipro baseball. Semipro baseball was an attraction driven by freewheeling personalities and high-strung competition and rivalry. Just as heroes of major league teams attracted throngs of fans to huge stadiums in cities, thousands of others played the game at the humble little fields before the crowds of small-town America. They played for recreation, for sport, or for love of the game, from the time they could hurl a baseball to the time when they simply couldn't run with the young boys any more.

Semiprofessional or semipro was a term handed down through years of town teams that offered food, living quarters, and a small stipend to keep a player in town. It is probably as accurate an adjective as one could find to describe this brand of baseball. There was little money in most semipro baseball. Many players were paid only part of the time, and the mode of payment for "money players" came in many forms and in a wide range. The people who were bold — or crazy —

enough to put up the cash to start a team made little money. They usually operated on a shoestring budget.

The players, of course, carried a wide range of talents. They were boys and men from high school age to age 40 … or even 50. Some were good enough to play professionally, and others were just talented enough to hold their own against a good curveball. They were as fast as lightning and as slow as a glacier. They would run through a fence to snag a long drive or let a slow grounder go right between their legs — neither to anyone's surprise.

Their reasons for choosing a particular town were different, too. Some were wanderers who, like mercenaries, played for whoever offered the highest pay. Others were town boys, totally dedicated to making their hometown a winner and somehow becoming heroes along the way. They were the most free of free agents, because there was little to keep them on one team from year-to-year, or even week-to-week. The agreement to play with a team was usually closed by a handshake rather than a contract. The players liked it that way, because many of them had already signed contracts of organized professional ball and often didn't like them. They didn't like the rigors of playing six days a week for small salaries with the only reward for outstanding play being a trade to another strange town maybe hundreds of miles from home.

But their reasons for playing the game itself were usually the same: they loved it. Love of the game seems clichéd and almost abstract. But there is little abstract in the personality of a guy like Elbert Adams, who succinctly stated that when he was young, he "would rather play baseball than eat." Or in the comment of Rexwell Adams, who sized up the summer life of a farm boy from Angier: "To crop tobacco in 100-degree weather, then go out and play a game of baseball, well you had to love it." And why would a pitcher like Carlton Mangum start in both games of a double header in one town and then drive 60 miles to pitch in the night game in another town? And why, for that matter, would 12 men carpool 1,300 miles to play a bunch of strangers?

Of course, you didn't have to play in the game to love it. The organizers of these semipro teams were not exactly prospecting for gold, either. They simply wanted to have the best team around; better than the boys in the next town or crossroads. It would often cost them more than the day's gate would bring in, if there was a gate at all. But that was OK, if it meant bringing a little excitement and pride to a tiny town.

The semipro leagues were loosely constructed and informal enough to be called bush leagues. But this was also baseball in its most pure form because of that informality. They went by league rules, which were usually broken. The only real rules that concerned anyone were the rules of the game itself, which by the 1930s had been defined, refined, and practically set in stone. Scorebooks were kept, but recorded statistics were rarely published or otherwise distributed. So, other than the community buzz that followed some players, there was little to judge a player's worth until he took the field, the mound, or entered the batter's box. The scene harkened back to the years of baseball in its infancy, when men of the community gathered to take on the boys from down the block, across town, or in the next community.

There were usually bigger, faster semipro leagues in other regions of North Carolina, leagues built around larger towns or cities that had the backing of textile mills or tobacco markets. But the leagues in which the Angier teams played had the geographical advantage of being located near the state's largest colleges and universities, which produced much of the summer semipro talent.

Baseball was a big attraction then, not only because baseball is a fun game to play, but because it was one of the few forms of recreation, particularly in a small town. That is why a big game could generate excitement in Angier. During the Depression years, when Angier's official population was under 1,000, as many as 2,000 people would be at the town park for a July 4th game or a game that carried significance in league standings or playoffs. These numbers would decline as the years passed and the relevance of baseball itself declined. But until the last games were played in Angier, there was enough interest in the game to keep it alive in a small town, and certainly enough men who wanted to play.

Responding to the community's enthusiasm, the town's baseball leaders brought in the best talent a small town could afford. At least 30 players who donned the uniforms of Angier and its adopted baseball community of Pea Ridge were pros at some point. Nine of those made the major leagues. Together the teams won 12 league pennants and playoff championships in addition to two state semipro tournament crowns.

That includes the one bold season — 1946 — in which Angier

banded with Fuquay Springs to have a professional team. All of this was going on in this tiny farming community.

But as the decades passed and the hometown boys named Adams, Gardner, Price, and Ellen were playing out their baseball days, the town game itself was fading as was baseball's importance. By the 1950s, the unchallenged American pastime was about to take a backseat, lost in an array of new games to play, sports to follow, and things to do. The men who had witnessed the hometown game as kids and played it as adults, could never quite pass down the baseball-playing tradition to their baby-boomer children.

That is why this story is nearly forgotten.

Webster Lupton

Beginnings

Webster Lupton

Chapter 1 - Raised on Baseball

Men Help Boys Learn

Angier was a baseball town. As in thousands of American towns in the 1930s, the people of Angier craved baseball. It was their pastime.

About 25 miles south of Raleigh, Angier was close enough to the city for comfort, but far enough to be sheltered from urban trappings. And like other towns of that time, it was closely knit, conservative and generally peaceful. It was compactly structured, with a crossroads business district that stretched no farther than a block in any direction. A railroad passed through, running parallel to one of the main streets.

Everything seemed to have its place. There was a post office, fire department, drugstore, movie theater, barber shop, repair shop and blacksmith, three churches, two schools, a boarding house and several stores of general merchandise. The town was the heart of a surrounding rural community of farms; most of them small, for it was still a time when a few arable acres of tobacco could support a family.

The lives of the people in and around Angier were structured, too. They farmed tobacco or provided goods and services for tobacco farmers. That was pretty much it. Oh, there were remnants of the timber milling that had started the town and brought the railroad through. And a few folks might work at the textile mill in Erwin, the tobacco market in Smithfield, or have a plant job in Raleigh. But the town's world of commerce largely revolved around tobacco. They grew it from seed in winter, transplanted it in April, harvested and cured it in July and August and took it to market in September, coddling and pampering it every step of the labor-intensive way. And it was labor intensive. On the tobacco farm, a man's wife and children all pitched in to help harvest the crop. And if the family wasn't large enough, there was the black sharecropper and his family helping, too. On many days during harvest, it was a five-in-the-morning to eight-at-night job. But when the cured, golden leaf was auctioned at the tobacco warehouse and the check came in, it was worth it to the farmer. That check would feed and clothe his family through the winter. His income might be supplemented by the corn or cotton crop harvested later in the year. A vegetable garden and a little livestock may help keep the family in food. But it was tobacco that provided most of the farmer's sustenance until spring planting came again.

Folks in and around town still found time for the few distractions a small town could offer. There were a few social and civic clubs, churches, the movie house, and a seasonal street dance or outdoor cooking to help keep their minds off of the hard work and worry of the Depression.

But during the summer, few of those activities captured the passion of folks around town the way that baseball did. The 1930 census listed 740 people living within the town limits, but the true size of the community became evident on game day. It was nothing for 500-600 people to show up for a baseball game, more than a thousand for special days like July 4th, or as many as 2,500 when a title was on the line. [1]

Baseball, you see, offered the town people a chance to size their community up to others in the vicinity. The size of the town had little to do with its competitiveness and audacity when it came to baseball. Angier was often in a league with towns twice its size or bigger, such as Sanford, Erwin, and Smithfield, which were larger textile-mill towns and tobacco-market hubs.

Baseball seemed to be everywhere at the time. During the summer the game dominated the national sports headlines, even over boxing and horse racing, the other popular sports of the time. In the fall, baseball headlines would give way to college football, which had become a stadium-filler in the South. But football was considered too rough a sport for most who contemplated playing it, and basketball was not even on the radar screen of most sports enthusiasts.

North Carolina itself was crawling with semipro baseball teams. To the east, the Coastal Plain League would form during the '30s in tobacco-market towns such as Ayden, Kinston, and Greenville. To the west, textile towns such as Concord, Kannapolis, and Gastonia would be part of a semipro league so strong that it managed to steal some of the best professional players from nearby minor leagues.

13

There were certainly enough players to fill every roster in every corner of the state and nation. That was baseball's advantage and the thing that maintained its moniker of national pastime. It was still *the* summer game for young and old.

The 1930s were years of rugged, choppy infields and expansive parks that often offered the opportunity for triples or in-the-park home runs. Pitchers took the mound without the slightest notion of pitching less than a full nine innings, and managers were in uniform because they were also players. They wore short-billed caps, heavy flannel uniforms, and they ran on steel spikes that became weapons in feet-first slides into the fluffy-looking canvas bags that were bases. Players left their small gloves at their positions in the field when they came in to bat.

This was the town and the baseball that young boys named Adams, Ellen, Gardner, and Price grew up in. They learned the game from their fathers, men born at the turn of the century and raised as big-time baseball was overtaking the big cities and turning stars into household names.

Some of those fathers could still be found spending their spare time in the roughhewn fields of baseball. Harold Ellen kept the image of his father, Irvin, pitching for the town team in the early '30s. He kept the image because it was a bizarre thing that caused his father to lay the game aside. "He broke his arm throwing a curve," Harold said. "I was too young to remember it, but I've been told the story. One guy said it sounded like a rifle going off when it broke it. People ran when they heard it." But that didn't keep Irvin from teaching Harold baseball. And it didn't keep Harold Ellen from pitching — or throwing a curve.

When the boys weren't learning from their fathers, they were learning from each other. And that was more like fun. For small towns like Angier, there were no little leagues, at least in the organized sense. The games these kids played were grab-a-glove-and-go sandlot games.

"We played all the time when I was a kid," Frank Gardner recalled. "My daddy, Mack, was a baseball enthusiast and taught me the game. We played boys teams, against Lillington in the fifth and sixth grades ... There were two teams in town, one from my side of town, and another made up of Kenneth Williams, Kenneth Jackson, Linwood Herndon, and some others. My team had Vernon Brown, my brother Jim, Harry Dupree and some others."

Marshall Price referred to them as baseball "get-togethers," because there was no real organization. After the first few warm weekends of spring, it seemed the kids knew where to gather to play their pickup game. Marshall had his own roll-call of baseball pals. "There was Kenneth Williams, J.E. Dupree, myself, David and I think maybe R.C. and Etheridge Burch," Marshall said. Frank and Marshall both had two or three brothers to start the warm-ups with. And brothers were a big thing — brothers, cousins, and such.

And for the Adams family, you could always depend on a brother or cousin to show up for a game of catch, since there were four sets of Adams brothers growing up in one rural area during the 1930s.

They all adopted a game that had become one of tradition, handed down through generations. By the 1930s, baseball had nearly 50 years of legendary heroes for young players to emulate. From the first soft days of April to the first chilly breezes of September, kids with a bat, a ball, and sometimes gloves, converted schoolyards and rough farm fields into diamonds of drama, playing out the heroics of Ruth, Gehrig, Foxx, Grove, and Dickey — the legends they had read about or heard about from their fathers. For these youngsters, a place to play was rough. They carved out their own diamonds in whatever cleared lot or field they could find. With a few feed sacks for bases, a warm-up would turn into a full-fledged hard-pitch battle. The rough field would produce the worst of bad hops on grounders, but it would teach them to block the ball, even if it meant taking a sidewinder squarely to the chin. A hard drive into right field might damage Mom's neat rows of gladiolas, but it would teach them how to chase a long hit to the fence and how to use the relay throw. A rainbow into the nearby tobacco field was definitely ground-rule stuff, though, since tearing into a tobacco field could bring severe punishment. "A tobacco leaf is a dollar," farmers used to say, though it was more like a penny during the early Depression years.

The other rules were there, soundly entrenched for at least 50 years with little change. They were the rules of baseball, and everyone knew them. Though, for these games, it was easy to fudge on balls and strikes. And no bunting, please.

Those pickup games would be the skills camps for these boys, and the Adamses, Ellens, Gardners, and Prices would be among the most serious learners. By the time they became teenagers, they would know a little something about baseball.

They took in as many aspects of the game as they could, from the dramas of their major league heroes, down to the feats of the local semipro stars. They read what newspaper stories they could find about their heroes in the majors, were sometimes lucky enough to hear a big-league game on the radio, and sometimes even luckier to actually see a play or two on a newsreel at the movie house.

Baseball helped teach them to read, because to them, learning to frame a sentence about the exploits of Dean and Jurges was more important than learning one about Dick and Jane. And they learned math by studying the box scores and calculating batting averages and earned run averages. It was a big part of their young lives.

While their stickball contemporaries were squeezing into the major league parks of the big cities, these young boys, their schoolmates, and pals were trying to find standing room at Angier's little baseball park. It was game day, and that was something special.

Game day was when these boys had a chance to actually see the game played by men who played it well. There was no television, and radio descriptions of games were rare in small-town North Carolina. Traveling to see a minor league game was a "maybe" proposition, and going a major league city was practically out of the question. So when the town semipro team took the field, getting a good place to sit or stand was important to a kid, because it gave him a chance to see the big boys playing good baseball. And there was always good ball being played in Angier.

The boys were growing up during the Great Depression, which took a toll on practically every aspect of life. For rural America, it meant an already-rare dollar was even harder to come by. Farm prices had taken a tumble: tobacco from 47 cents a pound to a low of 8 cents; cotton from $150 a bale to $13 — if anyone was buying. [2]

But it seemed Daddy usually had a dollar, enough to treat the whole family to a home game. Even if it was one of his last dollars, everyone went home happy — at least if the home team won.

The Depression was not all bad, at least to a fan of the semipro game. Minor leagues had cut back operations all over the nation, which meant there were good baseball players wandering the countryside, looking for an extra buck during the summer. [3] For those who couldn't find work on one of the many barnstorming circuits, there was semipro baseball in places like North Carolina, a state full of small towns.

Many of these players would head for mill towns of the Piedmont, where they could get on the mill payroll without having a real job other than to play baseball. Others would end up in the Coastal Plain towns and cities to the east of Angier. These were tobacco-market hubs of around 10,000 people or more.

The Coastal Plain and The Carolina Textile leagues were the "fast" semipro leagues in the state during the Depression years. They were the semipro leagues that paid players good money and captured the attention of plenty of fans; fans driven by bragging rights in the rivalries with nearby towns. They were also leagues that were supposedly structured, with roster-limit and salary-limit rules. But the unwritten rule in semipro baseball was that rules were made to be broken. And that they were.

The players who didn't find work in the fast leagues, found their way to smaller, lower paying semipro leagues, and to teams and towns that weren't in leagues. These non-league teams essentially played exhibitions, which attracted good players only by guaranteeing a portion of a good gate.

In the early 1930s, Angier's semipro baseball teams were not in a league. As a matter of fact, a town game resembled the informality of a schoolyard game. Towns that didn't have league teams had bare-bones operations that struggled from weekend to weekend to schedule games and scrap together enough boys to play and maybe justify a decent take at the gate, if there was a gate at all. And the town-team organizers were always competing for players, against the fast leagues in the bigger towns and cities.

For the most part, Angier seemed to have a good supply of baseball talent. There were enough hometown players who knew the game, and there was always a shot at getting a man from one of the major colleges within a couple of hours of Angier.

When players such as Doc Smith, Woody Upchurch, and Bill Holland were in town for the summer, the talent factor went up a notch or two. They were local boys who were good enough to play professionally. When they donned the Angier uniform in the early 1930s, it would start a snowball of interest in the semipro game that would subside only when bombs fell on Pearl Harbor.

Doc Smith

Doc Smith was the eldest of that trio and was a man who took baseball seriously. He had learned that baseball was a mental game, one of strategy. It came from his years as a catcher, years of squatting behind the plate, calling pitches and directing the infield. His learning began at an early age, when he was taken in and raised by a family near Angier. One of the first things young Herbert Clarence Smith learned was that the place behind the plate was where he wanted to be. He later learned that catchers were a hot commodity for baseball teams and that if he mastered the craft of catching, he would have something of value.

By the time the 1930s rolled around, Herbert was a veteran of the game, complete with a nickname, though no one quite remembers how he came to be called Doc. Just off of a couple of successful seasons in the professional Texas League, Smith had become one of those players in the network of baseball talent. Since statistics on semipro or even some minor league players weren't readily at hand in those days, people in this informal network relied on each other for information on players. If you were in on this network and needed a player, you knew who to call to find one. If they didn't have someone, they knew who to call. It was one big decentralized databank of ball players, where reputations lived and died.

Doc Smith was in the network. Baseball people had heard his name and knew he could be relied upon to serve time behind the plate and put up decent numbers at bat. He had batted .283 in 1927 and .306 in '28, playing with Fort Worth and Wichita Falls of the Texas League. ₄ He had also played in the Piedmont League and, somewhere along the line, had hooked up with the Pittsburgh Pirates organization, though no major league roster ever listed him. He was certainly a player of reputation, and being in the network kept him on the road summer after summer.

But he managed to spend time at home, too. He married, became a father, mentored players, and coached and managed, his chief duties on the diamond as the years passed.

Doc had become somewhat of a legend in and around Angier. The younger boys in town hadn't actually seen Doc play ball when he was at his best. They only knew what their fathers and uncles had told them. And they knew that his absence during the summer meant Doc was off somewhere playing "big-league ball."

The spring of 1932 didn't bring Doc a baseball job, though. So that year Smith was the manager of the Angier Outlaws. That was an appropriate name for a semipro team, considering the derision "organized baseball" took toward the semipro game. The governing body of the minor leagues (National Association of Professional Baseball Leagues) was on the verge of an outright war with some semipro leagues and teams. The Depression, having put a dent into the number of minor leagues, was helping point many ballplayers toward the semipro ranks.

Players were actually paid better by some of these "outlaw" semipro teams. This was not something organized baseball could tolerate, because good players brought paying customers to their minor-league parks. And if these players were being siphoned off to the semipro game, so was income. It encouraged the nasty business of blacklisting, or keeping a player from returning to the minor leagues after having dipped into the semipro till. 5

Smith had no-doubt witnessed this when he named his team. Mostly high school and college kids, the Outlaws were nothing the NAPBL had to worry about. But Smith was likely displaying the banner with pride.

There is no indication that the Outlaws ever charged admission to their games, so the team probably didn't even come under the definition of semipro. They were mostly boys from around town who played just enough to refine their skills. Mason Bugg, Wales Blalock, Tally Dupree, and Mike Crawford were the stars of the team, and Doc probably got help from his son, Larry, as well as others he could round up from nearby towns.

The Outlaws took the field on June 3, 1932, and were shelled in Lillington, 16-4, Angier bats being held off by a pitcher from nearby Campbell College named Pee Wee Hight. The team struggled through the season, clubbing Lafayette, 14-6, splitting a pair with Buies Creek, and whipping Fuquay Springs. Most of these towns and communities were within 15 miles and were no bigger than Angier, so it wasn't until the Outlaws traveled to Dunn and won 11-6 that they knew they had a team. Dunn was about three times Angier's size and usually had a barn full of players.

Bugg was Angier's most effective pitcher, but these games were not 3-1 duels. The scores were more like 14-3, 12-9, or 11-6. The general rule in these battles was that if a pitcher held a team to single figures, he had a win. Dupree, Blalock, and Crawford provided much of the punch for Angier at the plate that year. The Outlaws played into August, mostly on weekends, against other communities in Harnett County and an occasional industrial team from Raleigh.

Smith didn't finish the season with the team. The network called, and he was back on his summer road, this time to the minor league town of Clarksburg, West Virginia. He would play in 39 games there, and bat .258.

But Doc Smith's tutoring that summer would pay off for the Angier boys who played for the high-school team. The following spring, 1933, Angier High School's baseball team would reach the Eastern Class B finals of the state playoffs before being defeated by Roanoke Rapids. Bugg, Dupree, Elmo Johnson, William Gardner, and Doc's son, Larry Smith, were all on the school team.

That spring season of 1933 was one that the players, their baseball fathers, and town fans wanted to continue, and they would see that the season carried into summer. But they needed a field; a place to play that didn't require permission of the school board or would be taken up by other activities. They needed a place to play baseball on Sundays.

A Home for the Town Team

In a small town in the South, there were only certain things a person could partake in on Sundays with the blessings of the local church. Semipro baseball was not necessarily one of them. Baseball carried with it the burden of a reputation. Gambling, drinking, and fighting were the type of things that supposedly followed semipro baseball, and this sort of mayhem was not to be tolerated in a Bible Belt community. Having a semipro baseball game at the local school field would require the permission of a school board, and no elected official was about to publicly favor baseball on Sundays.

So Angier's baseball backers found a few acres of land on the west side of town, owned by the Gardner family. In May of 1933, that land became the home of Angier semipro baseball. The Gardners had their own motives for such generosity. They had seen one of their own, William Gardner, a left-handed pitcher, play well for the high school, and his right-handed pitching brother, James, was becoming a star in his own right. They themselves could be the nucleus of a decent semipro team, town fans believed. There were other players from the high school team that could help fill a roster, and they could probably pick up some players from Campbell College's team. Campbell, a junior college in nearby Buies Creek, had put in a 14-3 season and won the state junior college title that spring. And with the help of few other locals who had played in the professional ranks, a formidable team could shape up.

An early May edition of the *The News & Observer* of Raleigh announced "Angier's Big Day," promoting the opening of the new baseball park on Saturday, May 9. [6] The town team took on the 17th Field Artillery of Fort Bragg in the morning that day, and Norfolk Southern Railway club of Raleigh in the afternoon. A barbecue dinner was held after the games for the folks who paid the 25 cents admission.

The Angier team split games that day, and though no attendance figures were announced, the gathering was apparently big enough for the home folks to think they had some potential in that little field. As *The News & Observer* put it, "A crowd which jammed the park, viewed the ball games and enjoyed the 'cue."

The new park itself was rather meager. The property's relationship to the neighborhood called for a small field, with short home run targets down the left and right field lines and no more than 350 feet to center for a round-tripper. The infield was dirt, or "skin," as the ballplayers called it. The first base line was too close to the parallel road to offer much more than space for a dugout, a board fence, and standing room. Most of the seating, enough for maybe 300, was situated on the third-base side of the backstop. As the park grew, a small wooden shelter would be built to cover most of that. It was a standing-room park for the big games.

But the park's small size didn't keep Angier folks from thinking they could have a place in a bigger semipro baseball world. With honest-to-goodness gates, they could actually bring in good players — and pay them.

Angier was entering the semipro baseball scene, and the town team would get the services of a couple of legitimate stars from nearby towns to certify it.

Pitchers Hit the Mark

Angier's new park would become the home to left-handed pitchers that season. Woody Upchurch was one of them. From Buies Creek, Upchurch was a farmer's son who had on-target control over his delivery. Upchurch had ridden the rails of the minor leagues, playing two seasons in Muskogee and Vicksburg, before Durham hired him in 1932. He played for mediocre teams there and lasted only through May of the 1933 season, his inability to make a breakthrough to the majors sending him back toward home.

But professional baseball's loss was again semiprofessional baseball's gain. Angier manager Roy Young was willing to give Upchurch a chance, and the lefthander would not fail him. Young's and Doc Smith's faith in Upchurch would restore his reputation and even get him a short run at the majors.

Bill Holland of Varina, a post-office farm community just across the tracks from Fuquay Springs, also improved Angier's prospects in 1933. He was only 17, but he was refining a baffling curveball that dropped just before arriving at the plate like it was falling from a table.

His brother, Chester, having the benefit of knowing where the pitch would end up, was one of the few catchers who could handle Bill's pitches.

The performances of Holland, Upchurch, young William Gardner, and "old" Doc Smith would put a spark into Angier's baseball fortunes that season. Tally Dupree, Mike Dupree, Charles Adams, and Mike Crawford would be others who provided much of the hitting punch.

Later in May, Holland and Upchurch put forth sterling performances, and Angier's knack for scoring runs became evident. Angier clobbered Pilot Mills of Raleigh, 17-3, with Holland on the mound, and Upchurch struck out 16 in a 10-3 victory over Dr. Pepper of Raleigh. Mason Bugg, Doc Smith, and Tally Dupree led a lineup that got consistent hitting through the summer, as Angier managed to schedule dates as far away as New Bern, 100 miles to the east. Teams from Rocky Mount and Durham were also coming to town to take on Angier.

Rocky Mount and New Bern, though much larger cities than Angier, were among a number of eastern North Carolina baseball cities with plenty of baseball players, but without a league. The Great Depression had spoiled the two years of the Class D Eastern Carolina professional minor league, which started in 1928, and organized baseball was not anxious to return a professional league to that part of the country for the time being. The result was a number of struggling independent teams in cities of 10,000-15,000 population, such as New Bern, Kinston, Greenville, Wilson and Rocky Mount, all within about a 70-mile radius and trying to field teams to play for territorial bragging rights.

Farther to the west and closer to Angier, were the slightly smaller towns of Smithfield and Sanford, which were also fielding teams. All of these towns and cities were jockeying to obtain the college talent from the Raleigh area's four big colleges as well as the "traveling" talent in the state.

Playing teams that were backed by industries, military units, and larger towns and cities, opened a door to the baseball world for Angier. As the summer of 1933 progressed, word spread that the little park in Angier was a place to find good baseball competition, and sometimes even good gates. And good gates meant something to traveling ball players, many of whom were more like mercenaries than men putting in a good effort for the home team. Players and managers usually divided the gate on game day, so it was important to draw a big crowd. Teams from Raleigh or Rocky Mount or even Smithfield would not even consider playing in a town the size of Angier unless they were assured a good turnout. With men like Upchurch, Holland, and Smith playing in town, a good gate was usually assured.

So, just as reputable ballplayers were in a network, Angier was climbing into the network of reliable stops for traveling non-league teams. Angier was becoming a place to play.

In the summer of 1933, Angier struck up a couple of series that helped the town solidify its baseball reputation. One series was with the Battery D team of New Bern. The New Bern team, which was sponsored by veterans of a World War I National Guard artillery unit, had network talent, too. The team was anchored by pitcher Bill Ferebee, who had a successful career at the University of North Carolina before spending five seasons in professional ball. His brother, Ham, was a catcher on the team.

Angier and Battery D first hooked up in New Bern on June 16 in a 3-2 game that was decided in the bottom of the tenth inning, Upchurch yielding the game winner. The game generated enough excitement for an interesting rematch nine days later in Angier. About 1,200 filled Angier's little park to see Upchurch and Smith return the favor against the Ferebee brothers by the same 3-2 score. The two teams played at least three more times over the summer, Battery D winning each time.

In mid-July, as Angier's boys were proving their worth on the diamond, a team from the nearby mill town of Erwin challenged Angier to a series that became billed as the "semipro baseball championship of Harnett County." Erwin's team had the backing of the huge textile mill there, which meant that some of the "workers" there were essentially hired baseball hands. The team was a good one also because Woody Upchurch played for the team when he wasn't in an Angier uniform.

In fact, the Angier-Erwin series that year was an example of the mercenary practices of players and organizers in non-league semipro ball. In the second game of the series, Upchurch pitched for Erwin. Angier countered with a "big name" of its own by bringing in pitcher DeWitt Perry, a popular professional who had played for Durham, Raleigh and Wilmington the previous three seasons. In the last game of the series, Upchurch and Smith were the pitcher and catcher for Erwin, so Angier recruited old rivals Bill and Ham Ferebee from New Bern. With those big names, a decent draw was assured for each game. This recruitment of big-name pitchers for one-game deals may have been good for the gate, but it wasn't a hit for Angier fans; Erwin swept the series in three games, all of them decided by four or more runs.

The important thing, however, was that Angier had put its new baseball park to good use, playing a lot of games and making a baseball name for itself at home and in the state. And the town had sparked a rivalry with a nearby town that had a good baseball reputation.

But nothing was easy in semipro baseball, and things were about to get tougher for little Angier.

1934 - Heading for the Coastal Plain

While Angier was getting new legs as a baseball town, some of the larger and more established baseball stops in eastern North Carolina were making their own moves forward.

In 1934, the semipro Coastal Plain League formed, with Kinston, Snow Hill, Ayden, New Bern, Greenville, and Tarboro aboard. The new league answered the region's yearnings for competitive baseball with a semblance of organization. A league offered some financial stability for the baseball teams in those towns and spiced up the regional rivalries. Financial stability was not necessarily a guarantee, since the drive to get the most exciting players and win baseball games almost always overcame any financial considerations. But at least the issue of who had the best team in eastern North Carolina could be settled.

The organization of the new league affected little Angier by drawing more of the best young prospects with better pay and a regular schedule. These young players were usually college boys from Duke University, the University of North Carolina, North Caroline State College, and Wake Forest College, the state's major colleges. The league would eventually draw Doc Smith, Woody Upchurch, and Bill Holland away from Angier, but it did not deal a knockout punch to the town's now-vigorous baseball following.

Smith went to Ayden to manage in the Coastal Plain League, and he would stay in the league as it grew from semipro to professional. Angier's two best lefties, Bill Holland and Woody Upchurch, were about to go their own ways, too. Holland, who was now working his way through Louisburg College, played the summer of 1934 in that town.

Upchurch stayed around for Angier's 1934 season, but was about to make a new name for himself in the Coastal Plain League, with Doc Smith's help. Upchurch and the younger William Gardner proved to be a strong combination of southpaws for the Angier team that summer.

They took the field with Mike Crawford, Tally Dupree, James Denning, and an assortment of players from the high school team and from nearby towns that year, still not in a league but playing enough games to keep Angier's interest up. They locked horns with traveling "all-star" teams, industrial teams, and occasionally a team from the Johnston County League, which consisted of Lillington, Selma,

Smithfield, Benson, Wendell, and Clayton.

The team's management apparently changed hands a couple of times that season. With Doc Smith hired out to Ayden, the team that he helped to establish in Angier floated on its own through June. The home team got a break when Woody Upchurch, who had ventured to South Carolina during the spring to pick up some extra cash, returned for a special game with a Durham team. He helped draw 1,200 to the park, and Angier won, 6-1, over U-Drive-It. Upchurch struck out seven and hit a home run.

Garland Adams took the reins of the team in July, but by the end of the month, S.H. Gardner and D.W. Denning were in charge of things.

It is not clear why the management changed, but the names themselves were significant. It seems that in Angier, a Denning, Williams, Young, or Gardner were always involved with baseball. Shake any of those family trees and a player, manager, or major financial backer would usually fall out.

By August, the Angier team was hitting stride, the pitching getting better and the hitting slacking up very little from previous seasons. The Angier boys whipped Lewis Sporting Goods of Raleigh, 8-4 with Nick Dupree, Wales Blalock, and William Gardner getting three hits each. Gardner was on the mound and gave up seven hits. Upchurch and those three headed a lineup that included Doc Smith's boy, Larry, Charles Adams, James Denning, Elmo Johnson, Bill Collins, Elmo Hockaday, and Tally Dupree.

The big game for the team that year was when Doc Smith

brought his Ayden team to town the next week. Smith's team was in the thick of the Coastal Plain League race at the time, and folks in town knew that if the home team could show something against a team from a "fast" semipro league, then they were pretty good. The Coastal Plain was already becoming an attraction to scouts, some who claimed the league was as good as many minor leagues.

Upchurch tossed a four-hitter and Angier claimed a 4-2 victory over Smith's Aces that day, the first of three wins that closed out Angier's season. Upchurch took the mound against Apex the following week and claimed a 9-5 win. Then on Sept. 10, the Washington (N.C.) All-Stars visited and could manage just five hits against Upchurch.

Upchurch and Angier ended the season proving they could compete with some of the best semipro outfits in the state, which meant good things for both the pitcher and the town.

Upchurch's performance that summer brought him good individual notice. On Aug. 11, 1934, the *Kannapolis Independent* published a statewide semipro all-star team, selected by managers and writers from across North Carolina.

Upchurch was on the team, and he was in good company: Cooleemee first-baseman Jim Poole had batted .288 for the Philadelphia Athletics in 1925-27; pitcher Orlin Rogers of Kinston was on his way to the Senators; Don Padgett of Hickory would nearly win the National League batting title in 1939; Buzz Phillips of Newton had pitched 14 games for the Philadelphia Phillies; and Lute Roy of Shelby had pitched for four major league teams. The all-star team also included outfielder

Gilbert Woodworth, who played for North Carolina State College and for Erwin, just 12 miles from Angier. [7]

The fact was that Angier was beginning to show up on the baseball map in North Carolina, thanks to the help of Upchurch, Holland, and Smith. If Angier was drawing more than a thousand people to some of its games, then there was a little money to be made from playing there; and more good talent would head Angier's way. And if these high school-age players, some who were headed for college or professional ball, could stay together a while, Angier had a legitimate shot of being in a fast semipro league.

The new park, the solid players, the teams from bigger towns, the admission, the Sunday games. They all added up to make Angier's baseball prospects encouraging. Despite the Depression, summers of the early 1930s weren't too bad in tiny Angier after all. Having a winner on the baseball diamond seemed to take the sting out of the battle to survive tough times. Baseball talk was buzzing through the winter now and filtering down to little boys named Gardner, Price, Adams, and Ellen, who were just picking up baseball gloves and learning to swat at a ball. For them, the best was yet to come.

Doc Smith

Herbert C. "Doc" Smith caught for Wichita Falls in the Texas League in 1928. He also played at Fort Worth that season and batted .306. He went on to play, coach, and manage in semipro and minor league baseball in eastern North Carolina for years.

(Photo courtesy of the University of Texas-Arlington Libraries)

Bill Holland

Bill Holland's curve ball would win him accolades in Angier and take him through four years of professional ball, including a short shot at the major leagues.

(Photo courtesy of the East Carolina University Athletics archives)

Chapter 2 - The Tobacco State League

The Ups and Downs of a Semipro Circuit

Spring planting was more hopeful around Angier than it had been in years. Tobacco prices had begun to recover in 1934, and it looked like 1935 could be even better. Other crop prices were also bounding back, and the pinch that had stung rural America seemed to be easing.

Baseball had suffered with the rest of the economy but was beginning to pull out of trouble, too. In North Carolina, professional minor leagues were making a comeback. The Piedmont League had not regained its old territory in Winston-Salem and Durham, but the new Bi-State League was putting more minor league dots on the state map. 8

The semipro leagues just seemed to be getting stronger. To the east of Angier, the Coastal Plain League was established enough to expand, adding Goldsboro and Williamston to make an eight-town league. *The News & Observer,* in its preseason coverage of the Coastal

Plain League, dubbed it the best semipro league in the state. [9] That could now be stated, since the strongest of the old semipro leagues had now become fully professional. Despite the fact that it was not an officially certified professional league, the Carolina Textile League in the Piedmont region was now regularly courting professional ball players for their rosters. The competition had become so fierce in the league that the NAPBL's invitation to make the textile league into an "organized" professional minor league was spurned. Any notion of salary limits that organized ball would bring them didn't set too well in Concord, Kannapolis, Cooleemee, and the other towns of the league. They were getting the best players around as it was, and making money, too. The league of mill towns had become an "outlaw" professional league, which didn't set well with organized baseball. [10]

The more immediate area around Raleigh had a six-team Tri County League and a six-team Central Carolina League competing in the semipro ranks. Now everyone seemed to want to get their team in league competition.

Barnstorming and exhibitions were finding their way to North Carolina now, too. Baseball would get a jump start in the state in 1935 from none other than Babe Ruth. The legendary player, who had his first home run as a professional in Fayetteville in an exhibition game for the Baltimore Orioles in 1914, returned to the town in April 1935 as a player for the Boston Braves. Schools and businesses in Fayetteville closed early for folks to see the Braves take on N.C. State College's team in an exhibition game. The game drew about 4,000. [11]

Angier was still getting its baseball legs but was not unlike the rest of the state in furthering its ambitions. Baseball talk had started even before the first tobacco plant had been placed in the dirt. Angier's baseball talent, and its following, was earning some respect. For two seasons the little park on Gardner land had been host to enough good players and fans to generate talk of better things. By August of 1934, fans came to expect to see a good game at the park, thanks to the interest Doc Smith, Woody Upchurch, and Bill Holland had helped generate.

Winter brought word of a new, fast semipro league in the making, and the baseball backers in Angier figured their town was ready to take that step. Though the 1934 season had not been very well organized, the Angier team had managed to play enough games to feel confident about a June-through-August semipro league schedule. The turnouts had been good, because fans came to expect at least one home game a weekend. With a regular schedule, there was no reason that Angier couldn't field a league team. Whether or not it could be a financial success was apparently never in question.

It all made the spring of 1935 a busy one around town, and not just because of planting.

Three nearby towns had tossed their hats in the ring with hopes of forming a new league and were looking for a fourth. The new league hopefuls included the mill town of Erwin, 12 miles to the south of Angier, and another mill town, Sanford, about 30 miles to the west. To the east, approximately 25 miles, were the sister towns of Smithfield and

Selma, which had decided to combine to have a team. These towns were considerably larger than Angier and were willing to play three or four games a week in a June-through-August regular season designed to accommodate the large number of college players expected.

Each of the towns had its own rich tradition of baseball, Erwin itself boasting 14 hometown boys on semipro and professional rosters. Ten of them would be on the Redbird team, making Erwin the solid favorite when the league season began.

But Angier would prove that there was plenty of solid interest in its hometown team. In April the town started a ticket drive with a goal of selling 2,000 tickets for a May 28 opening game. It was an ambitious goal, considering the town's size. And even with such an opening-day crowd, this business of having a real league team would be a tricky one. There would probably be no profit in this baseball enterprise. There rarely was. Semipro baseball was a game that thrived almost entirely on pure passion; the passion of owners and fans to field the best, most exciting players in the interest of winning. This often meant offering players more money than a team could afford. It was a losing proposition as far as pocketbooks were concerned. But if it resulted in wins on the field, the expense would be well worth it to the town and its people.

A four-team league was a risk in itself, because if one team had to drop out for some reason, the league could not continue. That's why a persuasive deposit was usually required of each team. The league also handed down rules on player eligibility, stipulating that players could not have been under contract with any professional team within the last year.

A monthly salary limit was placed on each team, too. The league wanted to make sure that the playing field was level across the board and that all of the teams had a good chance of playing out the season without failing financially. Trouble was, there was no guarantee that these rules would not be stretched, bent, or broken from time to time. Enforcement was another matter, ambitions of the team owners and yearning of the fans to win being too tempting. [12]

The new Tobacco State League, as with most professional or semiprofessional leagues of its sort, was starting out on shaky ground. Not only would the organizers have to deal with the financial prospects of maintaining teams and a league, but they had the semipro leagues around the area to compete with when it came to finding players.

The bigger leagues took a toll on Angier. The town team would have to do without Smith, Upchurch, and Holland in 1935. Upchurch and Smith had gone their ways, Smith taking up the banner in Ayden and calling on Upchurch to help the Aces' cause. Holland would put in a few games in Angier before heading off to play with some higher-paying semipro teams. Later he would start picking up minor league money.

But the baseball organizers in Angier, headed up by Roy C. Williams, announced in early May that they had sold 1,000 tickets for the first game, well on their way to the goal to be reached by the end of the month.

Williams was a contemporary of Doc Smith, and if Smith was Angier's baseball father on the field, Williams was certainly the paternal figure behind the scenes. An avid fan of the game, Williams was a farmer, merchant, and owner of the local livery stable. Though he wasn't technically the sole owner of the team, he was the person the town turned to during the 1930s for leadership in any baseball enterprise. He was usually on the team's board of directors, and he had tapped into the network of players and coaches enough to be a good judge of talent.

Thanks to Williams' leadership in the 1935 ticket effort, Angier proved enough promise to earn a spot in the new league. Now the honest-to-goodness work of putting together a real team could proceed.

Angier entered the Tobacco State League, and the four league partners strove forward with their plans. On the first weekend in May, a sort of combination exhibition and tryout started the process of putting a team on the field. Clayton and Angier played a Saturday-Sunday twin bill and split the pair of games. The series featured a few of the players who would play for Angier that year, but it was chiefly an exhibition to help perk fan interest. Doc Smith put word out that he was trying out players for his team from Ayden, and that contingent would form the Angier team. The Clayton team was made up of players trying to make Tick Poole's Coastal Plain League team in Goldsboro. In the Sunday game, George Turbeville, a UNC and Coastal Plain League star on his way to the Philadelphia Athletics, took the mound for Angier and faced Bill Herring, a Wake Forest College star. They dueled to a 2-1 Clayton victory. Angier's own Nick Dupree caught the game, and Angier's best hitter that day was Elmo Fish, an infielder who had come over from Fuquay Springs.

Over the next few days, Roy Williams sought an on-field

manager. DeWitt Perry, the veteran Piedmont League pitcher who had played for Angier in its series with Erwin in 1933, was hired to take the reins. He went to work finding more players to fill an 18-player roster limit. He saw pitcher Tommy Williams and shortstop Leroy Spell in action when Campbell College came to town for an exhibition, and he signed them two weeks later. Left-handed pitcher Joe Talley, who was from Roanoke Rapids and had put up good numbers at Wake Forest College, soon joined the team. Fish and Bennett Bullock agreed to come from Fuquay Springs to help in the infield, and local high school star Mason Bugg would play at a number of positions. Bill Holland would start the season, and Doc Smith's son, Larry, would be a catcher.

As the season progressed, there were, of course, a number of trades and acquisitions that changed the face of the lineup drastically. Along the way, Angier would acquire Tom Lanning, Frank Melton, and Jim "Chubby" Dean, all players who were considered professional prospects.

The rosters of all of the Tobacco State League teams were pretty much the same in terms of the mixture of hometown, college, and mercenary talent. So the season appeared to have the promise of competitiveness.

The Sanford contingent was led by an up-and-coming pitcher named Zeb Harrington, who was on his way to a minor league career and to becoming a bit of a Doc Smith-type legend in that town. Smithfield-Selma had a solid outfielder in Harvey Pittman, another pro prospect, and the Twins would later acquire Spencer Bruce, a former Piedmont

League hurler. But Erwin appeared to have the team to beat going into the season, with 10 semipro veterans led by pitcher Mickey O'Quinn and fielders Babe Bost, Duke Tew, Lee Norris, and Jake Owens.

Angier played a few more games before the May 28 opening date against Erwin.

The Angier Bulls took the field in their white flannel, red trimmed uniforms that afternoon before the sought-after 2,000 fans.

DeWitt Perry and Bill Holland had trouble with the hard-hitting Redbirds that day, and despite Bennett Bullock's home run and double, Angier lost a 10-7 decision.

It was an inauspicious start to Angier's first league season, and things would not be easy for Angier or the new league. Though the league openers were big draws, with 1,000 showing up in Sanford to watch the Spinners play Smithfield-Selma, and North Carolina Lt. Gov. A. H. Graham tossing out the first ball in Smithfield's home opener a day later, things seemed to go downhill from there.

Angier played through the summer, dividing wins and losses almost evenly, making trades along the way, but never quite able to press the league-leaders in Erwin and Smithfield. As June turned to July, the novelty of the league season would wear off in Angier, and the team would not produce enough wins to guarantee a good crowd at every game. Manager Perry's team apparently did not have the players to offer an entertaining afternoon to the baseball-savvy Angier community. More than that, the Bulls failed to consistently beat the teams from down the road, something Angier folks did not readily accept. So Perry was the first of four on-field managers the team would have that year. They ended up with Wake Forest catcher Porter Sheppard, and he even tendered his resignation as manager at one point in late July. Williams and the Angier team's board of directors would not accept it. [13]

At the end of July, Smithfield-Selma had the league lead with a 23-15 record. Erwin was second at 21-19 and Angier third at 19-20. Sanford was the last-place team, at 15-24.

Meanwhile the Angier team tried everything to get fans to show up in lieu of a lackluster season. They made trades not long after Sheppard was hired and quickly won six of their next seven games, before going into another slump. They even promised a post-game vaudeville show for one Friday date. Nothing seemed to work.

On August 24, the Tobacco State League announced an abrupt end to its inaugural season, one week short of the scheduled finish. Why the league could not complete the few games left was not made clear, but a number of factors were suspect. The practicality of getting out-of-state college players back to school may have been one of them. More likely, though, was the simple issue of finances. The league had been competitive enough for all of the teams to be within mathematical striking distance of the pennant down to the last month. The last-place team finished 13½ games back at the end of the season. At least one of the teams, in a make-or-break push to obtain better players and make a winning impression on the league and the home town, had probably overspent, under drawn, and could not afford even one more week's salary. The other teams would then have agreed to end the season early.

Erwin claimed the regular season title, as expected, with a 34-20 record, Smithfield-Selma was 4½ games back, Angier third, at 26-32, and Sanford was last place, at 22-35. The league did manage to stage a title series between the top two teams, Erwin and Smithfield. Erwin claimed the first Tobacco State League crown by, winning the series four games to two.

League baseball had been exciting, but it had been a struggle for the towns of the Tobacco State League. Still there was too much fondness for the game of baseball for league ball to be forgotten, and 1935 would be the start of a long relationship between each of the towns and the Tobacco State League.

The players of the Tobacco State League would become the heroes for the young boys in Angier, too. But the league, like the boys, had some growing pains to endure.

Chapter 3 - From Town to Town

A Place to Play was Often Down the Road

For a Depression-era man looking for work, $20 a week was nothing to sneeze at. [14] Considering the fact that you could get a nice pair of shoes down at Young's Department Store in Angier for $5, the salary for a semipro baseball player in town seemed to be good summer work. A mill hand made as little as $10 a week, and if a farmer brought home $1,000 from the tobacco market in September, his family might not have to worry about making it through another year.

Twenty bucks was a nice piece of change, alright. But a player had to be pretty good to get that, and teams had to be willing to pay that to get the kind of players who would draw a crowd in the 1930s. Anything less, and a player would look elsewhere. Local players were a different thing. A local player may not get more than the experience of playing a good brand of baseball and becoming a town star. After all, a town boy didn't have to worry about the expense of a boarding house and meal money. And a town boy was always there, usually kept around home by his farmer-father, who needed him for work when he wasn't wearing the home colors. That's why they called it semipro baseball; some were paid, some weren't.

The best of the traveling ballplayers may have gotten a whopping $40 a week and also may have had the luxury of finding a local family to board with during the summer. Avid fans of the local team were always willing to offer a spare room or bed for the summer.

And there was even bonus pay, or "fence money," as the players called it. That was when a grateful and rather wealthy fan slipped an extra bill to a player for an exceptional performance or a big play in a game. Sometimes fans would pass the hat to pay a player for outstanding play.

Semipro ball could offer a summer of downright extravagance.

Problem was, there were no guarantees. Owners of league teams didn't always have the money in hand to make the payroll each week or month. For team owners, it seemed the expenses were always there, but the income wasn't a sure thing. Teams in small towns at the time generally charged 25 cents admission for adults, 15 cents for children, and a dime for "Negroes," if any blacks attended at all. So a good draw was crucial to making ends meet at the end of the week or month. If you drew 300 folks to a game four times a week, you could barely pay a 15-man roster, about 10 of which demanded salary. This is all not to mention the start-up costs at the beginning of the season, which entailed uniforms, equipment, maybe a lease on the park, and a forfeit deposit if a league was involved. There is no indication that anyone except the best ball players made money out of the whole deal.

That is why there was no guarantee that a town would have a league team each year, and even if it did, no certainty that the team would last through the year.

The financial nature of this semipro baseball kept men such as Doc Smith, Woody Upchurch, and Bill Holland on the road through much of the 1930s. Each would usually give Angier a shot in the spring. But if the gates weren't good, or there was no notion of a stable league to play in, they took their talents elsewhere.

In 1935, while Angier was struggling through a so-so summer in the new Tobacco State League, Smith and Upchurch were having a better go of it in the more-lucrative Coastal Plain League. The average pay in that league was about $25 per week, and teams in that league played a 60-game schedule. They could afford it in the bigger towns.

Smith was managing the Ayden Aces, and Upchurch was one of the best in his pitching rotation. Though the team hovered around the .500 mark all season and finished fourth in the eight-team league, Smith's Aces would stun league-leading Greenville in the first round of the playoffs, thanks largely to Upchurch.

Ayden had finished nine games behind the Greenies in the league standings, but the Aces would send Upchurch to the mound on two consecutive days in August and clinch the series, three games to two. Upchurch won the second of those games on a five-hit shutout.

Ayden lost the title series to Kinston, but Upchurch's

performances that summer grabbed the attention of the Philadelphia Athletics venerable "baseball man" Connie Mack. The A's organization had lost the aura of the title teams of years before, because Mack, by now the majority shareowner of the club, lacked the wealth of the Shibe family, co-owners of the glory years of the 1920s. The Athletics of the 1930s were among the worst teams in the American League.

Mack had to pinch pennies here and there, and he became a raider of the semipro ranks to gather less-expensive talent. One of the places to which he consistently turned during the mid-1930s was the Coastal Plain League, where he picked up at least 10 players. [15]

Upchurch was the latest in the parade of semipro stars to be coaxed to Philadelphia by Mack. It would be a less-than-glamorous major league test.

Upchurch debuted on Sept. 14 in Philadelphia, and he kept the A's in a 2-2 tie against the Chicago White Sox until the ninth inning, when the Sox scored two runs on three hits and two errors. Upchurch shouldered the 4-2 loss, allowing nine hits, one walk, and striking out two.

The lanky lefthander would pitch in two more games that season and finish the year with an 0-2 record and 5.06 ERA. He would perform just well enough to get a return trip to Philly for the spring of 1936, but that would not last long. He appeared in seven games with the Athletics to start the 1936 season, but with little success. He posted an 0-2 record and had chalked up a hefty 9.62 ERA. It was in late May, after Upchurch took the mound and suffered through a 15-1 shelling at the hands of the

New York Yankees, that Connie Mack let the lefthander go.

He would then make a couple of appearances in Angier, bounce back into the Coastal Plain League, and again help Ayden in a playoff run, this time all the way to the championship. But early in 1937, before the season began, his pitching career would be cut short. A car accident injured his left arm enough to make him virtually ineffective on the mound. He would continue to be a fixture around baseball diamonds in Harnett County for years, mostly as a manager and pitching coach. But, at age 26, his best pitching days were over.

Bill Holland's left arm took him even farther down the baseball road. In fact, his four professional seasons would take him up and down the Eastern Seaboard. After pitching for two years at Louisburg Junior College and playing his summer seasons in Angier, he enrolled in East Carolina Teacher's College in Greenville in the fall of 1935 and played for the school team the following spring. He played semipro ball for the Greenville Greenies of the Coastal Plain League in 1936. He pitched the summer of 1937 in Angier and completed school at East Carolina before going professional in 1938, a busy season for the young lefty. He started his pro career in Orlando with the Florida State League, was picked up by Greenville, South Carolina, of the South Atlantic League, and finished the 1938 season in Charlotte with the Piedmont League.

He had a good enough start to the 1939 season in Charlotte to gain the attention of the Washington Senators, another of the basement dwellers in the American League. The Senators were on their way to a sixth-place finish when they gave Holland a chance late in the season. It would be a short major league career. Holland didn't start a game, pitching four innings in three appearances. He would later note that Detroit Tigers great Hank Greenberg helped make his term in the majors so short, swatting one of his 33 homers that year against the youngster from Varina. ₁₆ Holland gave up six hits and five earned runs in his four innings of work and was back in Greenville, South Carolina, the next spring. Then it was Springfield of the Eastern League and Pittsfield of the Canadian-American League before Holland was through as a professional, after the 1941 season. None of his pro seasons was spectacular. His only winning year was his first, when is posted a 5-4 record (2.44 ERA) at Orlando. He finished the minors with a 26-37 pitching record.

Holland, like Upchurch, would never be too far away from a diamond, and would later be recognized for his play at East Carolina. He was the first player from that school to don a major league uniform and is a member of the East Carolina University Athletic Hall of Fame.

Doc Smith's traveling days were behind him by the 1930s. He had been a Texas League and Piedmont League player in the 1920s, but baseball very rarely took him out of North Carolina after that. He was unsure of his job in Ayden in 1936, because March had been full of rumors that the Aces team could no longer continue with the Coastal Plain League. The league's problems bled over into the Tobacco State League, because Smithfield-Selma was one of the teams considered as a replacement for Ayden.

It was not until late April that Ayden made a last-minute appeal to get into the Coastal Plain League, and by that time, Smith was already trying to organize a restart of the Tobacco State League, or any league for Angier to play in. Smithfield-Selma, Clayton, Wendell, and Sanford were other teams mentioned in a *News & Observer* story stating that Smith was trying to organize a new league "where the Tobacco State League left off." [17]

But nothing ever emerged from Smith's efforts, and by late May it became evident that Angier and the three other teams that made up the Tobacco State League of the previous year were left with a summer of spotty non-league play. As it turned out, things would work pretty well for Smith. As the door closed on a league for Angier, Smith got a call from New Bern of the CPL. It would start a long association between Smith and the New Bern Bears.

His leadership in Ayden, where he managed the Aces to the Coastal Plain League title run in 1935, had boosted his reputation in the league. As a semipro and minor league player-manager in New Bern, he would bring that town its first Coastal Plain League title in 1938, winning the pennant and sweeping both playoff series. He would be at the Bears' helm on and off for five seasons. In 1940 Smith left New Bern briefly to manage the Raleigh team of the semipro Tobacco State League, but for much of the rest of the decade he managed in New Bern or coached Harnett County's American Legion teams. He even spent a short stint as manager for Angier's only minor league team in 1946. He spent his winters in Angier tending to his woodworking business downtown.

Smith's playing and coaching accomplishments would be remembered in town. The Doc Smith Award came to symbolize courage and ability on the Angier High School athletic fields for years.

It was that kind of life for many of the players who got their starts on the diamonds of Angier. Mason Bugg, Tally Dupree, Larry Smith, and others all went where the best games, best money, or a shot at fame would take them.

Bugg, who had been a star pitcher for Angier High's baseball team, became a star at N.C. State College, being named captain of the team for 1937. He played part of the summer of 1936 in Angier and part in Snow Hill of the Coastal Plain League. After graduating from N.C. State, he took to the road and didn't return to play again in Angier. He played three successful minor league seasons, in 1937 and '38 at Alexandria of the Class D Evangeline League, where he batted .288 and .328. He had 91 RBIs that rookie season. He made his way up to Class C ball the next season, playing for Charleston, West Virginia, of the Middle Atlantic League.

Doc Smith's son would eventually hit the road for good, too. Larry Smith's semipro seasons were at Angier and Erwin, and in 1939 he signed a pro contract that would take him through the South Atlantic League and all the way to Kansas City of the American Association in 1943. The catcher's five-season career batting average was .274.

Tally Dupree would always come back to Angier, but not before he had his flings: Elm City, Erwin, Raleigh, New Bern, Kinston, and a few other stops. The Wake Forest College star was one of those who carefully calculated his young career with baseball in mind. He chose to be a teacher, as did many players in the heyday of semipro ball. The school year and baseball season worked so well around each other. Dupree's last stop was Angier, and he would carry his talents to the Angier fields up until the 1950s.

There was a certain freedom that semipro baseball offered those men who traipsed the countryside playing for anything from no pay to a whopping $140 a month playing the game they enjoyed. [18] They could pretty much come and go as they pleased, not worrying about being owned by anyone until, of course, they signed that contract to be a real pro ball player. They could be heroes in their home towns or adopted heroes down the road. They could move from team to team in groups with their college pals or take out on their own, if the network called them to a high-dollar game or two.

If a league team wasn't looking for talent, there was always a shot at a weekend exhibition game and hopes that the gate would be big enough to make the trip worthwhile.

But the uncertainty of where to play next week also meant feast or famine. The best thing to do was look for that nice town with a nice host family and the $20 or so per week.

Webster Lupton

Chapter 4 - Down but Not Out

The TSL Struggles Back

Angier had proven itself ripe for baseball. Despite all of the uncertainties the semipro game posed, the town had produced some good local talent, had shown a good following, and had even made a go at league ball. But Angier was still a small town, and the bigger baseball world around it was uncompromising when it came to letting small towns into the mix. That was the case in 1936.

The Tobacco State League itself had been a limited success, coming to an abrupt halt in August of the previous season. A number of things had to be settled before the young league could continue. The league needed to make ends meet for at least four teams for at least three months, and this was the chief roadblock.

But the troubled conclusion of the 1935 season carried over into the next spring, and despite the efforts of Doc Smith in Angier and baseball leaders in the other towns, there was no Tobacco State League in 1936.

The other semipro leagues seemed to have all the push and most of the talent. While the Coastal Plain League seemed to be the magnet for players in the eastern part of the state, out west, the Carolina Textile League, now made up of Charlotte and seven Piedmont mill towns, had become an independent professional league. Teams in this league were employing the best players available, including college players, and they were paying top dollar. The league became so ambitious that it was regularly luring players out of the minor leagues. This prompted the governing body of minor leagues, the National Association of Professional Baseball Leagues, to threaten to "blacklist" players who signed with Carolina League teams. Some players, too tempted by the independent league's offerings, would take the chance in the Carolina League anyway and even play under assumed names. [19]

The Coastal Plain League was still thriving chiefly on college talent, and it appeared to be drawing the vast majority of the good college players from the University of North Carolina, Duke, Wake Forest, N.C. State, East Carolina, and junior colleges such as Campbell and Louisburg. What talent it didn't get was grabbed up by the Tidewater League, the Peach Belt League, or the Tobacco Belt League, other semipro circuits in eastern North Carolina. The eastern region of the state just didn't seem to have enough room for another full-fledged semipro league in 1936.

For the former Tobacco State League towns, the pickings were few, but not enough to keep a town team completely off of the diamond. Angier, Erwin, and Smithfield-Selma all had baseball teams that summer, though the dates were nowhere near as frequent as league play had offered. Sanford went to the Peach Belt League for 1936.

In Angier, folks had had their taste of baseball excitement, and despite the absence of a league, they wanted to see more.

So Angier would get in some exciting dates during the summer of 1936. Some of the best would turn out to be exhibitions before the other leagues started their seasons. During the last days of May, when the Coastal Plain League was yet to open play, Angier would again prove to the baseball region that if the players were on display, Angier folks would show up for a game.

The excitement started on the 24th when Bill Holland took the mound to strike out 16 batters, and Doc Smith's boy, Larry, crushed a grand slam home run in Angier's 7-0 win against Sanford.

That whetted some appetites for a big Memorial Day game the next weekend. It happened to be the weekend after Woody Upchurch had been slain by the Yankees and shown his way to the train station. Upchurch was back in Angier, and news of his return generated a buzz among people who didn't care what the Yankees had done to him. They just knew that their old friend, fresh out of the big leagues, was coming back to Angier to pitch. Doc Smith, who had not yet been hired by New Bern, quickly spread the news that the former major leaguer would pitch the Memorial Day game. A couple of former Angier High School stars,

Tally Dupree and Mason Bugg, were back from college and would be available for action. Dupree was the starting shortstop for Wake Forest College by that time, and his team had captured the Big Five title that year. [20] Bugg was over at N.C. State, and though he wasn't a pitcher there as he had been in high school, he had shown his worth as a hitter. Some of these players would probably be out of town for much of the summer, so local folks realized they might not get another shot at seeing them perform at home.

The fact that the opponent would be Snow Hill of the Coastal Plain League made the game more attractive. Snow Hill was a town about the size of Angier, located about 70 miles to the east. It had a baseball following big enough to sponsor a team in the fast league and would prove later to have the support needed for a minor league team. The Billies were playing a final warm-up before their league season began.

The word-of-mouth promotion, the best marketing tool for small towns of the time, worked magic. About 2,000 folks crammed Angier's park that Sunday to see Upchurch and company deliver. They did. In a thirteen-inning game full of fireworks, Upchurch claimed the victory by pitching the win and hitting the game-winning home run. Larry "Little Doc" Smith also hit a home run, and Bugg, Bennett Bullock, and Elmo Johnson also had key hits in a thrilling 6-5 Angier victory.

The Angier folks went home happy after that long, exciting afternoon. But the jolt of dramatics they got would have to carry them through the rest of the summer. It was a preseason buildup to an anticlimactic season. The bulk of the local talent was now headed for the greener outfields that league ball had to offer. Upchurch, Holland, Bugg, and Doc Smith were all off to the regular play and consistent pay of the Coastal Plain League.

The stars left behind a pretty good group to tackle the rest of the summer in town. Angier's high school team, led by James Denning, James Gardner, and Larry "Little Doc" Smith had had a successful spring before losing to Lafayette High School in the Harnett County championship game. Those three players, along with Elmo Johnson and Tally Dupree, would be leading players during the on-and-off summer season. Of course, there was not even a guarantee that those players would always be available. The higher paying league teams could call them into temporary service from time to time.

Still, the independent Bulls had their share of exciting games against reputable teams. Wilmington of the semipro Tidewater League came to town on June 14, and the hitting of Bullock and Elmo Johnson keyed a 4-2 Angier triumph. In July, the Bulls split a pair of one-run games with Lumberton, including one in which Erwin veteran Mickey O'Quinn pitched.

But there was no league title to play for, no regular schedule to count on, and no guarantee of a level of talent on the field on any given game day. It became evident toward the end of that season that Angier would have to get in a new league or re-form the old one for any hope of getting back some of the flavor of competitive baseball of any quality or quantity.

During the long winter months that led up to 1937, folks in Angier contemplated and committed to a revival of league semipro ball when spring again arrived.

With the warm days, more changes arrived in the surrounding baseball world. Minor league baseball was continuing its revival, and that would pay off for semipro baseball in eastern North Carolina. Over the winter the Coastal Plain League, which had financial problems of its own, had decided to go professional, opting for the stable salary structure of minor league ball. This meant one thing for hopeful little baseball towns like Angier: more college talent. Since a college player was not allowed to sign a professional contract, the minor leagues were off limits to any player who wanted to be on a school roster the next season. The semipro leagues in central and eastern North Carolina had many of these players on regular salaries — and pretty good ones — during the summer, but that was because the teams were not technically professional teams. When the Coastal Plain League went professional, dozens of North Carolina college players, who would normally look to the CPL, now had to turn elsewhere, at least to play in the state.

It all opened the door for a semipro league, and Angier was ready to again take a chance. There was still a financial risk, but baseball was worth the gamble for a town like Angier, and Angier baseball men were willing to try.

The Tobacco State League was brought back to life in 1937, even though it was again a four-team league and left team salary limits open. "No salary limit was made since it was seen in 1935 that it could not be controlled," reported *The Independent* of Fuquay Springs in a story about a preseason league meeting in May. No players under professional contract were eligible, the story stated, and that included players from the "high-salaried" Carolina League, the Piedmont mill league that was kicking dust on the shoes of organized baseball. The newspaper account also noted some discussion about playing league games on Sunday:

"The officials voted to have four games a week on Thursday, Friday, Saturday and Sunday. All teams were in favor of Sabbath ball, but Clayton was the only team holding out for league ball on that day. The other teams wanted the games to start on Wednesday, with exhibition games on Sunday, thereby taking care of games postponed by rain, etc." [21]

Apparently the real issue here was not whether to actually play baseball on Sunday, but it was whether or not upstanding, church-going men of the community should sign their names to a document officially sanctioning Sunday baseball. They did, because they knew that more guaranteed weekend dates resulted in more guarantees of income. Clubs such as Angier wanted to take full advantage of having a league team.

The Tobacco State League embarked on its new season with Angier, Erwin, the Johnston County town of Clayton, and a team called Wakelon, a hybrid name for the Wake County community of Wakefield and the nearby town of Zebulon, on board.

In Angier, the 1937 season brought some second chances for some of the town's prodigal baseball sons. Woody Upchurch was no longer the pitcher he once was because of the car accident that winter.

He could still throw on a limited basis as he would prove during the year, but he would never find the plate the way he once did.

Folks in Angier still had faith in the "old" lefty's ability to work with players. Club President J.W. Gardner appointed him manager of the team. Bennett Bullock of Fuquay would be his assistant, and the hard-hitting first baseman would bring some of his buddies from Elon College in to help the team.

Bill Holland, who had played with Greenville of the Coastal Plain League but was still at East Carolina Teachers College and no longer eligible for the CPL, also brought his services back to Angier. He led a pitching staff that included Tommy Williams and Andy Fuller from Elon, and James Gardner of Angier and Wake Forest College. Pee Wee Hight, a Buies Creek pitcher who had played at Campbell, would also help.

Larry "Little Doc" Smith was behind the plate, Bullock at first, Elmo Fish at second, and Leroy Spell and Tally Dupree switched at shortstop and third base.

A newcomer, Jeff Bolden, would be one of the first true journeymen to play regularly for Angier. A native of Georgia, Bolden had found his way to the powerful Carolina League of the Piedmont in 1935. There he had gained a reputation as a slugging outfielder for the Concord Weavers. In 1936 he went into a bit of a slump, and the Weavers released him in early July as they jockeyed for position in a tight league race. [22] He apparently wandered throughout the region playing for semipro teams here and there before finding his way to

Angier to start the 1937 season. Though his height and weight were not listed in any publications, newspapers always referred to him as Big Jeff Bolden, and the few people who remember, recall him as being around six feet and 230 pounds. His fiery character would get him into trouble from time to time, but Bolden would be a good addition to the Angier lineup. He would play outfield and lead the league in home runs in 1937.

Howard Smith, who had played for Angier in 1935, and a newcomer named Hoot Gibson rounded out the outfield with Bolden. Considering that six of Angier's regulars had played or would play on the professional level, the lineup looked formidable.

But Angier was considered the second best team in the league as the season started. The Erwin Redbirds were again considered the favorite. The Redbirds were led by slugging first baseman/manager Gilbert "Bummer" Woodworth, who had played at N.C. State and in the Coastal Plain League the year before. On the mound, they sported hometown star Johnny Wilbourne and one-time Elon star Art Fowler. [23] They also had former Duke standout Babe Bost, along with Mike Crawford, who had been an Angier standout in years past, and Jim Sessoms, a three-sport athlete at Emory and Henry College in Virginia. Colorful pitcher Mickey O'Quinn, a veteran semipro player, was on the Erwin roster for part of the season. For one exhibition game, the Redbirds even got the services of legendary Clinton hurler, Rube Benton. A fifteen-year major league veteran, Benton was fifty at the time and only months away from his death, but he was still effective enough to help Erwin top the CPL pros from Kinston, 8-5.

The Erwin faithful were more than anxious to get the season going, as evidenced by their early start in the exhibition season. The Redbirds had played at least nine exhibition games when the Tobacco State League campaign started, a head start that would help them in the early part of the schedule.

In Angier, the Bulls played three exhibitions as they scrambled to get their final roster filled by the June 10th opening date.

Angier's opening game was a true workout for everyone. Wakelon batters sifted through five Angier pitchers on the way to a thrilling 11-10 win over the home-standing Bulls. Leroy Spell was the Angier leader at the plate, getting two doubles and a single.

The Bulls would stretch out to a slow start in June, but the rest of the season would bear out the predictions. The day after the opener, Erwin came to town and slugged out an 8-6 triumph over the Bulls. Angier would suffer another loss before getting its first triumph of the season, a 3-2 home win over Wakelon, with Hight on the mound.

Angier's big win of June came on the 24th, when Fuller took the mound in Erwin and struck out thirteen batters in the Bulls' 5-1 triumph. Jeff Bolden clubbed a homer in the victory.

Much of the rest of the season was a two-way battle. The Bulls and the Redbirds waged war atop the league standings, neither able to stretch more than a three-game advantage. It was not as if Angier and Erwin could distance themselves from the other league teams, Wakelon and Clayton. Up until the final month of the season, each of the teams had genuine hopes of finishing in first place. This of course was good for attendance, keeping the interest high in each of the communities — and keeping the teams from folding. It may have set off a rash of high-dollar trading as each team jockeyed to keep the upper hand. Angier itself made a number of trades in July, some of the players staying for only a couple weeks at a time. But Woody Upchurch's boys ended up with a solid lineup for the last part of the regular season.

In late August, Angier swept a double-header against Clayton to end the season. But the Bulls, at 26-18, were still one game behind first-place Erwin and would have to play their way to the post-season finals to get another shot at their now-established rivals.

The playoffs, which included all four teams, set Angier and Wakelon to duel in the best-of-five-games first round. The Bulls did pretty much as expected, winning the series in four games. Erwin dealt with Clayton in much the same fashion, making the final series of the season the one that everyone had predicted and had wanted.

The seven-game series between the Bulls and the Redbirds would go even further than anyone expected because of a game that was actually played twice. The teams were hampered a bit by missing key players at various points in the series. It was September, and the college players had to return to school, which meant Erwin's Jim Sessoms and Angier's Bill Holland were off the rosters for much of the series. Angier slugger Jeff Bolden was also out of the picture for most of the games, and Tally Dupree came down with influenza after the first game of the series. Then there were times when the series was not very pretty, errors being key factors in three of the games.

But the match-up was an even one. The teams split the first six games, with even the mid-week games producing crowds of 1,000 or better.

Erwin came to Angier for the opening game and staggered the home team pitching almost from the start. Though Angier's Tommy Williams struck out the first three batters, the Redbirds clubbed him for four runs in the second inning and were off to the races. They added another two in the fourth before Andy Fuller came in. But it seemed the bleeding would never stop. Fuller surrendered another three runs to give the visitors a whopping 9-0 advantage. This was when Upchurch essentially threw in the towel for Game 1. Probably in an effort to rest the remainder of his pitchers, he took the mound himself and would finish the game. Erwin won, 15-4.

The opening game whipping and the fact that the next two games were on Erwin's turf didn't bode well for the Angier contingent. Of course that didn't prevent the line of cars and trucks on the twelve miles of road from Angier to Erwin the next day. It was a Sunday game, and 2,200 flocked to the Erwin park for Game 2. *The News & Observer* called it the largest turnout ever for a sports event in Erwin. [24]

The crowd was entertained. It appeared Angier was in for more trouble in the first inning as lefty James Gardner was tagged for a run on Mike Crawford's double. Angier tied it when Bennett Bullock drove in a run in the top of the third, before Erwin came to bat and answered with a pair of runs, Crawford again driving in one of them. Leroy Spell knocked in another Angier run in the top of the fifth, but the Redbirds made it 4-2 in the bottom of the frame on Babe Bost's single.

Upchurch then brought in Williams, who redeemed himself by holding the home team at bay for the rest of the game.

Meanwhile, Angier preyed on Erwin miscues in the eighth to begin a rally which would do in the home team. Lefthander Bob Green, who had started the game, walked two batters and surrendered a run on a throwing error. Green was pulled after his wild pitch brought in the tying score. Then Fowler was brought in and Larry Smith belted a single for what proved to be the winner in a 5-4 Angier win.

Game 3 was as close and even more exciting, particularly for the visiting Angier fans. Angier trailed by a run going into the ninth when a walk and an Emmett Johnson single set up Bennett Bullock with two outs. Johnson, acquired from Wakelon to sub for the ailing Tally Dupree, stole second before Bullock whacked a long single to give Angier a 6-5 lead. Andy Fuller stepped in to relieve Bill Holland in the bottom of the ninth and held the 'Birds at bay. Angier pulled out another squeaker on Erwin's home turf, 6-5.

The Bulls had done well by going to Erwin and stealing two games. One more win at home, and they would clearly be in the driver's seat. They got that win the next day, thanks to a combined seven runs batted in by Bolden and Gibson. Fuller went the distance and held Erwin to just four hits. Game 4's final score was Angier 9, Erwin 1.

Game 5 of the series presented a bit of dilemma when the playoff plan had to be ditched. The likely plan for the playoffs would have been to give each team two games at home and then to alternate home fields until the conclusion of the series or until one team had won the necessary four games. But, as it turned out, Game 5 would be played twice. The two teams — back in Erwin for the game — played for nearly three hours through eleven innings and were knotted at 8-8, when the game was called for darkness. Rather than resuming the game in Erwin the next day and playing it to the finish, the teams agreed to start over again the next day, playing in Angier in order to follow the planned scheduling of sites. The final two games would be played in Erwin if the series went to seven games.

That's how it turned out. Not only did Erwin go to Angier and take a 10-4 victory on the strength of Johnny Wilbourne's hitting and pitching, but they went back to Erwin the next day and forced a seventh game by squeezing out a 6-5 triumph. Wilbourne scattered nine hits in the Game 5 win and knocked in three runs on a double in the second inning. Angier had three errors in the fourth inning and was down 6-0 before even getting on the scoreboard. The Redbirds came from four runs down in Game 6 and broke a 5-5 tie in the bottom of the ninth on Bummer Woodworth's run-scoring single.

The title-deciding game was set for Sunday, September 12, and it drew another record crowd of about 3,000 to the Erwin park. However, there was little drama to keep the gathering entertained. Erwin got five runs in the second inning on a couple of errors, two singles, and Bummer Woodworth's two-run double to take the lead. Redbird pitcher Johnny Wilbourne went the distance and kept the Bulls scoreless until the eighth, when they tagged him for the only Angier run of the day. Erwin got in the last lick of the season, 5-1, and claimed the hard-fought crown.

Angier would have to stew all winter. But the team's popularity had grown during the year, and so had the league's. Despite the problems that had arisen from the "tie" game in the title series, it had stretched a seven-game series into eight games — at least as far as the ticket take was concerned. Since all of the playoff games were well-attended, there would actually be some money left to count at the end of the year, particularly at Angier and Erwin.

The league had been through the growing pains of a semipro organization, one that had seen both the good and bad league ball. It had been a rough and tumble experience, but now Angier and the Tobacco State League were drawing attention. Players young and old now had another good league to consider when looking for a place to play.

And for the youngest observers in Angier, kids who were still getting their baseball legs, there was a place just down the road where they could go to witness baseball drama ... and to dream. Their most memorable summer was on the way.

Chapter 5 - Tommy Byrne's Year

More Than Just Another Lefty

The young men named Gardner, Price, Ellen, and Adams were barely baseball fans as Angier evolved from a town of pick-up games into one of regular league competition. They were too young to actually see Doc Smith's best days behind the plate and Woody Upchurch's best pinpoint pitches. They relied only on the stories of their fathers. The tales would be relayed like finer points of baseball.

But when the 1938 season rolled around, these boys were around ages six to twelve: old enough to begin understanding this sandlot game but young enough to have tears when the home team lost a heartbreaker. They were now at the ages when they had something to look forward to, even if they couldn't get a sandlot game going on a summer day. The big boys were playing in town. Some of the youngsters would have an out-of-town player boarding at their home, and that was something special. Others might get to be a batboy on game day, and that was a privilege.

They were truly ready to take in the game of baseball and ready to have a new star twinkle in their eyes.

The 1938 season would be one they would all remember, not just because of the excitement of winning, but because they would see a group of players in Angier that they would follow for years, even until their own adult playing days. The upstart college players who would take the field in Angier that summer would eventually make their marks on the major leagues. One in particular became a stalwart performer for the famed New York Yankees.

The season would indeed be better than ever. The excitement of the 1937 campaign had not only brought good gates for the towns of the Tobacco State League, but it had also brought promise of a good future for the league, good enough for the league to expand. A six-team league would provide a cushion in the case of a team dropping out. The season and a four-team playoff could still continue.

With the minor leagues back on track in the region, still more college players would be available, making a bigger league feasible. The Tobacco State League was suddenly considered among the "fastest" of the semipro circuits.

Other than its size, there is no indication that the rest of the league setup would change. The success of 1937 left no notion of a feasible salary limit structure or the change in the roster size. There would be games on every day of the week except for Monday and Tuesday, those days being reserved for rain make-ups. The season would again be school friendly, running from June through August.

Angier and Erwin were in the league, and Zebulon essentially replaced Wakelon. The league turned south for newcomers, adding Sanford, which had been a charter member in 1935, Fayetteville, and Laurinburg. Fayetteville was large enough (pop. 13,049 in the 1930 census) to be considered of minor league potential. But the city had not had a minor league team since the late 1920s and would not again until after World War II, when the town's growth practically demanded a team. For now, Fayetteville fans would turn to Faytex, a local textile mill which had a new park in the Massey Hill section of town. Clayton, which had finished last in the standings in 1937, did not make another bid for a league entry.

The new setup made the Tobacco State League geographically huge by standards of the semipro leagues of the region. Zebulon, the northernmost member of the league, was about 100 miles from the new southernmost entry, Laurinburg. In fact Laurinburg's shortest road trip would be the 40 or so miles to Fayetteville. But Laurinburg, a thriving mill town and rail hub, was a bit larger than Angier, Zebulon, and Erwin and was willing to take part in what was now considered a fast semipro league.

In Angier, the fans and baseball leaders were simply anxious to put together another competitive season and pay back Erwin for the previous season's disappointment.

In May, the Angier Bulls team officers were announced, and the names familiar as Angier's baseball leaders — Gardner, Williams, and Young — were there. The newspaper listed them as T.H. Gardner, president; W.H. Hamilton, business manager; and Roy C. Williams, David H. Young, Otis Aiken, and Purvis Spivey, advisory committee members. All were merchants or farmers in the community, and all would be responsible for whatever money the team made or lost. But, again, Roy Williams was generally the man they turned to for any of the on-the-field decisions to be made because of his connections with baseball people outside of the community.

The group went to work, first by hiring an on-field manager. They picked Mickey O'Quinn, who had pitched in the area in recent years, performing mostly in Erwin. O'Quinn, apparently a happy-go-lucky sort, liked to be identified in the local press as having been a veteran of the Spanish-American War. But O'Quinn was still an effective pitcher, at least in relief, and his claims of involvement in the 1898 conflict would have put him in his late 50s or early 60s by this time, and even semipro pitchers weren't very effective at that age. [25]

The team members they would pick would be a strange mixture, at least geographically speaking. They would include a lefthander from Baltimore and a group of players from Louisiana.

In Angier they would be heroes, and for the youngsters in town who had seen the throngs of fans and exciting games of the year before, a few good heroes were a perfect recipe.

As had been the usual case in Angier, the heroics started with left-handed pitchers.

Tommy Byrne had just completed his freshman year at Wake Forest when he donned an Angier uniform. A native of Baltimore, he was quickly learning to like southern town life despite the fact that he was one of the few Catholic kids at a Southern Baptist institution smack dab in the middle of the Bible Belt.

Byrne had dreams inspired by his youth in Baltimore. In 1924, an exhibition game brought Babe Ruth back to his home town, and young Tommy's mother was lucky enough to know someone who knew someone. She got tickets for herself and her son, which would lead to an experience that would help turn the youngster to a life of baseball and a yearning to emulate a star. Before the game, Ruth took time to shake hands with young Tommy. It was one of his first memories of baseball, and it was enough for a lifetime.

"If you were a lefthander and you were from Baltimore, there's no doubt about who your hero was," Byrne said.

As a teen, Byrne was one of hundreds of kids who tried out for the local boys' Catholic school team. He excelled enough not only to make the team, but to become a hitter and pitcher who showed the stuff that attracted professional scouts: "I pitched through high school and never lost a game. Word got out that I could pitch and I could hit." The Yankees, Tigers, and Athletics all had an eye on Byrne during his senior year in high school. But to Byrne, a college scholarship was as valuable as a baseball contract and with more guarantees for the future. He wanted to go to college.

Dartmouth and Duke were high on Byrne's list of prospective colleges until Jim Weaver, the athletics director at Wake Forest College, came calling.

During Byrne's senior high school year, Weaver was in Baltimore buying athletic equipment and scouting for Coach John Caddell. The Wake coach needed a lefty to replace the graduating star, Joe Talley. Weaver quickly saw that Byrne could fill the bill.

Byrne had received a scholarship offer from Duke, a school that had become noted for baseball talent, but Weaver tipped the scales in favor of Wake Forest.

"I had never even heard of Wake Forest, and I told them that I had this scholarship offer at Duke, but that they wanted me to work in the cafeteria as part of the scholarship. [Weaver] said, 'Well, Tommy, if you come to Wake Forest, you won't have to work in the cafeteria,' " Byrne recalled. "I asked him more about the school, and when I found out that Wake Forest played Duke, I thought I would be better off going to Wake Forest and beating Duke. And it really transpired just that way; I beat Duke nine out of ten times I pitched against them."

The little town of Angier would also reap the benefits of Byrne's decision to attend Wake Forest. The Baptist college had developed a connection with the town through its recruitment of a number of players. James Denning, Tally Dupree, James Gardner, and J. Carl Young were other Angier players who were on the Wake Forest roster.

Byrne was beginning to learn the ropes of semipro baseball in the South too. He had spent a couple of weeks in the "outlaw" Carolina League. "They paid me $37 a week and room and board, which was good money then," he said. But, "they weren't pitching me enough. They had people jumping pro contracts to play on the team. Even the manager was working under an assumed name. But they weren't playing me, and I felt I was in the wrong place."

His Wake Forest teammates would convince him that Angier was the right place. Ray Scarborough, another Wake Forest pitcher who had played in the Carolina textile league, was headed to Angier to play. But it was Dupree who got a phone call from Coach Caddell to go and recruit Byrne for Angier and the Tobacco State League.

Dupree coaxed Byrne with a variety of persuasive propositions. Byrne would have familiar faces around him, a competitive league to play in, and Angier just happened to have a nice Catholic family to board him. And, provided he could control that sometimes-wandering pitch of his, Byrne would get plenty of playing time. "They didn't pay me as much as they did in Concord, but that was alright," Byrne recalled. "I enjoyed being there and in the activity."

But a lefty is a lefty, and though Byrne had plenty of zip and movement on his pitches, that movement would often direct a pitch out of the strike zone — way out. While he continually stumped batters, he would occasionally get wild and drive his catcher crazy with pitches that swooped, spun, and sailed to the dirt or to the backstop.

"I warned them," Dupree recalled. "He may throw a little wild at times, but if he's on, he'll whoop you."

The proposal was good enough for Roy Williams and company, who had made arrangements to surround his Wake Forest recruits with a group of boys all the way from the Louisiana Bayou. Williams had tapped into the network of players through an old friend, Larry Gilbert, of New Orleans. Gilbert was managing the minor league New Orleans Pelicans, and had spied some Bayou talent that was worth more training in a decent semipro league.

Williams was persuasive enough to get three Louisiana boys to spend their summer in North Carolina. Gilbert sent up his son, outfielder Charlie, infielder Connie Ryan, and catcher Bob Dexheimer. Pitcher Al Jurisich would also make the trip from down south at mid-season.

Bennett Bullock had signed into the professional ranks and was playing at Tarboro of the Coastal Plain League. But his home town of Fuquay Springs had another young player with talent, Elmo Fish, who could take over at first base. Williams got wind of another talented Wake Forest outfielder and coaxed young Fred Eason of Kenly out of the semipro Central Carolina League to play in Angier. Leroy Spell, who had played for Angier's 1935 team and had bounced around various semipro circuits since, returned to play, and slugger Jeff Bolden was back.

What was shaping up here was a team with talent the likes of which the little town of Angier had not seen. For the pitching rotation, they would have Byrne, Scarborough, Jim Denning early in the year, another Wake Forest hurler Hal Farley, and later, Jurisich. The Bulls would also have Stuart Flythe, once a reputable Coastal Plain League pitcher who had even put in 40 innings in the majors. The infield shaped up with Dexhiemer, catcher; Fish, first base; Ryan, second base; Spell, short stop; and Dupree, third base. Gilbert, Eason, and Bolden were in the outfield. As the season progressed, Angier folks would come to appreciate this combination of talent. But it would be years before their true talents would be born out. Nine of these men would become professional players. Five would make it to the major leagues.

Though the Louisiana contingent made Angier a bit of an unknown entity in local circles, the Bulls were considered one of the top teams as the season began. But recruiting so many out-of-town boys had its price. There wasn't a lot of room for local boys on the Bulls payroll, considering the fact that the out-of-towners had to be paid to keep them around. James Denning would start the season in Angier but would later head to Sanford and then to Erwin. Larry Smith took his talents to Erwin, where the Redbirds were planning to repeat with the nucleus of Fulton Sessoms, Jim Sessoms, and Johnny Wilbourne. Erwin had defections of its own. Babe Bost, the Duke star, was now in Sanford, another town that was considered a contender for the league crown. Bost joined N.C. State pitcher Vic Holshouser and former professional hurler Setzer Weston. Future pro Ike Cross was in the outfield.

Opening day was delayed by rain, but on June 4, Angier officially began a baseball season that would be spiced with controversy and ruled by Tommy Byrne's pitching.

Appropriately, the season opened with Angier in a two-day home stand against the previous year's league rivals from Erwin. Angier took the first game, but was paid back the next day when Larry Smith beat his hometown and former team with a game-winning hit.

Byrne's debut was precarious at best. At worst, it was a downright disaster. He took the mound on June 10 against Laurinburg, and his untamed pitches were way off the mark.

"In college and semipro the strike zone was a little bigger. I threw well, but I didn't always know exactly where it was going," Byrne recalled.

Exactly how many pitches the Baltimore boy threw that day isn't clear, but he couldn't have stayed in very long. The Bulls trailed 10-0 before they even came into bat, and a total of five Bulls pitchers took the mound in Angier before they finished on the bad end of a 20-3 lashing. The warnings about this Byrne kid had proven true, and there was now considerable doubt as to whether he could make the grade.

But the speed and movement of the lefthander's pitches were irresistible, and Williams and O'Quinn decided to take the gamble.

It paid off.

Two days later Byrne got his second try on the mound, a rain-shortened home game against Sanford. Byrne pitched the full five innings and allowed three hits while striking out 11. The game went into the books as a 6-2 Angier victory.

A week later he took over for John Wills in the second inning and went the rest of the way, striking out 13 and allowing just two hits in a win at Zebulon.

Then on June 23, Mickey O'Quinn took his Bulls to his old stomping grounds in Erwin and sported his new recruit. Byrne pitched his first full nine innings and his teammates, Dexheimer, Dupree, and Ryan, provided big hits on the way to a 6-1 triumph.

The Kids Watching

Tommy Byrne and the Angier Bulls were off to the races, and the summer of 1938 would be a big one in Angier, particularly for the youngsters who were just getting their baseball legs. Frank, Mack, and Jim Gardner were eight, ten, and twelve years old that summer and were privileged among the baseball loving kids of the community. Since the baseball field was Gardner land, they'd get into the games for free, and their father, Mack Sr., would see to it that they'd make about every home game on the schedule and some on the road. Little Mack was even given the honor of being batboy for the Bulls.

Marshall and David Price were ten and eleven and made it to most of the games too. Their father's local barber shop was a meeting place for men of the community, and the baseball players were no exception. Many of the players would go there to dress for the game and shower afterward. Marshall got the heavy work of hauling their equipment the few blocks from the barber shop to the field, a difficult chore for anyone but a kid who adored baseball and worshipped the local heroes of the diamond.

"We watched every single move those guys made on the field," recalled Marshall. "It was our baseball education."

It was a grand summer for the town and its youngest baseball fans. Byrne and Scarborough took the mound week after week, commanding respect of the league's batters by embarrassing them. The other Wake Forest boys, the town boys, and the contingent from Louisiana cracked out high scores at the plate, a home run over the Angier park's short left field fence being an easy mark.

Angier grabbed the league lead in a tight race during the week before July 4th , a huge day on the baseball calendar.

That was the day when just about every town that had a home team had a home game. The common practice on July 4th was for teams to play a morning game on one home field and the afternoon portion of the doubleheader on the other team's turf. This required considerable travel for the teams and the fans who had cars and wanted to make the trip, but it afforded each team the opportunity for a healthy holiday gate.

Angier was swept by Zebulon that day and emerged with only a one-half-game lead in the standings, just above Sanford. Each team in the league had played nineteen or twenty games at this point and all were within five games of the lead.

All of this was secondary in the minds of Angier fans. Their objective was to see their team prevail over the Erwin team that had carried off the league banner in the bitter title series the year before. A satisfying triumph would come with a weekend series on July 9 and 10. Whether by necessity or just to get more fans out in Erwin, O'Quinn put himself on the mound to start the first game. It was a rare start for O'Quinn, and probably a risky one, but he managed to put in enough work to earn a win in Angier's 3-2 victory. Byrne took the mound the next day in Angier and struck out 12 on the way to a 6-1 victory over the Redbirds and a weekend sweep. The Bulls had beaten Erwin in the

82

season opener, had used rookie Byrne to stump their heavy-handed bats in two other games, and had even beaten the Redbirds with a pitcher who had once been considered almost property of Erwin. But Byrne was just getting started. He had four more wins in four outings in July before Erwin came to town on the 28th.

The Baltimore lefty struck out 18 and allowed four hits in a 4-0 shutout over the Redbirds. Erwin fans had just about had enough.

Byrne and Angier's winning ways were making enemies all over the league. By the end of July, Angier's one-game lead in the standings had been stretched to five games, and it seemed everywhere they went there was controversy. Angier hosted Fayetteville on August 6 to take on the textile gang, and somewhere in the midst of a scorching 13-10 duel, Fayetteville's manager Slim Watson protested that tar and/or tobacco juice were on the Angier bats. That game and the next day's 12-0 Angier victory at Faytex were both played under protest. The following week, a league ruling backed Fayetteville in its protest of the first game, and Faytex was given a win by forfeit.

The next week, Angier made the twelve-mile trip to Erwin, where another set of mill hands were waiting, still steaming from the whippings they had taken all season. And as might have been expected, things got out of hand.

It appeared things would go Angier's way again after the Bulls' first at bat, which produced a four-run rally. But Erwin swiftly turned things around; three runs in the first, two in the second, and after a big seven-run rally in the fourth inning, the home team led 12-5. And the

Redbirds did not let up.

One could imagine the scene at the Erwin park that day, with rabid fans, mostly mill workers, having their day against the rivals that had gotten the best of them all season. It isn't clear what the umpire's call or series of calls set off the first altercation, but the *News & Observer* story the next day used most of its short length describing the fray.

"At one stage of play the Angier team had only eight players in uniform. Jake [James] Denning, former Angier pitcher, was drafted to fill in. The Bulls lost Bob Dexheimer, their only catcher, when base umpire Ray Caldwell decided that Bob's yelling from the dugout was unpleasant. They later lost Elmo Fish, infielder, when plate umpire Arrington decided Fish appeared unhappy about being called out at the plate." [26] Arrington's name would later come up in a spat during a play-off game in Angier.

Whatever close calls were disputed may have been secondary to the fact that Erwin was finally stomping Angier. The Redbirds were on their way to a 20-6 shellacking of the Bulls, and the out-of-control game, with the hooting and hollering of 500 or more mill workers, not to mention the verbal outpouring from the opposing dugout, were probably a little much for the Bulls.

With all of the commotion, the first four innings of the game took two hours. There were no newspaper accounts or records of any out-and-out brawls during or after the confrontations, but the bad blood between the rivals had certainly reached boiling point.

This sort of sniffing and stomping did nothing for semipro baseball's reputation except to put lines at the ticket table. A dispute-free semipro baseball season was almost unheard of. If a league put a ban on fighting, punctuated with a $5 fine, fans would simply pass the hat at the game — just in case one of theirs had to stand up for the team. [27] Pitchers liked to pitch at home, not just because of the fanatical support, but because they knew they could get the baseballs fixed just right. A phonograph needle slid into the stitches worked nicely if a pitcher knew how to work it. [28] Under the soft lights in a town such as Sanford, a hard hit might get lost in the darkness and then magically appear in an outfielder's hands for the play back to the infield. [29] Some of these shenanigans would be picked up by umpires. Some wouldn't. League rules were made to be broken, and fiery disputes on the field would light a torch that would burn in fans' memories until the next game. It all had farmers and textile workers scraping the bottoms of their pockets and coffee cans for ticket money.

During all of this turmoil, though, the thing that had Angier fans most excited was Tommy Byrne's pitching. In late July he mounted a strikeout-filled run that would amaze fans, embarrass batters, and carry the Bulls to the playoffs.

In July he posted two eighteen-strikeout performances, followed by a seventeen-strikeout showing in the first week of August. On August 10, Lefty Byrne fanned eighteen batters again in a four-hit victory over Zebulon.

"My ball naturally had a lot of movement. It would rise and go into left-handed hitters and away from right-handed hitters. And once in a while, I would get on top of it, and the ball would sail in, and a right-hander thinks it's gonna be out over the plate, and it's in there on the elbow. That's the kind of pitch I had in high school, college, and on up into the majors."

At Angier's park it became a custom for fans to make note of each Byrne strikeout.

"We used to sit in those old wooden bleachers," said Jim Gardner, who was age eight that year. "Everybody had a pocket knife, and you'd make a notch on that seat every time Byrne would get a strikeout. After the game you could go down those bleachers and see just lines and lines of those notches people had made."

And Byrne's bat was almost as dangerous as his fastball. Even at the bottom of the order, he was a threat to move runners or keep a rally alive. "To me, hitting was fun. Pitching was more like work," he said.

Fred Eason, who would later post two professional seasons batting .300 or better, recalled being disappointed once when O'Quinn gave Byrne the nod to pinch hit in Eason's place with the bases loaded and the game on the line. "Of course, Tommy lined one to the wall and won the game for us." Eason would not be alone. It was a harbinger. In later years, Byrne would be placed as high as sixth in the New York Yankees batting order, almost unheard of for pitchers, even in the 1940s.

But it was pure pitching that Tobacco State League fans latched onto when Byrne was on the mound during that August. On the 21st, as the season wound down and Sanford was making a last gasp for the

86

league pennant, 1,500 fans showed up in Angier to see the Wake Forest lefty continue his astonishing string. Byrne delivered with a seventeen-strikeout show and a one-hit triumph.

He had an 11-2 record at this point and was clearly pitching out of his league. He had led his team to a league-leading 31-16 record, four and one-half games in front of the Sanford Spinners. The Angier fans were seeing a player on his way to becoming a legitimate major league star.

Byrne was truly Mickey O'Quinn's ace in the hole, and the manager rode him as far as he could. Byrne pitched a five-hit win over Zebulon on August 26, striking out fifteen batters, to continue his winning ways.

Angier took a 16-2 victory over Fayetteville Faytex on the final day of the season and easily ended up with the league pennant. But there was plenty of post-season left, and the Tobacco State League officials tried their best to have as much as possible left to entertain fans and to make sure the league's coffers could support the prospects of another year.

First, the league scheduled a post-season all-star game, hosted by the previous year's champion, Erwin. It featured the best players from the North — Angier, Erwin, and Zebulon — taking on the top players from Faytex, Laurinburg, and Sanford. The 20-member North squad included Angier's Byrne, O'Quinn, Dupree, Spell, Ryan, Gilbert, and Dexheimer. One of the features of the game was league president Chick Doak's announcement that all six of the league's teams would be involved in the playoffs. This would seem strange, to award a team a chance at the post-season playoff crown no matter how badly it performed during the season. But again, the prospect of extra ticket sales to help balance the books would have trumped the fairness of giving the top four teams the privilege of being the only ones in the post-season. And two of the better teams in the league, Erwin and Angier, had reportedly insisted on the six-team playoff, probably because they each figured they had a good shot at making the finals and getting that many more home dates and because they probably had the highest player payrolls in the league. 30

With this playoff plan, two other problems arose to which unusual and somewhat confusing solutions were applied. First was the simple issue of having six teams, as opposed to having four, in a tournament/playoff format. A simple solution would have been to give the top two teams in the league byes, or exemptions, for the first round of the playoffs. But rather than deny the best teams the extra money, all six teams played the first round and a bye was awarded in the second round. Since the first-place team, Angier, had lobbied for the six-team format, the winner of the Sanford-Laurinburg series would be awarded the second-round bye. Then the league officials had to deal with the sheer length of the playoffs. The rosters were made up of college students, and the fall semester was quickly approaching. If two best-of-five series and one best-of-seven series were played, the championship wouldn't be decided until mid-to-late September, and the students, particularly the ones from out of state, would be hard-pressed to attend their first classes.

The solution was to cut the second-round series to a best-of-three, and the teams would play every day it didn't rain. The playoffs would be finished by September 9.

The first round of the playoffs shaped up pretty much as expected, though Angier got a scare from Zebulon. Byrne took the mound in the opener at home and fanned 15 in a five-hit victory. The Bulls' bats roared and Angier won, 12-2. But things became edgy for Angier fans when Zebulon claimed a 9-8 win at home and then went to Angier to win 9-6. It put the pennant winners on the verge of elimination. But Byrne took the mound again and struck out fourteen batters, pacing Angier to a 2-1 win to tie the series. The very next day, O'Quinn turned to his ace lefty once again. Pitching without even a day's rest was an unusual feat in those days, but not unheard of. The good pitchers were the durable ones. Pitching a nine-inning game was the rule rather than the exception, and if a good lefthander was what was needed the next day, then that was what the manager went with. Besides, Byrne was not the type to say no to his manager when given a chance to start the series-deciding game.

So Byrne took the mound for the second straight day and made the home folks happy by again striking out fourteen batters and leading the Bulls to an 8-3 victory and triumph in the first-round series.

Trouble was, the playoffs continued the next day, and Erwin was waiting, after having dispensed of Faytex in the first round. Byrne, whose arm was numb by now, was certainly not available, and O'Quinn was having to fill in other gaps on the team because many of the college players and school teachers were having to prepare for the fall term. The Bulls called on Ed Johnson, who had pitched for Erwin in past seasons, to take the mound against his old team in the first of the best-of-three series. It worked to the tune of a 6-3 win at Erwin. The series went to Angier the next day, and Jurisich was on the hill to help give Angier an 8-1 victory and the clincher against Erwin's star hurler, Johnny Wilbourne.

With their chief rivals out of the way, Angier now faced a Sanford team that was well-rested because of the second-round bye.

It appeared the grind of having played seven straight days had worn on the Angier team when they ventured to Sanford to start the best-of-seven title series against the Spinners. Jim Denning started the game for the Bulls and ran into trouble early. The Spinners cruised to a 13-2 win.

A rainy day brought a merciful break to the weary Angier team. But things didn't get much better for the Bulls the next day at home, not even with Tommy Byrne on the mound. Though Byrne struck out fifteen batters, he surrendered twelve hits and suffered through a 9-5 loss to the Spinners.

However, Angier turned the tables over the next three days, winning three straight games to take a 3-2 edge in the series. In the closest of those games, Mickey O'Quinn, in a desperate pitching situation, had to put himself on the mound with one out in the last inning and the tying run on second base. He ended the game by fanning two straight batters.

Angier's three-game sweep set up an opportunity for Byrne to clinch the title on Angier's home field. But with just six outs to go for Angier to match its regular-season Tobacco State League pennant with the league playoff championship, things went a little haywire. Byrne was clinging to a 2-1 lead in the eighth inning when a walk and a couple of singles had the lefty in a bases-loaded jam with two down. Then came disaster. One of Byrne's testy pitches sailed on him and got past Dexheimer. The Sanford base runners took off. One run scored, and Dexheimer in the rush to make the play, threw wild and allowed another run in. Sanford led 3-2.

That rally would prove to finish the Bulls for the day, but the sideshow to the whole thing was the commotion created by challenges to the umpiring. A call at first base in the middle of that eighth-inning rally brought O'Quinn out of the dugout and into the face of base umpire W.H. Arrington. The umpire was the same one who had ejected so many Angier players in Erwin a few weeks earlier, and apparently the hard feelings had not worn off. Things only got worse for Byrne, Angier, and even Arrington. The Spinners would end up with five runs in the final two innings, and Angier, down 6-3, would not even get to finish its half of the ninth. The game was reported in *The News & Observer* to have been called for darkness. But the story also gives clues to a much more disturbing situation:

"After the game, Angier's Big Jeff Bolden shouldered a bat and made threatening gestures at Umpire Arrington. A bit of persuasion was necessary to change Jeff's ideas, and a police escort accompanied

Arrington from the park after some fans decided that Jeff's ideas were excellent and decided to join him." [31]

The whole scene had turned particularly ugly, even for semipro baseball. But typical of semipro ball, the inmates were pretty much in charge of the cellblock. There is no indication that Bolden was suspended or fined as a result of the incident. Rather, the league ruled that the umpire would not be calling the next game, probably more out of consideration for his safety than anything else.

Angier and Byrne were unable to clinch the league title at home and now had to travel to Sanford for the seventh and deciding game without Byrne on the mound. The Bulls turned to Al Jurisich. The New Orleans hurler had been on the mound to clinch the Erwin series and had beaten the Spinners just two days before.

Jurisich faced Roy Boles, a sturdy performer who was on his way to a successful 11-year professional career.

But Jurisich got plenty of help from his Bulls teammates, still steaming from the previous day's confrontation. Tally Dupree cracked a homer on the first pitch of the game, and it was Angier's game from there. Dupree smacked another round-tripper in the second, and Bolden and Eason added homers as Angier piled on four more runs. The Bulls pounded out 12 hits that day, Jurisich got his second win of the series, and the 9-3 win gave Angier its first Tobacco State League crown.

The trip from Lee County back to Angier was a gleeful one for the young men who had brought a league crown to the little town. And for the younger kids who worshipped them, it was as if Christmas had come early. Nobody — not Erwin, not Sanford — nobody had as good a town ball team as we did, the Angier kids could say. For them, even the big league stars of the day, Lou Gehrig, Joe DiMaggio, Bill Dickey, Jimmie Foxx, and Hank Greenberg, couldn't match Ryan, Dupree, Spell, Bolden, Fish, Gilbert, Eason, Dexheimer, Scarborough, Jurisich, and Tommy Byrne. They were the names that would pop up when these boys remembered their own glory years of baseball. They were the players who inspired the youngsters to relish the notion of one day going to bat themselves.

For the town itself, Angier's claim of a small-town baseball reputation had been solidified with a league pennant and a playoff title.

Tommy Byrne

Tommy Byrne was the star of the 1938 Angier Bulls, who won the Tobacco State League title. But his claim to fame would come later, during his service with the New York Yankees. He would return to Angier in 1958 to play with the semipro Angier Braves of the Tobacco State League.

(Photo courtesy of Tommy Byrne)

Chapter 6 - Farewell - For Now

Re-tooling and Re-loading

The triumphant 1938 season left an impression on folks in and around Angier, particularly the young kids who made the players their personal heroes. But the season made a mark on some of those players, too. It gave Tommy Byrne plenty of mound work and helped him develop as a durable, hard-throwing and hard-hitting star. And being a star helped him develop more than the characteristically nebulous attachment semipro players had for their towns. The little town of Angier, North Carolina, was alright in Tommy Byrne's thinking. And he would not forget it.

But, as was the case with these wanderers of semipro ball, a new season often meant playing in a new town. Another place to play was always on the horizon, a place that offered as much in excitement and more in wages.

That's why the town team of one year was often nothing like the town team of the next. And that's why Angier's summer of triumph would be hard to repeat in 1939.

Byrne and Ray Scarborough went to play in Roanoke Rapids, which had a nice payroll and a reputation. The team, led by their old Wake Forest teammate Joe Talley, had won the four-year-old state semipro tournament in 1938 and had gone all the way to Wichita to play in a national tournament. The National Baseball Congress's state and national tournament setup was quickly becoming an attraction to town semipro teams who wanted to prove their worth at a higher level and get their players some exposure to professional scouts that gathered at these venues. So Byrne and Scarborough were off to prove themselves.

Charlie Gilbert and Al Jurisich took the professional route, Jurisich taking up work near home in the Evangeline League, working his way toward the New Orleans Pelicans and, after wartime service, a place on the St. Louis Cardinals roster. He would play for the Cardinals and the Philadelphia Phillies from 1944 through 1947. Gilbert began working on a .317 batting average in Nashville. The next year he'd be in Brooklyn to start a five-year major league career.

Tally Dupree sort of wandered to and from the professional ranks. He signed a contract to play with the Kinston Eagles of the Coastal Plain League, but found the minor-league life and a .179 batting average wasn't to his liking. He returned to Angier to play for part of June, but that got him and the Bulls in trouble. Since he had played more than ten games professionally in the same season, Dupree was ruled ineligible by the Tobacco State League. The Bulls were ordered to forfeit two games because of his services. He later went to Elm City and played for a semipro paycheck, but would be back in an Angier uniform before the year was out, apparently far enough from professional pay to make him eligible for the league again.

Fred Eason and Leroy Spell would be picked up by Sanford. Connie Ryan and Elmo Fish stayed in Angier for at least part of the 1939 season. And slugger Jeff Bolden just took off to parts unknown, maybe to any of the semipro outfits from North Carolina to his home in Georgia.

It would indeed be tough for Angier to defend its title, particularly considering the threat that was brewing in the town that had been the bridesmaid the year before — Sanford. Sanford had built a new ball park — with lights — and the Spinners' new owner, brick mogul Lewis Isenhour, was determined to fill it with top players. He would do this partly at the expense of Angier, where he went and swiped Eason and Spell. He also grabbed up three Duke stars for his infield, Eddie Shokes, Glenn Price, and Crash Davis.

Shokes and Davis were major league prospects. Shokes would be the target of a bidding war between the Reds and the Yankees the next year, and Davis was a year from the majors, not to mention more in the minor leagues, and the honor of having his name memorialized in the film "Bull Durham."

But Isenhour and his manager, Zeb Harrington, needed good pitching to carry the league. They started the season with veterans Setzer Weston and Floyd Elliott as well as high-school fireballer Lefty Ripple.

But before the season was out, they would have their own equivalent of Tommy Byrne. Porter Vaughan, a Virginia boy who played for the University of Richmond and was also on his way to the majors, would be the answer to the town's pitching prayers.

Angier's 1939 Bulls were nothing to compare. They started the season with O'Quinn, Dexheimer, Fish, Ryan, and a bunch of unknown, untested youngsters. The team again had a bit of a Cajun kick to it, with Dexheimer bringing another contingent of Louisiana players with him.

Dexheimer was named Angier's manager before the year started, but he would be called away at the behest of Doc Smith. It seems Smith was in a jam at the backstop position down in New Bern, and called Dexheimer to fill in. Dexheimer went to New Bern, but only for about three weeks. The Tulane University star, after finding that playing under the lights was not to his liking, was back in Angier by June 20. Apparently he did not play the ten games of professional ball that would have gotten the Bulls in trouble as in the Dupree case.

The Louisiana connection was maintained with pitchers John Clower and John Dirman and fielder Hal Bodney, a Tulane football star. The Bulls would get Renfro "Peanut" Doak from N.C. State and other Raleigh boys, Jack Holt and Aubry Pittman, who played at Oak Ridge Military Academy. Price Ferguson, another pitcher with professional potential, was also on the Bulls squad, and Mike Crawford, the hometown boy of years past, was back with the team.

Erwin returned pitchers Bill Averette, Johnny Wilbourne, and infielder Babe Bost, the Duke player who would manage the team. But it was almost Sanford's title before the season started.

Angier and Erwin might have had better teams had some of the best young talent not been on the powerful Harnett American Legion Juniors team. They included Angier high schoolers Herndon Wells, an infielder; James House, a pitcher; and Kenneth Jackson, a catcher.

Fayetteville and Laurinburg, who had finished in the last two spots in the league standings the year before, did not enter the Tobacco State League in 1939. So the league went with the foursome of Angier, Erwin, Sanford, and Zebulon.

The prospects were good for the upcoming league season. Baseball was beginning to pick back up where it left off before the Depression. The minor leagues were returning to life. The North State League had grabbed up the textile teams of the piedmont after the Carolina League's independent professional experiment had collapsed under the crush of high salaries and threats from organized baseball. The Coastal Plain League was cruising along in the tobacco market towns of the east, and the Piedmont League had picked up Rocky Mount, Asheville, Charlotte, and Durham. North Carolina now fielded twenty-three minor-league teams. [32]

The latest upshot of professional baseball left the Tobacco State League as one of the few semipro leagues in the state that made it worthwhile to the traveling mercenaries and college players. *The News & Observer* billed the TSL "the last survivor of North Carolina's fast semipro circuits," but that may have been stretching the truth, since there were still plenty of semipro leagues in the state. But the Tobacco State

League was still a close neighbor to Raleigh, Durham, and Chapel Hill, where much of the state's college talent was.

The league opened its five-day-a-week, sixty-game, June-through-August season with high hopes of repeating the previous year's success.

Angier opened on June 7 with an 8-3 home victory over Zebulon. But for the rest of the year, the Bulls could do no more than flirt with second place in the league. They tried to boost their hitting by acquiring Paul Brotherton and former N.C. State player Adolph Honeycutt, two pro prospects. And after the American Legion juniors season, they gave Elmo Fish's brother, Pate, a tryout along with Kenneth Jackson, the young catcher who was a sure shot to follow in Doc Smith's footsteps as the next Angier boy to star at the position. The Bulls also brought pitcher Bryan Hammett up from Louisiana.

But the big deal of the season came in the final two weeks when Tommy Byrne and Ray Scarborough finished their duties at Roanoke Rapids and hustled back down to Angier for service. When team boss Roy Williams pulled up to Angier's park with the two stars for a game in mid-August, Angier folks thought their prayers had been answered. The plans Byrne and Scarborough had for making a trip to Wichita for the National Baseball Congress tournament had not panned out. Strangely enough, Sanford would be the team to win the state semipro title. The Spinners, however, would decline the trip to the national tournament in Wichita, choosing to stay to clinch the TSL pennant instead.

Angier's 1938 pitching stars would do their best to boost the town's hopes in 1939. Byrne struck out a whopping twenty-two batters in a win over Zebulon, and Scarborough notched a couple of wins over Erwin before the regular season was done.

But it was too late. Nobody in the league could deal with Isenhour's Sanford squad. The Spinners stomped off with the league pennant, finishing with a 37-16 record, nine and one-half games in front of Erwin and thirteen and one-half in front of Angier.

Angier was matched with the powerful Spinners in the first round of the playoffs, still holding hope that, with renewed talent, they could pull an upset. But in the first game of the best-of-five series, the Spinners knocked the Bulls back on their heels. Their star fireballer, Porter Vaughan, went up against Byrne and out-dueled him in a 2-1 test of wills. The result irked Angier fans even more, since it was former Bulls shortstop Leroy Spell who hit the winning homer for the Spinners. Then Bryan Hammett lost a 4-2 decision the next night, and Scarborough was beaten 5-3 the following night, a sweep for the Spinners.   Sanford went on to plow through Erwin for the 1939 league title.

Byrne Moves On

The 1939 season would be the last for Tommy Byrne in an Angier uniform, at least for a while. The following summer would be a bittersweet one for the young lefthander. After his junior year at Wake Forest, Byrne could see a real future in baseball. He had been one of the leading pitchers among the Big Five schools and had actually led the league in hitting. Baltimore native and New York Yankee scout Gene McCann was among the major league representatives to follow Byrne throughout his college years and figured the time was ripe for taking him to the next level. In July of 1940 the Yankees offered Byrne an unprecedented $10,000 signing bonus. He was attending summer school at Blackstone College in Virginia — where he was playing semipro ball — and knew he could gather enough credits to take advantage of the offer and get his degree after a few winters. "I was just thinking about getting married and looking after my mother and other things. And I would come back to school. I had to come back three winters to get my degree."

But the good news was tempered by of the death of his college coach, John Caddell. He was able to tell the ailing coach of his good fortune with the Yankees. But days later, Byrne would be a pall bearer at Caddell's funeral.

Byrne was called to play at the Yankees affiliate in Newark, where he spent three seasons. By 1943, the Baltimore lefty would be a rookie in the dugout at Yankee Stadium, and after World War II, he would become a regular in pinstripes.

But Byrne would not forget Wake Forest College, the state of North Carolina, or the town of Angier, where he had honed his talents to the delight of the local fans.

He would long remember the summer of '38, the season of dazzling performances that helped him find his potential as a pitcher, and he would make friendships that would last for years. Byrne and Elmo

Fish, the boy from Fuquay Springs who had anchored first base in 1938, hooked up almost immediately. Fish would not let Byrne forget those Tobacco State League days. He followed Byrne through his years of pro baseball, reading clips, watching newsreels, and even showing up at the gates of major league parks on the east coast. Byrne practically came to expect to see Fish in Philadelphia, Washington, or even at Yankee Stadium, waiting with a smile and a handshake and always trying to get Tommy in on a business venture. The friendship and Fish's persistence would pay off years later. And Tommy Byrne's connections with the community would be even more closely bound. He met Mary Sue Nichols of nearby Coats during his playing days at Angier. They would marry in 1940.

Byrne would also leave a lasting impression on Angier and the crowd of young boys who never forgot and never waned in their desire to play baseball. He and the Angier players who brought home the town's first Tobacco State League title would be in the minds of those kids as they strove years later to become hometown heroes on their own.

But the more immediate future held sacrifice for the young boys and their big brothers, who would have to ditch baseball for war.

Webster Lupton

Chapter 7 - Baseball Changes Uniforms

War Brings Summers of Sacrifice

Baseball had recovered from the Depression by the end of the 1930s. Towns were picking up minor league teams again, and people were showing up for games. From the hills to the plains, semipro baseball was clinging to its roots in the rural areas of North Carolina. As usual, baseball followed the surrounding economy. Rural North Carolina's tobacco farmers got a boost from the price controls implemented in the mid-1930s, which put a little more money back in their pockets.

But it seemed that each time baseball made a comeback, there was something around the corner that determined its fate. The decade of the '40s would bring more change. By September of 1939, Hitler had begun his conquest of Europe, and it would soon become clear that the United States would have to play a role in saving the continent. By June of 1940, that conquest had reached Paris, and by mid-summer England would be battling for survival. From there on, things would be different in America, and baseball would begin feeling a sting.

For the next five years, there would be shortages of just about everything. As far as baseball was concerned, the shortages started with manpower. Draft notices began arriving in October of 1940, and with their arrival young men began departing, many of them handing over their baseball gloves to their little brothers — or sons.

With all sorts of rationing and recycling, and with Americans turning their attention to an impending war, recreations such as baseball began moving lower on the priority scale of everyday life. Everything became one big contribution to the war effort.

The Gardner, Price, and most of the Adams boys were reaching their teens now, and they knew the meaning of sacrifice. If the Depression hadn't taught them, baseball had. They knew a sacrifice was when a batter bunted or hit a long fly to score or advance a runner. They knew sacrifice meant giving something up for the good of the team. That's why they would come to accept the fact that there was no more baseball in town and that even if there was, many couldn't play or even watch. They would understand it when Angier High School discontinued athletics, denying them a chance at their first organized baseball. The nation couldn't afford the fuel and tires consumed by rural schools for athletics. If a young player was good enough, maybe he could make the county American Legion team, which managed to stay active. Otherwise, baseball meant heading back to the sandlots where they had learned. But that was alright with the teens around Angier. It was about all they had known. They would still have to wait to play in a real league, wait for the time when Angier would have another town team, if ever.

None of the heroes the boys had come to love were back for the summer of 1940 because Angier could not field a league baseball team. Oh, they could read the paper and find out that Tommy Byrne had signed with the Yankees, Ray Scarborough with the Senators, Charlie Gilbert with the Dodgers, or that Al Jurisich was now in the Cardinals chain.

But 1940 would not be a memorable year for baseball in town. Angier had represented itself pretty well in organized baseball for a small town. But a town of a thousand or so just about had to have the best team in the league to bring out fans game after game and to afford the cost of a fast semipro league. The 25-31 record the Bulls posted in 1939 was not much of a draw for local fans.

And besides all of the sacrifices of the oncoming war, there was a new trend circulating in the baseball world, one that would unfortunately keep Angier in the background of semipro ball. That was the onset of the night game. Lights had come to the major leagues in 1935, and even before that in North Carolina's minor league and semiprofessional ranks. Forest City, a semipro town in the western part of the state, played its first night baseball game in May of 1932. [33] Asheville's and Greensboro's minor league teams were playing under the lights in the early 1930s also. At least one TSL team, Sanford, had played night games in 1939. The convenience that night games offered working people, and the more cool, comfortable setting of night baseball, were hard for the bigger towns to resist. The trend caught on quickly.

It was not altogether an easy transition. Lights offered problems in the early years. First of all, baseball was, and always had been, a day game to most people. Just the notion of playing at night was a sort of heresy to traditionalists. The early lighting systems were also hazards of sorts. The hot, high-intensity bulbs were very sensitive to moisture and would pop if a few drops of rain hit them. Even the threat of a thunderstorm would mean the lights would often have to be cut off, even in the middle of a game. And the lights were simply not very bright, which would lead to all sorts of shenanigans on the field. Nevertheless, night baseball stuck, and the expense of putting up lights left Angier behind.

Angier still fielded a town team in 1940, playing only occasional games and missing the stardom that Doc Smith, Bill Holland, Woody Upchurch, and the 1938 gang had provided. But fans in Angier kept an ear to the baseball goings on, and there was enough elsewhere to keep them interested. They kept attuned to the Tobacco State League. The 1940 league adopted the night game with Raleigh, Sanford, Erwin, and the Moore County town of Hemp joining. Many of the players with which Angier fans had become familiar were still in the league. Crash Davis, Eddie Shokes, and Zeb Harrington were still in Sanford, and Erwin still had players such as Angier's Tally Dupree and former American Legion star Oliver Bass. One month into the season, Raleigh would hire Doc Smith to manage its squad, and Doc would recruit some former Angier players.

All of this didn't make the league a total success. It still only had four teams, and signs of instability began to show up relatively early. In June, the Raleigh team backed out of the league. The Raleigh Luckies had both sponsorship and manpower from the American Tobacco Company plant in Durham. On June 19, the team announced that it was leaving the league. Seaboard Air Line stepped in as a sponsor. The new Raleigh Meteors then hired Smith, whose 1939 season in New Bern had been a disappointment. Smith had to start the Raleigh team practically from scratch, and he went after former Angier stars John Clower, Tally Dupree (now with Erwin) and Leroy Spell, which brought some Angier fans to Raleigh's Devereaux Meadow.

That summer would be one of the first to show the wear of the oncoming war. Attendance was down across the board. The rising ticket price took its toll, as the first of a series federal defense taxes was being assessed. Tobacco State League ticket prices went from thirty-five cents to forty cents because of the tax, not to mention a levy on gasoline and tobacco, both of which affected the locals.

The issue that hurt Sanford's TSL participation actually came in the form of success. The team won the state semipro baseball tournament in July of that year and was seriously considering making the trip to Wichita, Kansas, this time, rather than staying to win the local league title. This combination of things added up to a July 24 announcement that the Tobacco State League was closing its doors, effective immediately. Sanford played a five-game title series with Erwin in early August, winning three games to two. Then the Spinners went on to the national tournament in Wichita and placed fourth, one of the best showings ever for a North Carolina team.

When the Tobacco Sate League pulled up stakes, folks in Angier and Harnett County turned their attention to the county's American Legion baseball team. The Harnett Hornets, which had a successful season in 1939 with a lineup including Angier boys Kenneth Jackson, James House, and Herndon Wells, were on their way to an even better showing by August of 1940. Coach Bill Averette's team still had Jackson and House, along with Shamrock Denning, Billy Holmes, Bobby Bryan, J.L. Reardon, and a number of other talented players from around the county. An indication of the talent on that team was borne out after the war when as many as twelve of its players found places on professional rosters. [34] Denning climbed all the way to Class B in the minor leagues.

The team emerged with a title in a district that included teams from Raleigh and Wilmington, and it roared through the early playoff rounds into the state title series. It ran into a strong Albemarle team in the state finals and lost the series four games to two. Albemarle went on to win the national Legion title that year.

The American Legion teams in Harnett County would continue to be competitive during the war years and would be about the only source of organized play for high school-aged boys during that time period. The team would reach the eastern district finals in 1943 under Coach J.R. "Dick" Cathey. Frank Gardner would find a place to play in 1944 with the Legion team, and in 1945 he would be coached by Doc Smith on the Legion squad. It would be just about his only outlet to organized baseball, but it would help him learn. Legion ball was about all Harnett

County fans had left in the early 1940s. The summer of 1940 would be the last in which most young men were at home.

In the summer of 1941, the summer before Pearl Harbor, most of baseball slowed even more, particularly in small towns. There was no Tobacco State League that season, and minor league teams were beginning to suffer. Three semipro leagues were prevalent in the area that season. Teams from old TSL stomping grounds, Erwin, Dunn, Benson, and Selma found homes in the Eastern Carolina League, the Central Carolina League, or the Central State League, none of which was considered to be on the level of the old Tobacco State.

Sanford bucked the trend and took its baseball success a step further in 1941. It entered the professional Class D Bi-State League, the first of two years it would have a minor league team before war finished the league altogether. It was that year that the Spinners signed Orville "Hank" Nesselrode, a hard hitting outfielder, who had been tearing up the minors. Nesselrode had batted .369 for South Boston, Virginia, the year before and had jumped all the way to the Class A1 Texas League, where his numbers fell off a bit. Sanford latched onto him July 7, and the outfielder cranked out a .320 average for the next forty-nine games. Folks in Sanford came to like Nesselrode so much that his wedding in the middle of an August 4 game that year drew 3,500 folks to Temple Park, the largest crowd in the town's baseball history. [35] After the war, Nesselrode would play three more professional seasons in Sanford.

After 1941, minor leagues continued to dwindle. In 1942, the number of league teams in North Carolina dropped from twenty-five to eighteen, then to just one — Durham — in '43. By the time 1944 rolled around, there would be a period when North Carolina would not have a single minor league team.

But baseball, as usual, never really died out during the war years. Nationwide, the game had a friend in Washington, D.C. Just as he had done during the Depression, President Franklin Roosevelt encouraged the continuance of the major league game during the war years, and it survived, though hurting a bit for manpower and talent.

And when the boys went overseas, baseball followed. Thanks to various efforts by major league teams, collection drives sent gloves, balls, and bats to troops overseas so that during their spare moments, soldiers could convert the flat spaces of England, France, or the Philippines into temporary baseball diamonds. Decks of aircraft carriers were almost big enough for full-fledged games, excluding the long ball. It was certainly common for a game of pitch and catch to start up on the deck of a ship. And ports of call meant other units against which to compete. It was one thing boys from New York, Wisconsin, Montana, or North Carolina all had in common.

At home, in places outside of the major league cities — places such as North Carolina — baseball simply changed uniforms. Though the traditional semipro town teams were pretty much off the board, World War II brought another interesting baseball phenomenon to the state — military teams. Military units had been fielding baseball teams for years. In fact, the Civil War is considered one of the springboards for the spread of the game's popularity. The fact was that military units were like any other concentration of American men — put fifty or so together and there would be a pretty good baseball team in there somewhere.

In the early and mid-1930s, Fort Bragg artillery units regularly played Angier teams and others in the area. Now, as the entire nation's manpower mobilized, there were plenty of guys at military posts looking for baseball games or anything else to distract them from the notion of dodging bullets. Fayetteville and Fort Bragg, of course, were crawling with manpower. Tank battalions, artillery units, infantry units, when they had spare time from training, were invading the countryside looking for teams to play. Of course, since most of the town men were themselves in the service, the units ended up playing each other. The Fort Bragg Reception Center team fielded a particularly strong lineup of former area college players, including Wake Forest star Fred McCall.

But Bragg wasn't the only baseball home during those years. In 1942, the Navy established a pre-flight school at the University of North Carolina to train pilots. It was an extensive project in Chapel Hill. The campus had to make room for about 1,800 cadets, so the college expanded Woollen Gymnasium, and built a new infirmary, recreation center (Navy Hall), and athletic field. The first cadets arrived in May of 1942.

Athletics were a big part of the program, and in the summer that meant baseball. The Navy Pre-flight School Cloudbusters came into being and played in a circuit called the Ration League with teams from local colleges. Proceeds from the games went to the war effort. [36]

The thing that made the Cloudbusters so popular was a roster that included some of the biggest names in baseball. Ted Williams played for the team, not to mention other major leaguers such as Johnny Pesky of the Red Sox, Johnny Sain and Louis Bremp of the Braves, Joe Coleman of the Athletics, and Buddy Hassett of the Yankees. This assemblage of players probably made the team one of the best baseball units ever to base itself in North Carolina.

With so much rationing and shortages, it was hard getting people to games during the war, but people found a way to beg, borrow, or steal to get to see the major leaguers on display. The Ration League games reportedly drew good numbers. And when the Norfolk Naval Air Station team was in town that was a must-see for fans who could find the extra fuel. That team included Peewee Reese and Hugh Casey of the Dodgers, Murray Franklin of the Tigers, and local favorites Eddie Shokes and Crash Davis, former Duke and Tobacco State League players.

The two teams played several games in North Carolina in 1943, with no fewer than 3,000 showing up at each game. One of the biggest games was July 14, in Raleigh's Devereaux Meadow, when 7,000 showed up and saw the Norfolk crew dump the flyboys, 4-2. The United War Fund benefited to the tune of $1,100. [37]

In Angier, neither the school field nor the park on Highway 210 saw much action during the war. Angier managed to get up a team in 1943 with Warren Gardner, Lee Brown, and Cadvil Adams as the featured players, but if they couldn't find an Army outfit or an industry team to play, Angier was pretty much out of business. And as the war continued, the boys of prime playing age left town for military service.

114

Kenneth Jackson, Tally Dupree, and some of the Adams boys would go. The younger town boys simply had to wait and hope for better days. This war-era baseball was just enough to keep that hope alive. With all the cutbacks and restrictions, the baseball scene faded but didn't go away.

Angier itself would go six summers without any league baseball. But the kids who had spent a good part of their teen years watching a war would get another jolt of baseball inspiration they hardly expected to see.

Webster Lupton

American Legion Baseball Team
Harnett County
1939

1939 Harnett American Legion team

The Harnett American Legion juniors teams would be competitve thoughout the 1940s due largely to the wealth of talent in the county. Six members of this 1939 team would go on to play professional baseball. Front row, left to right, are George Jackson, Mitchell Currin, Sheppard Bryan, Kenneth Jackson, Billy Holmes, and Buck Jones. Back row: Carl Fitchett, Granville "Shamrock" Denning, Herndon Wells, Joe Woodworth, James House, Frank McLeod, Art Vann, J.L. Reardon, Troy Godwin, and Coach Bill Averette. Three members of the team, House, Wells, and Kenneth Jackson, were from Angier. The 1940 Harnett Hornets went to the state finals, losing to the eventual national champion, Albemarle.

(Photo courtesy of Janie Jackson)

Chapter 8 - A Shot at the Pros

A New Game, A Sterling Performance, An Amazing Finish

Spring always meant something to Angier. Like any other rural community, it brought the hope and renewal for the growing season. And like any other baseball-loving community, it brought the same type of hope and renewal for the home team. But spring of 1946 arrived with more than just the normal hope for a good growing season and a good baseball team. World War II was over, and Americans could get on with their lives newly emerged from under the clouds of world conflict. America had a lot of catching up to do in the baseball world, and now there was nothing holding it back — no Depression, no war — nothing.

Things would never quite be the same as before the war; the lives that had not been lost had certainly been changed. But baseball was to follow the prosperity of the rest of the nation. As far as fans and players were concerned, it was time to throw the first pitch, hit the first homer, win the first game. Baseball was, after all, still America's game. The game bounded back after the war with an unprecedented boom. Professional baseball turned into something akin to a post-war fad. Everyone wanted in on the action. Organized baseball began grabbing up territory like a land rush, and every town, it seemed, was fertile ground for a pro team.

The National Association of Professional Baseball Leagues saw its membership swell from twelve leagues in 1945 to forty-three in 1946, fifty-two in 1947, fifty-eight in 1948, and fifty-nine (the highest number ever) in 1949. [38] North Carolina was no exception. Leagues and teams began roaring back in 1946 and didn't let up until about 1951. By 1948, an astounding forty-three towns and cities in North Carolina would have professional baseball teams. [39]

Semipro baseball was certainly still around. There were plenty of places players could go to make good money in the towns and industrial areas of the semipro game. In eastern North Carolina, where the Coastal Plain League was again the predominant professional league after the war, semipro players turned to the farming towns such as Edenton, Windsor, and Colerain of the Albemarle League for summer cash. In the piedmont region, where the Carolina, Tri-State, and Western Carolina leagues had professional teams in most cities and towns, there were mills and factories willing to hire baseball players to field semipro league teams. There were many baseball players around, and there were plenty of places where the restrictions of "organized ball" were not necessarily welcome. But the situation after the war seemed to beg for professional baseball, and Angier, the little town that had dared to compete with its bigger neighbors in the semipro games of the 1930s, was right in the thick of things.

The town's population, by the 1940 census, was over 1,000, and the end of the war brought promise for more growth. [40] Angier had ridden the tide of the semipro game in the 1930s and had proven its competitiveness on the field as well as its willingness at the ticket gate. It had proven to be a good baseball town, at least when the home team was a winner, and many of the folks around town still held the years of local heroes of the '30s close to their hearts. It was still rich baseball country.

The first spring after the war brought the notion that the old Tobacco State League, once strictly semipro territory, could be reborn in the midst of this surge of professional baseball. A plan for a new TSL was put forth by Raleigh promoter Sam Allen and Wilmington real estate broker Jimmy Wade. The plan was to get the old TSL towns plus a couple of other towns into a six-team league, the minimum size considered feasible for a professional minor league. It would be a Class D league, about the lowest on the minor league rung. [41] And it would take some doing.

The old league towns were still small in terms of the revenue needs of minor league franchises. The National Association of Professional Baseball Leagues, the governing body of the minors, considered population as a major criterion for establishing a league. So a plan of a partnership between neighboring towns was needed to boost the potential for bigger draws at the gate. The plan worked nicely for the

TSL community. Smithfield and its sister town of Selma had combined for a team in the old semipro days. Dunn and Erwin, though bitter rivals in just about everything for years, would come together in the name of pro ball, too. Clinton wanted in, and that team would eventually be called the Clinton Sampson Blues, bringing its draw from all of Sampson County. Wilmington was a large enough city with a minor league history, and Sanford had made its minor league team a success just before the war. That made five teams.

Angier, which was growing and had played on its own during the semipro days, was still too small for the professional ranks. The only other North Carolina town of comparable size that had had any success with pro ball was the Greene County town of Snow Hill, which had carried a Coastal Plain League team for four years before the war. But a couple of businessmen, W.B. "Red" Williams and W.H. Hamilton, were bold enough to give it a go. Williams, who had moved to Angier in 1936 in time to see the town's most popular semipro team, was one of those baseball men with just enough money in his pocket to make it happen. Hamilton was one of the town's old baseball backers, too. He had been the Bulls business manager in that memorable 1938 campaign. The two men remembered those years before the war and knew the town could proudly brag that those late-1930s teams had produced five major league ball players.

Fuquay Springs would be Angier's partner town in the enterprise. Fuquay Springs and Varina had been partners with Angier in baseball for years, with the Holland and Fish boys coming over to play and bringing their fans during the 1930s. With Fuquay Springs only eight miles from Angier, and a bit larger than Angier at that, the choice was an easy one. The businesses and fans in Fuquay Springs would support baseball as heartily as those in Angier, the entrepreneurs figured.

Getting fans to come over to Angier became the next issue, as Angier's ball park was to be the home of the new team. Fuquay Springs' high school ball field could not be made available for the entire season, and with the hefty schedule of a minor league team, night baseball was a necessity. So Williams and Hamilton, determined to make the project work, jostled a few local businesses and wealthy farmers of the two communities to help get lights at Angier's park. A persuasive and popular fellow, who would serve 12 years as Angier's mayor, Williams also had connections with Fort Bragg and used them to "requisition" materials for other improvements to the park. With the addition of bleachers, the Angier ballpark's seating capacity was pushed to 1,900. The deal was now set to bring a team called Angier-Fuquay into the professional baseball world.

In early May, a late start for a minor league season, the team called Angier-Fuquay became a member of the new Class D Tobacco State League. The combination of teams appeared pretty solid. Wilmington was a bit out of the way for a compact league, but it was a port city and railroad hub, and it had a tradition of baseball. It had been in the old pro leagues at the turn of the century and was a member of the Piedmont League in the 1930s. Wade, the Wilmington real estate broker, was anxious to get his city back into pro baseball. He had made a pitch for entering Wilmington in the Coastal Plain League, but his proposal had been rejected. [42] Clinton, a tobacco market town, had a bit of tradition, too, being the home of two major league pitchers from the old days — Roy Crumpler and 150-game winner Rube Benton.

With the low Class D classification, the quality of baseball would be practically on par with some of the better semipro teams the town of Angier had seen. The big difference was that every player was paid, not according to the loose stipulations of a fast semipro league, but according to the more strict regulations of organized ball, as established by the NAPBL. The salary limit was $1,500 per team per month, not including the manager, who was usually a player as well. [43] Teams in Class D also had to rely a lot on rookies, or first-year professionals. Like many other minor league teams of the time, the 1946 Tobacco State League teams did not have affiliations with major league franchises, so the personnel was decided locally.

Fielding an all-professional team could be even more of a gamble for a small town than fielding a league team on the semipro level. Making ends meet would mean bringing fans to the park consistently all summer, even on weeknights, for the home dates in the 120-game schedule. That, of course, would mean fielding a consistent winner. But a professional team was more certain of a budget than were the old semipro teams. Players were under contract, and their salaries set, though many players were untried and unfamiliar to the community.

Angier had a couple of players it could count on as "hometown drawing cards." Kenneth Jackson, the catcher who had so much promise starring with the Harnett American Legion team in 1939-40, returned to play with the new pro team. Jackson was among thousands of baseball players whose careers were interrupted by war. His father, who ran a corner market in town, was a fan who let his son pursue the chance at a real career in baseball. Kenneth had schooled in baseball at Buies Creek Academy and had shown the type of talent behind the plate that caused most folks to think of him as the town's next Doc Smith, or even better. He had displayed a blistering throw to second and a strong bat during his days with the American Legion team. In 1942, Jackson signed with the Brooklyn Dodgers and was sent to play with Johnstown in the Class D Pennsylvania State League. There he put in a .328 batting average for part of the season and was close to being moved up before war called. A knee injury had set aside his hopes for a career as a catcher. But where his hopes left off, his passion for the game took over, and his batting prowess could not be ignored. He would sign with Angier-Fuquay and would play two more professional seasons.

Pitcher James House was the other local boy on the home team. He had played for Angier High and the Harnett Legion team and had played a brief stint in the Class D Bi-State League in 1942, before the war closed down that league.

But professional contracts brought in a host of new players for local fans to become familiar with, and trades would maintain a continual parade of unknown talent. There would be a mixture of holdovers from before the war who still had hopes of a breakthrough into the big leagues, and there would be young up-and-comers with genuine promise.

The Angier-Fuquay group that stayed with the team the longest was typical of the mix of players that made up a Class D professional team. Former N.C. State pitcher Ray Hardee spent part of the season playing in Memphis, Tennessee; outfielder Andy Scrobola and pitcher Ray Bomar had played with Jim House in Leaksville; outfielder Otis Stephens was a rookie from Roxboro; infielder Roscoe Gentry had played in the Coastal Plain League before the war; Marvin Lorenz had spent his previous professional seasons in Iowa, Florida, and West Virginia; and Joe Mills was traded in from Raleigh.

The new TSL had some other players that fans recalled from the "old days." Zeb Harrington was in Sanford; Shamrock Denning and Eddie Bass were over at Dunn-Erwin; and Wilmington had a former Campbell College star, Hargrove "Hoggie" Davis. It would be memorable season in some ways and a forgettable one in others.

The new league was hastily organized and didn't begin play until May 11. The pitchers apparently arrived even later. Opening-day scores were: Angier-Fuquay 22, Clinton 18; Smithfield 17, Dunn-Erwin 9; and Sanford 29, Wilmington 4. It would be a high-scoring, hitter's league for sure. A total of twenty-eight players in the six-team league would carry batting averages of over .300. Some of those players remained in the league for only a short period of time. For instance, Angier-Fuquay short-timer Bob Mann batted at a .378 clip, playing only a limited number of games. Regulars Paul Dunlap (.361, 81 RBIs) and Marvin Lorenz (.338, 86 RBIs) were more representative of the heavy-hitting lineup for the team. Five players who played much of the season for Angier-Fuquay would bat above .300, though not all of them played together at the same time. Hometown boy Kenneth Jackson batted .292 and drove in sixty-four runs for the year. The league's top hitter that year among the regulars would be Clinton's Willie Duke (.393), and Sanford's "Hammerin'" Hank Nesselrode would be the top slugger in the league with a .354 average, 30 home runs, and 150 RBIs. It became clear early that a good solid pitcher would be a hot commodity in the swing-happy TSL. Clinton's Bob Keane (23-4) and Earl Mossor (21-8) and Sanford's Howard Auman (22-8) would be the only 20-game winners in the league.

The Angier-Fuquay team was competitive in May but slumped off for most of the rest of the season, battling for fourth and fifth in the standings and winning less than half of its games. This led to a number of personnel changes, and managers were not spared. Williams and Hamilton naturally wanted a winner and were willing to do what was necessary within the bounds of the team's pocketbook. They butted heads with managers. Paul Dunlap, a veteran outfielder who had played on practically all levels of the minors, started the season as skipper. He was replaced during the season by Doc Smith, whose last pro job had been in New Bern in 1941. Pitcher Ray Bomar was the man who finished the summer as the team's manager.

This was a pretty common occurrence in the league that year. At the end of June, Zeb Harrington replaced Gaither Riley as manager in Sanford. Riley played for Angier for just a few days and then moved to Smithfield to replace Mickey Balla as manager. In early July, Jimmy Guinn stepped down as Dunn-Erwin's manager, and the Twins hired Dwight Wall a few days later. Willie Duke of Clinton was the manager to stay the longest in the league, but he got a job scouting for the New York Giants in late July and was replaced by former major leaguer Van Lingle Mungo.

Of course players were also bounced around with regularity throughout the league. It was noted in *The News & Observer* that pitcher Dave "Porky" Odom, a former major leaguer, took the circuitous route from Sanford to Wilmington to Greensboro to Angier-Fuquay and then back to Sanford. Angier-Fuquay alone sifted through no less than fifty players during the season, mostly in the pitching department, where at least twenty-two different men took the mound at one time or the other.

But Angier-Fuquay managed to hold on to a core of players for several weeks, and the final combination of players would pay off. After shuffling through a stock of pitchers, the staff with which Angier-Fuquay finished would perform well down the stretch. Jim House and Ray Bomar would each get eleven wins during the season, and Ray Hardee (9-8) highlighted the staff's season with the league's first no-hitter on July 12, as the Angier-Fuquay topped Clinton and former Brooklyn Dodger, Mungo, 13-0.

All of the personnel changes never amounted to much in the regular-season standings for Angier-Fuquay. As a matter of fact, the team had to struggle down to the last week of the season to reach fourth in the standings and qualify for the post-season league playoffs. Angier-Fuquay ended the season with a 57-62 record, a full fourteen games behind pennant winner Sanford, which finished at 71-48, one half game better than Clinton at 70-48. Smithfield-Selma ended up third at 58-62, and Wilmington at 52-66 and Dunn-Erwin at 48-70 were out of the playoff picture.

The fan response in Angier during the regular season was equally lackluster. By the end of August, it was evident that the professional baseball experiment in Angier was not working financially. It was all Red Williams and W.H. Hamilton could do to come up with the player salaries at the end of the month, not to mention the light bill and all of the other fees. It would take a huge payoff in the post-season for Williams and Hamilton to be able to keep pro baseball in town. The playoffs would be one of the more remarkable feats in the town's baseball annals.

The Playoffs

The Sanford Spinners faced Angier-Fuquay in the first series, confident after having finished the season fourteen games better than Angier-Fuquay. But as the best-of-seven series progressed, the A-F squad gained more confidence and proved that a streaky team on an upswing could be a threat. Kenneth Jackson put up the first roadblock in the Spinners' hopes for the post-season title by knocking a home run over the right field fence and playing what *The News & Observer* described as "brilliant fielding in right field." [44] About 2,500 fans in Angier cheered pitcher House to a 5-1 win, and Angier-Fuquay led the series.

Jackson hit another homer in the second game, and Ray Hardee tossed a five-hitter to lead a 4-1 victory. Sanford battled back with star hitter Hank Nesselrode getting four hits and five RBIs to win, 10-1, in Sanford. The Spinners tied the series the next night when former Angier-Fuquay catcher Bruce Hedrick drove in the winning run in the tenth inning, and Sanford won 7-6.

Controversy arose in Game 5. The game was up for grabs in the eighth inning when an umpire's call at second base infuriated the Angier-Fuquay camp so badly that the game was delayed for a thirty-minute argument. With Sanford trailing by one run, Spinners shortstop Joe Nessing had reached on a walk and went to second on a grounder to short by Bob Pugh. Nessing was ruled safe, but Bomar disagreed and threw enough of a fit to extend the game to the edge of Sanford's Sunday curfew law.

The Spinners ended up scoring on a two-run double by Bob Wicker to take a 7-6 lead, but the game was stopped after the eighth because of the curfew. It remained under protest, a status that Angier-Fuquay made official the next day before league directors. The league ruled the game "no contest," taking away Sanford's apparent victory. A *News & Observer* story stated: "The league directors ruled that the umpire was in 'no condition' to handle the contest." [45] Exactly what "no condition" meant was not made clear, and the newspaper did not dare name the umpire, probably because the worst interpretations could have been libelous. (Umpires were not named in the published statistical boxes that ran with the game stories in those days — and probably for good reason.) All of the controversy guaranteed a packed house the next night in Angier, and 2,000 showed up to see Angier-Fuquay back its protest with a seventeen-hit barrage and an 11-6 victory.

Angier-Fuquay brought a small piece of baseball history to Sanford's park on the night of Sept. 10, 1946. The regular-season champion Spinners had their backs to the wall, down three games to two, and called on their ace to take the series to the seventh game. Howard Auman, at 22-8, was one of three twenty-game winners in the Tobacco State League, a league that had clearly lacked strong pitching. He had allowed ten hits in the 5-1 loss in the opening game of the series in Angier, but at home he would be the man to put a stop to the upstarts — at least that's what the Sanford faithful had hoped.

He faced Angier's own Jim House, one of those players who had put in a year of minor league time before the war. House had struggled every inch of the way through a 10-10 season but had managed to four-hit the Spinners in the opening-game win. Whether it was House's ability to measure the Spinners' batting order, catcher Bill Ratteree's ability to measure House's ability, the weather, the convergence of celestial objects, or just plain dumb luck — it was truly House's evening.

Angier grabbed the lead in the fourth inning by loading the bases and scoring a run on Ratteree's sacrifice play. Ratteree and Marvin

Lorenz drove in two more runs in the sixth inning to give Angier a 3-0 cushion. Meanwhile, Jim House sifted through the Sanford batting order that night, out after out, grounders, pop-ups, hard drives with hit-prohibiting fielding plays. He allowed four batters to reach on walks, but going into the final inning, he had not allowed a hit. Sanford could do nothing to get the best of House. Third baseman Joe Mills expertly played a drag bunt for the twenty-sixth out of House's masterpiece. Then Kenneth Jackson charged back and crashed into the right field fence to hold onto a fly ball. Final play, final out, series clincher, and a no-hitter for Jim House.

It was a remarkable feat for a pitcher in a hitter's league, particularly against the league's top team. The Spinners had three .300-plus hitters in their lineup that night, including the powerful Nesselrode, who didn't have a hit at four at-bats.

The Clinton Blues, the second-place team in the regular season, were next in line. They had whipped Smithfield-Selma in the first playoff series and eyed the Bulls as easy pickings. The series would go to a late-September seventh game, with big crowds in Angier and Clinton showing up for each contest. The series opened in Clinton, and the Blues brought their bats, hammering Angier-Fuquay by a 13-4 score. Back in Angier the next day, Marvin Lorenz crushed a two-run homer in the fifth inning to give Angier a 4-0 lead. Pitcher Ray Hardee held off a late rally for the 5-4 victory. Clinton hosted game three and pulled out a squeaker, scoring the game winner in the seventh inning for a 6-5 triumph. The Blues led the series two games to one. Lorenz would be the star again the next night before 2,000 fans in Angier. His two-run single in the eighth proved to be the game winner as Angier-Fuquay pulled out an 8-7 win to knot the series again. Then Clinton returned home and pummeled five Angier pitchers with sixteen hits and an 18-8 win to take a 3-2 lead in the series.

Rain and scheduling were challenging factors for the rest of the series. A rainout cancelled the game in Angier the next day. Then the circus had a date in Angier for the weekend, probably scheduled long before there was any notion whatsoever of Angier-Fuquay stretching its season far into September. So Angier's next home date was played in Dunn on September 21. That apparently was alright with Angier pitcher Hardee. He tossed a four-hit shutout as his team rolled up six runs and Angier-Fuquay evened the series at 3-3.

The seventh and deciding game, on September 22 in Clinton, drew 2,300 fans with Clinton ace Earl Mossor (21-8) facing off against Angier-Fuquay's newfound star, Jim House. The pitchers delivered a duel that only a steady rain could dampen. Pitcher House hit a solo homer in the third inning, and his catcher, Bill Ratteree, knocked a two-out homer with none on in the fourth to make it 2-0. But a trickle of rain turned to a steady shower, and by the time the seventh inning arrived, players splashed mud with each step, and pitchers were slipping on the mound. Finally, when Clinton player-manager Bill Campau thudded through the mud to first on a single with two down in the bottom of the seventh, umpires called the game. It was enough for an official game and enough for the Angier-Fuquay boys to return home with the first professional Tobacco State League playoff championship.

The finish to the season was little short of amazing for a team that had played a so-so regular season. But because of that so-so regular season, team owners Williams and Hamilton had less to crow about than the local fans. Unfortunately for the home folks, the team had not done well enough at the gate during the sub-.500 regular season to bring the owners much money. Despite the gates of 1,500 or better that had been the rule during the playoffs, Angier-Fuquay's professional baseball experiment had not been a financial success.

"I remember Red saying that after they had looked over what had happened, playing seven games in each playoff, they just broke even," Jim Gardner said.

While few minor league franchises, particularly in small towns, made money, "break even" apparently was not in Red Williams' vocabulary. He saw little promise on the horizon and took the route that offered the most. He and his partner sold the team during the off-season. They knew that making a profit meant putting more than 500 folks in the seats night after long, hot minor league night and during the week, to boot. That had not happened in Angier. While the big home dates had been good money, those midweek regular-season games had not even paid the light bill. The lights, equipment, dugouts, benches, bleachers, bases, home plate, everything went with the deal to send the Angier-Fuquay team to the Duplin County town of Warsaw for the 1947 season.

This experiment was the only time the town of Angier would have a professional baseball team. But more than that, it was the last time an Angier team of any sort would play in the town park that had been the scene of excitement since 1933. Angier was left without a town team. Its now-empty park had been the scene of heroic performances from players such as Doc Smith, Bill Holland, and Woody Upchurch to the stars of the 1938 campaign — Byrne, Scarborough, and Gilbert — to the professionals House, Jackson, Stephens, and the rest.

The professional Tobacco State League continued for four more seasons. Clinton, Sanford, Smithfield-Selma, and Wilmington would remain with the league until it folded after the 1950 season. It would actually grow into an eight-team league in 1947 with the addition of the league's first two teams with major league affiliations, Lumberton (Cubs) and Red Springs (Athletics). Dunn-Erwin would continue through 1949, replaced by Whiteville in 1950, and Warsaw would later be replaced by Fayetteville, which was in turn replaced by Rockingham. [46]

Unlike some of the players of the 1930s, who were now making their ways through the major leagues, the 1946 Angier-Fuquay professional team would never produce a major leaguer. The players went their own ways, with only Otis Stephens and Andy Scrobola following the team to Warsaw. Joe Mills, Ray Hardee, and Marvin Lorenz would reunite in Raleigh the next summer, with Mills going on to six more teams in the next eight years. Hardee won eighteen games in Raleigh, but it was his next-to-last season. Jim House and Kenneth Jackson were also at the end of their relatively short minor league careers. House put up a 9-8 record in Sanford in 1947 before leaving the pro diamond, and Jackson ended his pro career with a .317, 103 RBIs performance for Dunn-Erwin the same year.

But Angier baseball, it seemed, was never completely done for, largely because of the boys who had grown up to love the game in their little town. They had seen too many hometown heroes and had had too much fun playing sandlot ball to let the town game go by the wayside in Angier. The young boys who had witnessed the heroes of the 1930s were now well into their teens. Some of them had missed playing high school baseball because of the restrictions during the war, but that did not keep them from carrying their passion for the game down to the Angier park, even during the long summer that produced a win one day and losses the next two nights.

Ben Price was one who fit the Angier-Fuquay baseball games into his routine: "I worked for my father at the barber shop. I'd quit shining shoes and say 'Daddy, I'm going to the ball game,' and I'd take off about eight o'clock and walk down to the park."

There may not have been more than 200 or 300 at the park to join him, but there were dozens of memories provided by men such as catcher Bruce Hedrick, whose gags on the field got him into trouble more than once. He had a habit of concealing a nice round Irish potato under his catcher's garb as a tool for fooling base runners. The pitch would come in, the potato would come out, and Hedrick would fire the object to third, just late enough to make the runner think he could beat the return throw home. But the real ball would be mysteriously awaiting him for the tag at home plate. Hedrick would have to beg the umpire to

134

stay in the game. He did it once during an exhibition game, and the opposing players stomped off in a fury.

Price also recalled the night Bill Ratteree proved he could play just about any position. Ratteree had spent five minor league seasons as a pitcher in the Tidewater areas of Virginia and North Carolina. As his pitching arm faded, he became a catcher and a utility man. He was a true utility man during that one twenty-run shootout during the season. In what was surely a scorekeeper's nightmare, he caught, pitched, played infield, and played outfield.

"Those names still come back to me," Price said. "Any time you get so wrapped up in something like we were [about] baseball, and you're interested, and you love the game, you can remember things like that."

It was those memories and the memories from the years before the war that would carry baseball in Angier. Just because the pro team was gone and the park was closed down, it didn't mean baseball had left town. The Prices, Adamses, Gardners, and others would find a place to play and would get up their own game if they had to. They had seen the blood-and-guts game at the park and had played it on their own little sandlots. Now it was time for the Gardner, Price, and Adams boys to go to bat for Angier baseball.

1946 Angier-Fuquay

Angier and Fuquay Springs fielded a shared team for one season, the only time either town would be involved in professional baseball. The team had a lackluster regular season but won the Tobacco State League playoff championship. Front row, left to right: Ray Hardee, unidentified, Harry Fortune, Sam Sellers, Paul Hunt, Kenneth Jackson, and Gus Rogers. Back row: Andrew Scrobola, Ray Bomar, Otis Stephens, Roscoe Gentry, James House, Marvin Lorenz, Joe Mills, and Bill Ratteree.

(Photo courtesy of Chris Holaday)

Angier-Fuquay	Ab.	R.	H.	O.	A.	E.
Mills, 3b	3	0	2	0	1	0
Scrobola, cf	5	0	1	4	0	0
Gentry, 2b	5	1	2	1	0	0
Jackson, rf	4	1	3	3	0	0
Lorenz, 1b	4	1	2	7	1	0
Ratteree, c	4	0	1	6	0	0
Stephens, lf	4	0	0	0	0	0
Hunt, ss	4	0	1	1	1	0
House, p	4	0	1	0	0	0
Totals	37	3	12	27	4	0

Sanford	Ab.	R.	H.	O.	A.	E.
Butcher, 2b	3	0	0	3	1	1
Guinn, 3b	4	0	0	1	3	0
Shoffner, 1b	3	0	0	4	1	0
Nesselrode, 1b	4	0	0	1	0	0
Hedrick, c	3	0	0	3	0	0
Pugh, lf	3	0	0	0	0	0
Nessing, ss	3	0	0	1	3	0
Gales, cf	3	0	0	2	0	0
Auman, p	2	0	0	0	4	0
Totals	26	0	0	27	10	1

Score by innings:

Angier-Fuquay	000	102	000—3
Sanford	000	000	000—0

Runs batted in: Ratteree 2, Lorenz. Two base hit: Mills. Three base hits: Lorenz. Base on balls: House 4, Auman 4. Strikeouts: House 4, Auman 4.

James House's no-hitter, TSL playoffs, 1946.

(From the News & Observer)

The Pea Ridge Miracle

Chapter 9 - Starting from Scratch

A Family Builds a New Place to Play

To look at the small plot of land now, it takes some imagination to see the outline of a baseball field and even more imagination to see a center of community activity on summer weekends. It is just under three miles outside of Angier, just around the bend from where Doc Smith was raised, and smack in the middle of farm country. A few houses, farm ponds, and tobacco and bean fields dot the area. Not a lot has changed in that respect in the last fifty years.

A few miles farther, Benson Road merges with Johnston County Road and rides a ridge along the Johnston-Harnett county line. The ridge is so sandy, legend has it, that little more than peas can grow there, and a sort of informal name evolved. Pea Ridge has no borders, no community center, fire department, post office, or even a signpost marking its existence. It isn't on any map or listed in any gazetteer, but most folks who have lived in Angier for any amount of time can point a stranger in the right direction. "Just go out Benson Road, past Old Stage Road and the old ball park on the left," they'll say. "It's out that way."

The old ball park itself is now overgrown with tall grass and pine trees. It was a pasture for livestock in 1947 when Clyde Adams ran a country store just across the road. That was two years after the end of World War II and a year after the local professional team had won a title, drawn up stakes, and left town. And it was the year Angier baseball would start almost from square one to rebuild its baseball reputation.

Adams, his brothers, cousins, and a few others in the Pea Ridge community conjured up the idea of playing baseball near their homes, there in the country. Clyde and his brothers, Wayron, Hayden, and Claybourne, were one of three sets of baseball-playing Adams brothers that lived in the community. Elbert, Rexwell, Connie, and Odell Adams were another set; Gerald and Raythell Adams were brothers in the other family. That was ten, just enough for a baseball team with, say, a relief pitcher to spare. All they needed was a home field.

For the boys in town, the Angier High School field served as a summer baseball playground, the old town park on Highway 210 having been stripped by the exiting professional team. But the way the Adams boys saw it, there was always plenty of land for another baseball field. They didn't need anything big, just a good clearing for a diamond to use for warm-ups and maybe even a few pickup games. Clyde, who was running the country store for his father, pointed across the road to the pasture. "Tell you what I'll do," Clyde told the Adams boys. Clyde was on his way to becoming a shrewd and enterprising businessman, and

140

people would come to know that when he prefaced a conversation with, "Tell you what I'll do," it was likely that something was on its way to being done. He was that persuasive and that determined.

Clyde's proposal was to use the pasture across the road from the store, which was owned by C. M. Dupree. It was just big enough and just flat enough. Through the generosity of Dupree and the hard work of the Adams boys, it would soon become a place to play baseball. Those three or so acres of land could have been used for crops or livestock. An acre of tobacco was worth about $600 a year to a farmer at the time. 47 The idea of building a baseball field there may have seemed strange to some and downright silly to others. But to the group of Adamses who held the game of baseball close to their hearts, it would be a place to play.

Country baseball fields had popped up from time to time in other places. The Johnson boys from Lillington and Buies Creek had tossed the ball around at their little pasture field called Twin Oaks at a crossroads not far from Buies Creek, and schoolhouse fields at crossroads communities such as Cleveland and Boone Trail, were pretty common. However, Clyde Adams had no idea that he had pointed his kin in a new direction for Angier baseball. He only knew there were enough baseball-loving Adams boys to at least play a few pickup games.

The Field

It was logical that grown men would want to fulfill the childhood dream of building a baseball field. As kids, many of these fellows had to build makeshift baseball fields in order to bring any sense of reality to their backyard game. But those were diamonds of tow-sack bases and a kid's imagination. Why not put their adult ingenuity to work? So, over the course of a few months in 1947, the Pea Ridge "park" began to take shape, as the Adams men resorted to whatever it took to build and maintain it.

"We just took the Cub tractors, scrapers, mules, harrows and went to work," said Rexwell Adams.

"We hauled all sorts of stuff in there, sometimes on tractors and trailers — dirt, sawdust, whatever we could," Elbert Adams added. "Won't a thing to it."

Actually there was something to it. They disked, graded, leveled, mowed, measured, built a mound, strapped down bases, and plugged in a plate. They harvested trees to craft fence posts and begged, borrowed, and otherwise "acquired" yards and yards of what they called chicken wire for an outfield fence and a backstop. Like the old town field, there wouldn't be much space down the first base line — just enough for a bench before a ditch and then the road.

And like the old town park, the field would be small. Crop land beyond left field and stands of hardwoods around right and center would limit the expanse. But ballplayers would come to like it for its offensive and defensive aspects. The ballplayers estimate that the roughly assembled right and left field fences were about 290 or 300 feet from the plate. Center field was 320 feet away … maybe. It was safe to say that a drive to left or right did not have to be too long for a round-tripper, but it

142

wasn't any shorter than the right field at the Polo Grounds.

"In one game, I hit two home runs, if that's any indication," said Carlton Mangum, a slender pitcher, known more for his breaking ball than his long ball.

A more accurate measure of hitting power was a pond a few yards beyond the center field fence. If a hitter plopped a ball into plowed ground beyond left, rattled the low limbs in right, or floated one in that pond, it was considered a home run worthy of note.

"There was a big old oak tree past the fence near the right field line there, and I once hit the limb that hung over it, about twenty feet up, I guess," recalled Tommy Byrne, who played exhibition games there after his retirement from the majors.

The small confines of the field virtually prohibited triples and even became a little dangerous for swift outfielders accustomed to covering more ground at larger parks. James Stevens could hardly forget the outfield fence because of a close encounter: "It was a chicken wire fence, had six-inch board across the top, all the way around it," he recalled. "I ran through the fence, I mean, clean through it. About the time that ball hit my glove, I hit that fence."

And, of course the infield was skin, skin swept smooth enough to, as Marshall Price put it, "make us all look a little better."

Over the years, the little park would grow with the team. Benches became "dugouts" with wooden posts holding up a tin top. A small bleacher seating section was constructed behind the tall wire backstop; the Adams boys put up posts with chicken wire on top, and covered the wire with straw for shade because, "there was no place hotter than the Pea Ridge field on a Sunday in July," as Roger Honeycutt recalled. The straw shade "was great until it rained hard," said Harold Ellen. "Then, there was that drip, drip, drip." It was as close to a grandstand as the little field would ever have.

Upkeep sometimes required resourcefulness. Danny Watkins, who helped with equipment for the team, recalls acquiring a nearby road roller, when the state highway department wasn't looking. "We just hitched it up, hauled it down there, and rolled the field good and flat and hauled it back. No one was using it. We figured we could."

Play Ball!

No one remembers now, exactly when the first real game was played at Pea Ridge. That's how meager the beginnings were. There was hardly a notion of a real baseball team out there, just a place near home for the Adams boys to play pitch-and-catch. Clyde Adams had no reason to believe Pea Ridge would ever be any more than just a field for a little infield practice.

However, during that summer of 1947, the Adams boys got up a loosely organized team and began taking on all comers. The few games they played did not go down on any league record and weren't recorded in a scorebook or phoned in to the newspaper. By all accounts, the scheduling seemed as if they were kids again, going around the neighborhood asking their buddies to come out and play. Clyde would somehow find any group of nine or more guys who had spare time on a Saturday afternoon. They might come from Angier or Kipling or as far away as Boone Trail, slam on the other side of the county. Sometimes they would even play an organized league team, which was OK with Clyde, because on game day he could be real formal and submit a lineup card. In 1947, Clyde submitted lineup cards that were very simple: Adams lead-off, Adams at two and three, Adams cleanup, Adams at the bottom of the order. Oh yes, the late sub or relief pitcher — that would be Adams. There were games in which Adams was the only name in the home team roster.

The team could have been nicknamed the A's. The first roster, according to an Angier town history *More Voices of Yesteryear*, lists these players: Clyde Adams, Claybourne Adams, Wayron "Pete" Adams, Hayden Adams, Raythell Adams, Gerald "Butch" Adams, Odell Adams, Connie Adams, Rexwell Adams, Elbert Adams, and Winfield Adams (umpire). With Winfield Adams as umpire, it was safe to say that all questionable calls at the Pea Ridge field would most certainly go to the home team. Otherwise, Winfield would get a shy helping of barbecue at the family reunion in the fall.

Submitting an all-Adams lineup and then sending the visitor's home with their tails between their legs was part of the fun that Clyde got out of having his own little team. And it was — and would be — his team. Clyde was one of the elders of the Adams cousins who played out at Pea Ridge. A World War II veteran, he would make his way in business in the Angier community, and good business was usually foremost in his thinking. But the Pea Ridge baseball team was more like his hobby, and he would use the same persuasive powers that made him a good businessman to eventually build the team. Over the course of the next ten years he would repeat the phrase "Tell you what I'll do," hundreds of times, and he would make it mean something.

It was Clyde Adams who put the team in uniforms, Clyde Adams who came up with money for equipment, Clyde Adams who found players and other teams to play, and Clyde Adams who passed the hat around Angier as the Pea Ridge team garnered a following. Clyde became the team's business manager, sometime field manager, and sometime player. If one were to consider the Pea Ridge team as a franchise, Clyde Adams would have been the owner and general manager. When the players living today are asked about any sort of organizational matters involving the team, its league affiliation, or financial backing, the answer is always the same: "Clyde handled all that stuff."

"He was the man who made it all go, financially and every other way," said Roger Honeycutt, who played for Clyde for two seasons. "He was really Pea Ridge baseball, to my mind. It was his project and he looked after everything."

With Clyde as manager and general unifying figure of this makeshift team, the other cousins and brothers would fall into various positions on the diamond. The talent level varied, which meant there were plenty of surprises during a game. Most of the boys could play just about any position on the field, but there were some positions that were favored by certain ones and rarely disputed. Gerald "Butch" Adams was always pitching, and his brother Raythell was catching. Hayden Adams was at first base, the position he would hold for the ten years the Pea Ridge team existed. There was a bit of a contest at third base, where Connie and younger brother Elbert both wanted to play. Connie won this tug-of-war, finally yielding in later years, as Elbert matured more at the position.

The rest of the field was filled in by whoever was available on a particular Saturday. Weekday games were out of the question, for it was the growing season, and these boys were sons of farmers. In the coming years, the Adams boys would come and go for various reasons. But for the life of what would become the Pea Ridge team, there would always be an Adams on the field, and there would always be Clyde behind it.

The Team in Town

The Pea Ridge ball field wasn't the real home for baseball in the Angier community in 1947, and it wasn't the only place the Adams boys played. After all, Pea Ridge in the beginning was just a place in the country situated near the Adams homes and used for pickup games. In town, many of the town players were competing in a regular league. To the town boys, the Pea Ridge field was simply a practice field.

The Cape Fear League, an informal recreation-type league made up of teams from communities mostly in Harnett County, formed and began a weekend schedule in June of 1947. The eight-team league consisted of Angier, Erwin, Buies Creek, Anderson Creek, Lillington, Kipling, Godwin, and Fuquay Springs, a perfect setup for summer ball for men and boys who had competed against each other at various high schools in the same towns and communities.

The league was open to anyone who wanted to play, but unlike the fast semipro leagues of the old days, there was no acknowledged salary for players. This did not mean that at least some players were not paid. Like the old days, there was little enforcement of any league regulations regarding pay. The league was considered amateur, but if a player hit a home run or made a spectacular fielding play, there was nothing to prevent an avid and grateful fan from offering some sort of gratuity. In fact, some town businesses that were team sponsors openly advertised rewards of a carton of cigarettes or a tank of gasoline to stars in special games. How could a league president actually prevent a community leader from calling in a good pitcher from out of town with the promise of ten or twenty bucks for a game? Rosters were not set in stone, and players seemed to come and go as they pleased, much like in the old days. About the only generally accepted rule in these leagues was that a team was prohibited from bringing in a "ringer," or a player who was under a professional contract.

It is almost certain, however, that there was no balancing of books in this type of ball. Players played for fun and competition, and folks in the various towns or communities simply stepped forward to foot whatever bill there was at the end of the day. "Owners" such Clyde Adams or Chester Holland in Fuquay usually forked out their own

148

money to put a team in equipment, and players usually got no more than a free dinner or gas money. Everyone, however, got to see — or play in — one or two baseball games a week, and that kept everyone happy.

Communities and their teams seemingly had no commitment to being in the same league the next year or even to playing out the current league season. Forming a league consisted of little more than scrounging up at least four teams from communities within an hour or so driving distance, choosing a league "commissioner" and board to rule on certain issues, devising a schedule, and giving the organization a name that somehow reflected the geographic region in which it played.

The point of all this informality and lack of organization was just that. To organize a semipro league with the same type of rules and salary restrictions that were in minor leagues would have defeated the purpose. This was really baseball for fun, and any strict adherence to rules cooked up by some league commissioner took the fun out of it. Those matters seemed to work themselves out during those days, anyway, because it really was a good time to be playing baseball. The players with real ambitions who wanted to make a buck could turn to any of the dozens of minor league teams that were popping up in North Carolina around that time. The Tobacco State League was still active, and the Coastal Plain League was still going strong. The Carolina League, North Carolina State League, Blue Ridge League, and Tri-State League also had minor league teams in the state. Those leagues ranged in classification from D up to B. [48]

If a player didn't particularly like the restrictions and enslavement of organized professional baseball, he could turn to the next rung down, the fast semipro leagues that still existed. Down east, the Albemarle League would set a good player up in a beach house for the weekend and send him home with a wad of bills. In the piedmont industrial leagues, teams would dip deep into the local plant payroll to compensate a good player. And if that wasn't enough, there were plenty of leagues like the Cape Fear League — towns and communities in the Peach Belt, Eastern State, Eastern Carolina, Tri-County, and Central Carolina leagues were all within about an hour's drive of most CFL outposts. That's what made things so good for decent baseball players in North Carolina. A man with a glove could find just about any level of the game to play on a Saturday afternoon without having to miss supper back home. Teams, players, and usually fans were just about everywhere.

In Angier, the Cape Fear League entry was what was left to carry the town's baseball banner, a banner that had been lowered for the war and nearly dropped completely with the exit of the 1946 minor league team. The Angier team didn't have a high caliber of talent. The town's best ball player, Kenneth Jackson, who had been the star of the Angier-Fuquay Bulls the year before, was still playing pro ball in the Tobacco State League. He and another local favorite, Granville "Shamrock" Denning (.333, 96 RBIs), were helping the Dunn-Erwin Twins into the playoffs.

As usual, there were some up-and-comers on the Angier roster that season, with one of the Price boys providing much of the punch. David Price was one of four sons of Lyda and Romie Price, who owned and operated the town barber shop. All of the brothers played baseball in Angier at one time or the other. David's older brothers, Marshall and R.C., had been tossing baseballs around town for years, and his younger brother, Ben, would in a few years be a member of one of Angier High School's best baseball teams on record.

It was only natural for the Price boys to be baseball men. Being a son of the local barber might have meant a lot shoe polishing, but it certainly had its privileges when it came to baseball talk. When the town men weren't bantering about politics while the clippers buzzed away, they were usually sizing up the sports scene. During the semipro days before the war, Marshall and R.C. were just old enough to cherish the afternoons when Tommy Byrne, Charlie Gilbert, Connie Ryan, and the rest would parade into the barber shop where they showered after the game.

David was the star of the show in 1947. Playing for the high school team, he had pitched eight straight victories before losing a game, striking out ninety batters along the way. His team had gone 16-2, missing the state playoffs by a hair. He and brother R.C. both played for the town team during that summer. Price would be a name on the town team lineup for years. So would Adams and Gardner. Gerald "Butch" Adams pitched for the 1947 Angier team, and Jim Gardner, who was just out of his first year with the high school team, played at most any position he was needed.

The team also had "old timer" Tally Dupree, the former pro and third baseman on that memorable 1938 semipro team. Dupree had playe´

two minor league seasons in 1940 and '41, before joining the Marines for the war. He was now a school teacher, but at age thirty-one, he still had the legs to get around a diamond and was always up for a baseball game when the opportunity arose. He and David Price played well enough to make the league all-star game that season.

The team also had Kenneth Williams, Harold Wells, and fleet-footed Ray McLeod, among others. Angier opened the league season in June with a 5-4 victory over the rivals from across the Wake County border, Fuquay Springs. But Angier was at a disadvantage to Fuquay and the league's other power, Buies Creek. Those teams had strong college talent and would lead the league all year. By August 20, Angier had a 6-12 record in the league, seven games behind the leader of the division, Fuquay Springs. Woody Upchurch's Buies Creek team, with Louis and Johnny Johnson leading the way, went on to defeat Chester Holland's Fuquay gang in the league championship series, three games to two. Kipling and Lillington were also in the playoffs.

The pickup games at the Pea Ridge field and the league games in town represented a humble return to town ball in Angier, but they had filled a void for the Adams, Price, and Gardner boys of the professional team. The league team and the little warm-up field in the country were notice to the town that baseball was not about to go away. There was no longer the high-strung, well-paid, out-of-town talent and competition that folks had become used to before the war, but the boys who had grown up with that fire were now getting their chance at bat. They had built a field in the country and had played league games in town. And even though the world was changing, to them there was no reason Angier baseball couldn't grow again.

Webster Lupton

Chapter 10 - A Town Team out of Town?

Two Names for the Same Home Team

A new name showed up in the Cape Fear League standings in 1948. It wasn't really a different team, though. The names on the lineup cards had not changed that much. Adams, Price, and Gardner, which by now encompassed more than a dozen players, were always on the list. And their opponents simply considered the team as "them boys from Angier." However, as league games started being played at the Pea Ridge field, the Pea Ridge name was in the standings instead of Angier, and datelines in the small newspaper stories began reading PEA RIDGE. For the first time, Angier's town game was actually being played out of town and at a place no one could really point to on a map. It didn't set too well with some of the town baseball people. Baseball had always been played in town, and the town folks were reluctant to surrender their baseball identity just because Clyde Adams and his cousins had decided to carve out a ruddy little field in the country.

The whole thing created a bit of an identity problem for town baseball around Angier, and for a while, folks didn't know whether the same set of ball players would be called Angier or Pea Ridge in league standings each year or whether they would play home games at the high school field or the one the Adams boys built in the country. In one way, this identity issue would divide the town's baseball talents. Veterans Tally Dupree and Kenneth Jackson would never play league ball for the team called Pea Ridge. Nor would Ben Price, who said, "[I] didn't go over there much to see them play. I reckon I had a little envy in me, because I wanted to form something here in town."

In another way, the situation united talents. Playing at Pea Ridge wasn't enough of an issue to deter most of the town or country boys from summers of playing baseball around town. If the nearest game was being played at the Pea Ridge park, so be it. They just wanted to play. That **was** all Clyde Adams and his cousins had ever expected at the little **field** across from the country store — guys who just wanted to play.

Marshall Price

Marshall Price was one of those guys. Though the small complication of maintaining a rigid identity for the town's baseball team managed to smolder for a few years, it wasn't something that bothered boys like Marshall. To Marshall, it didn't matter if he were playing for a team called Angier or Pea Ridge. To him, the issue was finding a baseball game to play on Saturday afternoon. And if the nearest one was out in the country, that's where he'd go. He was always in search of a baseball game. It had been that way since he was a kid, out there with the rest of the gang in backyards and open fields of the country, learning the game. He started playing at age six, and having brothers helped. In fact, it had been pickup games most of Marshall's life. In 1948, Marshall was just out of the Army, one of the thousands of troops to help Europe back to its feet after a devastating war, and the one person in his unit that had the wherewithal to figure a way to get up a game. He had missed seeing Angier's only professional team, but that didn't mean he'd miss playing baseball.

While in Europe, Marshall had a problem understanding that a group of men could be together without a ball game breaking out from time to time. Even post-war Germany offered a few breaks from the chaos.

"When I went overseas in '45, we didn't have an organized league, and everybody was wanting to do something. So they wanted to know if I would see the company commander. I went to him and told him what we had in mind. I said, 'We don't have any uniforms, athletic equipment, don't have a ball field, nothing.' We sat there and talked for a little while, and he said, 'You go down to the motor pool and tell that sergeant that I said to furnish you with all the machinery you need to build a ball field.' And we did. The boys got so interested in it, we formed a league and we had ball that summer. I was almost ready to re-enlist."

That was the way Marshall was; always looking for a game

somewhere. He was a bit reluctant to go out to Pea Ridge to play until he "found out how much fun they were having out there." And he wasn't about to spend his first summer back from the service without a glove in his hand on a game day. He would make his time to play ball and pretty much make himself a fixture in the team lineup for the next nine years, valued largely for his ability to send a curveball over the left field fence. Marshall patrolled the outfield and was one of a cadre of players who formed the nucleus of the team down through the years.

The Gardners

The Gardner boys were others. The summer of 1948 was also the first in which more than one Gardner would take the Pea Ridge field. Frank played his first year with the team, splitting time with a semipro team in Benson, where he was getting some notice from pro scouts. That notice would keep Frank away from home for much of the next two summers. Then military service would keep him away for four more years.

Brother Jim had just gotten out of high school and played for three more years before heading off for a career in the Air Force. Jim was what one would call a utility player, a versatile member of the lineup, who could swat the ball well enough to keep him in the batting order, and he could play just about any position. He would come to admit that he wasn't quite as good at the game as his big brother, but he *knew* just as much, if not more.

For Frank, there was only one place on the diamond. He was not the hitter that some of his teammates were. It seems he either led off because of his smarts, or batted way down in the order, behind the harder hitters. But the area at the top of the baseball diamond that most people call second base, Frank Gardner called home. Any park, any time, Frank Gardner was ready to trot out to his special spot, sweep the ground with his cleats, warm up, and stand in half crouch — ready to play second base, ready to guard the bag, ready to work magic with his best friend, the guy at shortstop. He said, "Second is what I always wanted to play, or short. It was what I always thought was the liveliest part of the infield."

If he were called on to play another position, well, that was alright with Frank. It was still baseball. But the hard liners hit by left-handed hitters, the spinning choppers from right-handers, the grounder over the middle, and the double play ball — these were what Frank Gardner lived for on game day.

He had grown up playing sandlot ball and watching Angier's Connie Ryan, Leroy Spell, and others work the top of the diamond. At home, he'd grab up the newspaper and check the boxes to see how Bobby Doerr had performed the day before. All professionals, consistent, in a quiet way. All second base. "I tried to pattern myself after Bobby Doerr," he said. Typical second basemen. They never got the press the other infielders did. The hard hitters were at first and third; fancy, strong-armed fielders were at short; and catchers were in a world of their own. The Hornsbys, Robinsons, and Gehringers — true stars at second —

were few and far between. But a crafty fielder — not a slugger — who wants to find his place on a diamond has to go somewhere. And Frank Gardner found his little niche.

He had spent his formative teen years during the war without the benefit of high school ball but with the advantage of playing with the county American Legion team and playing for Doc Smith. "I was out of school by the time I was sixteen. There were only eleven grades, and my mother started me when I was five," he said. "We used to kid her about trying to get us all out of the house early." The American Legion experience was Frank's first with what one would consider organized baseball, and he played with some the best young players in the county. Eddie Jackson, Billy Harrington, Lefty Ferrell, and Jack Stewart were other boys on those Legion teams who would go on to play professionally.

For now, Frank was biding his time, getting in good workouts with pretty good local players and thinking maybe his time would come for a chance at playing professional baseball.

The Adams Battery

With the Price and Gardner names added to the list of Adamses on the roster, Pea Ridge was becoming a bit more diverse and representative of the community. That trend would continue for years. But the Adams name, it seemed, would always be central to Pea Ridge baseball, and in 1948 it started with the pitcher-catcher combination of brothers Butch and Raythell.

Raythell had just gotten out of the Navy, a seaman first class on the USS *Missouri*, a battleship with certainly plenty of space but not enough for much more than a game of pitch and catch. He had managed to find a game of baseball in port, though. His crew faced off against crews from others in the fleet. Considering the *Missouri* had a crew of more than 2,000 to draw from, Raythell was usually on the winning side. His service with the Navy had taken Raythell Adams around the world. But upon his return home, he found a little brother who thought he knew just about as much as Raythell did — particularly when it came to baseball. This was the family situation that for a few summers formed the battery of the Pea Ridge ball team.

The battery is the pitcher and catcher of a baseball team, always named first in the bare linescore of a baseball summary. That's because the pitcher and catcher are the soul of the defense; the pitcher, for obvious reasons, and the catcher because he's the man who decides the pitches, calls the cutoff throws, and is the captain of the defense. He glares through the web of a mask and sees the entire field. He is a human backstop for all sorts of curving, dipping, and sliding projectiles that hit the dirt, bound off the plate, deflect from the bat, and sometimes even hit squarely in the mitt behind the blinding whiff of a batter's frustration. The catcher gets credit for the putout when a player strikes out. He deserves more. He spends half of the game squatting, and in heavy gladiator-like garb. And through all of this thinking, targeting, and chasing, he's expected to spring up the instant a base runner jumps for second and throw a rocket to the shortstop's glove waiting a foot high and just off the bag. Then if a guy barely gets his bat on the ball and fouls one over his head, the catcher has to toss off his mask, find the ball, watch for the screen, and call off a charging pitcher who is yelling, "Mine, mine!"— all at the same time. But catchers never get respect they deserve, particularly from pitchers, who think they know best. When a pitcher leans forward before his windup and starts shaking his head, that's when he thinks he knows better. When a catcher takes his mask off of his backwards cap and strides to the mound, that's when he's out to correct that notion.

And here were Butch and Raythell, brothers and pitcher and catcher; one always thinking he knew better than the other. To watch them in a conference on the mound was like watching two boys in the backyard arguing over whose turn it was to take out the garbage. It was certainly disgruntling to everyone on the field when the two demonstrated their differences of opinion right there on the mound. And there were such demonstrations. More than one account had Butch simply throwing up his hands and walking off the mound in frustration over someone's fielding error or his own pitching mistake, as pointed out by his catcher/brother.

One such series of tales describes Raythell strolling to the mound to confront Butch about his control. The exact words of the argument vary from story to story. But the gist was this: "If you think you can do better, here, take the ball." Butch and Raythell switched positions. Each of them thought they were getting the upper hand in that exchange, because each figured his brother would learn what it was like to play a *really* difficult position. Of course, neither would actually start a game at the other's regular position. The battery in the newspaper linescore usually read: "B. Adams and R. Adams," the way it was supposed to.

Elbert Adams recalled this instance about his cousins: "Butch took a guy to a 3-0 count. Before the next pitch, Raythell kept signaling and signaling and Butch kept shaking him off. Then Butch rares back and throws a knuckleball that hit the dirt and had Raythell scramblin' for it. Raythell went to the mound and said, 'What in the hell do you think you're doing?' Butch looked at him just as straight-faced and said, 'Just experimentin'. ' "

Hijinks aside, the brothers did have an array of abilities that helped the team considerably. Butch was a clever hurler with good high school experience who won many more games than he lost. And at the plate, he had a knack for pulling screaming liners down the third base line. "He had a hit that, well, if you placed a bucket beside third base, he would knock over nine out of ten times. He was that kind of a pull hitter," said Walt Whittington, who saw most of the high school team's games in the late 1940s. Raythell was a strong-armed monitor of base runners. He would have plenty of heroics from the plate, too, and his overall ability would give him aspirations for playing professionally, another in a line of Angier catchers that had passed from Doc Smith to Kenneth Jackson. An injury to his throwing arm at a baseball camp in Florida kept that from being a reality. These Adams boys, the Prices, and the Gardners were the foundations for a solid team, one that would make its mark on the Pea Ridge team starting in 1948.

1948 Season

With the Gardners, Prices, and Adams all lined up for a uniform, the Angier baseball story was truly one of familial relationships. But the baseball relationships went further than the immediate families. Bobby Gardner, a cousin of Jim and Frank, put in his first year for the town team that summer, and Ray McLeod was one of the Price boys' cousins. And there were others.

These various sets of brothers and cousins embarked on the Cape Fear League season as Pea Ridge. Businesses in and around Angier chipped in to help with uniforms for the team. They were white with red trim, and each uniform shirt had the name of a business on its back. The fronts displayed "Pea Ridge" and in later years "PR." Butch teamed up with David Price for pitching duties, with Wayon "Pete" Adams and Jim Gardner relieving. Raythell caught, Hayden Adams anchored first base, and Marshall Price began being the fixture in right field. The other positions would have various players — usually an Adams. Clyde Adams sometimes played, but he was largely relegated to "business management" duties. He called on pitcher Bill Watkins, another Angier boy and career soldier, to be the field manager when Watkins's military duties allowed him to be close to home, namely at Fort Bragg.

The Pea Ridge team was one of ten in the Cape Fear League standings in 1948. The team stayed in the top part of the standings most of the summer. Other teams in the league were Buies Creek, Lillington, Boone Trail, Cleveland, Pleasant Grove, Coats, Godwin, Linden, and Kipling, another tight arrangement of town teams, most from Harnett County.

It was a competitive and high-scoring league, but the pitching was apparently not too reliable as a rule. Teams in informal weekend leagues like this had little adherence to what one would consider a pitching rotation. Having good pitching on Saturday or Sunday depended largely on whether or not the one or two real pitchers on your roster showed up healthy and relatively sober.

In a July 4th game at Pea Ridge, Godwin visited, and the two teams put together a fireworks display of thirty-eight total hits. Pea Ridge won, 21-10. A week later, Hayden Adams homered in a five-for-five day at the plate as Pea Ridge whipped Linden, 16-7. Hayden would repeat the five-for-five feat in the last game of the season, this time with two home runs, as the team defeated Godwin, 16-4. By the first week in August, not long before the league playoffs, Pea Ridge had a 16-7 record, in second place and two games behind Buies Creek, another hard-to-beat team under Woody Upchurch. Lillington overtook Pea Ridge for second place in late August, which positioned the two teams for a series in the post-season playoffs. Buies Creek, the first-place team, played fourth-place Cleveland in the other semifinal series.

The Pea Ridge-Lillington best-of-three series was a rousing contest. The teams exchanged victories before a September 2 third game that was played in Kipling. Pea Ridge pitcher David Price suffered through a four-run Lillington rally in the first inning of the deciding game before settling down. He ended up pitching the entire ten-inning contest. In the bottom of the tenth, Ray McLeod singled, stole second, and was sacrificed to third. He scored the winner when Butch Adams lined to center field.

Pea Ridge went against Buies Creek in the finals, a best-of-five series. The teams played to a fifth game with Marshall Price and Raythell Adams supplying thirteen hits between them in the first four games. But they could not find a way to whip Buies Creek ace Archie Lynch. Lynch, a lefthander who pitched at Campbell College, tossed a one-hit shutout in Game 3 of the series. Then, in the deciding game, on September 11 at Lillington, Lynch tossed a five-hitter to lead his team to a 9-4 win and the title.

1949 Season — Back in Town

In deference to the support that came from town, the slight brewing of controversy that had arisen, and the need to have Kenneth Jackson and Tally Dupree in uniform, the 1949 team was again called Angier in the league standings. The other names in the lineup were pretty much the same, making the team essentially the same as it had been before.

Frank Goes Pro

One name missing from the Angier lineup that year was Frank Gardner. Frank's struggle to become a top-notch second baseman was beginning to pay off. Playing with some of the best players in the area during his summers of Legion and semipro ball, Frank's baseball education flourished. The squirrelly grounders and flips to the shortstop for double plays with which he had battled as a youngster were becoming second nature to him now. He could almost play the position with his eyes closed.

Baseball scouts, practically everywhere at the time, liked the looks of a good, solid infielder, and it seemed the dozens of minor league teams in the state at the time always had a spot to fill. Glenn Lockamy was one of the scouts who took notice of young Frank Gardner's play, and Frank was a cinch to recruit. Lockamy took Frank to Raleigh to sign a professional contract, the first of many changes ahead in Frank Gardner's baseball life.

For a kid who had been raised in baseball, the temptation of a professional contract was hard to overlook. The pay would not be sparkling, but the way Frank saw it, neither was the pay for Connie Ryan when he was in Savannah or Bobby Doerr in Hollywood. The big change for Frank was that he would be playing almost every day, measuring his strengths against other pros. Baseball every day, and getting paid for it! How much better could life be? That was always the draw for a kid at the time. Few knew exactly what they were getting into.

Frank took the basic rookie salary of $150 per month and headed for Rocky Mount that summer to play with the Leafs of the Class D Coastal Plain League. ₄₉ It would be a good season. He played with league stars Bill Stanton, Walt McJunkin, and Jim Reges, who led the team to the 1949 pennant. Frank had a second baseman's batting average, .258. It would be his best pro season.

But he didn't get back much to see folks at home. They worked you in professional baseball. You played practically seven days a week, spent much of the non-playing time either taking batting practice, riding the team bus, or sleeping. "There wasn't a whole lot of spare time then, unless it rained. You usually played six nights a week and on Sunday afternoon," he recalled. "You had to be at the park at four thirty or five for batting practice. Then after the game if you were on the road … In the Coastal Plain League, we never stayed away over night…. You slept on the bus a lot. It was tiresome, but you were young."

Angier's Season

Back in Angier, the rest of the local lineup was much the same. Butch and Raythell Adams were the usual one and two in the scorebook, with Hayden at first base and Connie and Elbert Adams at the left side of the infield, switching off at short and third. David, Marshall, and R.C. Price all suited up, and with Jackson and Dupree on board, Angier appeared to have a formidable crew. Jim Gardner was splitting duties as player-manager with Bill Watkins.

The trouble was, all of those players did not play together all of the time for various reasons, farming usually at the top. Angier struggled in the early part of the season. In mid-July the team was 5-11 and fifth in the standings. But the team rallied in the second half of the season to finish second and make the post-season playoffs. It took league-leading Cleveland and a wild three-game series to finish Angier's league season in late August. The final two games of that series each went to eleven innings. Winfield Adams singled in the winner in a 12-11 Angier victory, but Cleveland claimed a 6-5 victory in the last game.

It was in that last game that Butch Adams had one of his conniptions, playing to the hilt his role as the toiling, unappreciated pitcher. "Cleveland had the bases loaded after a couple of errors," recalled Jim Gardner. "I went to the mound and had the infield come in. The errors had made Butch mad, I think, and he said, 'Here, Jim, you take it.' Just like that. So, I did. I warmed up, and my first pitch was hit a roller toward third; Raythell kind of bobbled it trying to turn the double play and, well, we lost the game." Buies Creek went on to defeat Cleveland and ended up taking the league crown for the second straight year.

Angier/Pea Ridge had been frustrated a bit in trying to reestablish the title-winning ways fans had become used to when players were on payrolls. In four post-war summers, Angier's baseball faithful had seen a professional team come and go, a park to play lost and another gained, and a group of memory-filled men and boys try to establish some semblance of what they had known town ball to be. Their quest had been three shaky seasons of juggling players, struggling for an identity and trying to recover prestige as a small-town baseball hub. But as long as these Adams, Price, and Gardner boys were in town and could throw hard and wheel around the bases, there would always be a town team. Angier's next decade of baseball would be just as shaky in some ways but somewhat remarkable in others.

"We watched every single move those guys made on the field. It was our baseball education."

- Marshall Price

"Second base is what I always wanted to play..."

- Frank Gardner

```
   Score by innings:        R. H. E.
Angier  ....... 010 000 000—1  8  0
Kipling ....... 101 010 00x—3  8  1
   Adams and R. Adams; Brown and
Matthews.
```

A bare linescore with batteries.

Chapter 11 - Let the Good Times Roll

New Decade, New Challenges, New Foes

There was a whole new ball game when the decade of the 1950s rolled around; not just the town ball game in Angier, which had gone its own way. But it was a new day for the young men who had been raised on baseball. Little tykes of the sandlots and students of the high-powered semipro players, they were teenagers of the war and the town's one minor league season. These boys had become men and would soon face the responsibilities of college, military service, marriage and families, or honest-to-goodness jobs — sometimes all four.

Outside of the tiny world of Angier baseball, there was a bigger world that was beginning to change drastically. This was the beginning of a decade of prosperity these young men had never known as boys. It would become the time of television, fast cars, rock 'n' roll, drive-in movies, *Peyton Place,* and *The Power of Positive Thinking*. Though their parents, who remembered the trials of the Great Depression, were reluctant to spend, this new generation was marching into a world of shrewd marketing and advertising that put them into a carefree buying mode. The world's richest and most powerful nation was now full of kids who wanted — and knew they could have — much more than their parents had. This new generation was, in fact, ready to let the good times roll. Two years of war in Korea would put a damper on these good times, but it was only a speed bump along the way.

All of this was beginning to have its effect on baseball in one way or another, and from top to bottom. Sure, the major leagues were still popular, and minor leagues were still riding a post-war resurgence, though not for long. A semipro player could still make a good buck in certain places, but things began popping up in the sports world that were grabbing the attention of fans. The popularity of college football now had a solid tradition of its own in the South, and the professional National Football League was expanding. Closer to home, stock car racing was revving up in the Carolinas, with the establishment of NASCAR in 1949. Even closer to home, North Carolina State College would become home to a huge arena that could sit 12,400 fans for basketball. [50] Baseball was no longer the sole proprietor of a North Carolina sports fan's heart.

Baseball was struggling in the smaller minor league towns in the state. Dunn-Erwin's Tobacco State League team did not last through June of 1950, being sold to Whiteville. The league cited poor attendance. As it turned out, the league itself was on its last legs. The six towns whose teams finished the 1950 season would not see professional baseball again. It had become clear that towns the size of an Angier or a Fuquay could no longer support the baseball business. The end of the five-year run of the Class D Tobacco State League now indicated that towns of 5,000-10,000 people, such as Clinton, Lumberton, Dunn, Smithfield, and Sanford could no longer maintain professional teams. By the end of the 1952 season, even the Coastal Plain League, with its cities of 10,000 or more, would disband along with the Western Carolina League and the North Carolina State League in the western part of the state. Members of the Carolina League and the South Atlantic League, which sought venues in cities of over 20,000, would be the only survivors of the 1950s. [51]

It was a similar decline to that of the 1930s and the 1940s, only this time there was no war or depression to blame. In fact, it could be said that progress and prosperity were the culprits this time. Things such as television, air-conditioned homes, faster modes of travel, and the growth of competing recreations and sports were all chipping away at baseball's dominance on the American scene. Baseball was left to the guys who wanted to play for the fun of it and the fans who still had a little pride in the town team. While communities such as Angier still had plenty of young men who wanted to play the game, fan support was another matter. Small town baseball would never see the crowds of avid followers it had before World War II.

Change at Home and On the Road

All of this didn't mean a whole lot on a baseball diamond in Angier, at least directly. The boys who had been raised on baseball were going to play baseball no matter what. Yes, they were taking over the responsibilities their fathers once had — jobs and families of their own. But baseball was their recreation as long as their legs could carry them and as long as they could still put the bat on a good curveball.

Guys such as Marshall Price played on. He had followed his father into the hair-cutting business, and he got married in 1950. But even that didn't cause him to break a stride in his pursuit of the summer game. The man who had pursued ball all over Germany with his military unit announced to the love of his life, Mattie Agnes Matthews, "I am going to play ball. You may come out and watch, if you want. But I am going to play ball." Mattie would accept it and fall into the routine. "Marshall would cut hair on Saturdays until right before the game, come up to the apartment, put on that hot, wool baseball suit and go out and play ball, and come right back after the game and go back to cutting hair," she said.

Frank Gardner hadn't married yet, but he had enough life changes in the world of baseball to keep him occupied. Another transition was on the way for him that would make 1950 a big year. The spring renewed Frank's hope of making a break in the world of pro baseball. His Rocky Mount team had finished the 1949 regular season atop the Coastal Plain League standings, before being surprised by Greenville in the first round of the playoffs. He had batted an acceptable .258, but his hopes rested on his ability to make the good fielding plays from the position he loved, second base. Frank was no longer a rookie, and he was making more than that rookie salary now. He figured he earned every bit of it, for these were hard-work months.

Despite the long days, lots of travel, and lots of time away from home, Frank was willing to give baseball — and himself — a chance. The way he saw it, there were worse things in the world than having to play second base every day, and he knew that the man at the top of the diamond needed only to prove he could consistently make the catch and the flip. A .300 bat was hardly a necessity for a second baseman. If he could just get that bat off of his shoulders and find a way to bat maybe .280, there was even a chance a moving up.

But as the season unfolded, his batting numbers went in the other direction. His average slumped by more than twenty points in the early weeks of the season, something that does not bode well for any player, even on a Class D minor league roster. In this classification, a second-year player in a slump was usually wondering about his future in the professional game; even a good-fielding second baseman and even a guy who loved to play.

Then, on one July night in Rocky Mount, Frank made an uncharacteristic mistake, and the incident that followed caused frustration to turn to total disillusionment. It was a simple mistake, one that wouldn't even be recorded in the scorebook as an error. Frank charged in to field a bunt on the first base side. Trouble was, the first baseman had charged too, and it was Frank's duty to cover first base. For a second baseman, it was an unacceptable mental error. Dumb, dumb, dumb. Frank knew it, and so did Red Benton, the Leafs' manager. But Frank never thought he should have gotten the on-field dressing down Benton gave him, right there in front of everyone. "There must have been about 2,000 there at the game. I was young, and it kind of hurt my feelings. I jumped the team and came home." Benton had not given much thought to the chewing-out he gave his young second baseman, and Frank had given even less thought to how much he loved playing second base each day. He was on the road that night.

It was in the coming days that Frank would give baseball more thought, and he decided to give the pro game another chance. A new contract took him to the Virginias and another Class D league, the Appalachian League. He played out the season with manager Worlise Knowles, a former Coastal Plain League star who had played for Doc Smith in New Bern. The evening of the last game of the season, Knowles, seeking a reunion with his old manager, gave Frank a ride home to Angier. It was that night Frank learned he would soon be hitting the road and donning a new uniform. In Angier, on his father's desk, awaited a draft notice. Within days of his last game as a professional baseball player, Frank signed another contract, this one for a term in the United States Air Force.

The Korean War began in June of 1950, and for the next two

years, some of Angier's young men would be signing up. Frank's brother, Jim, would start a career with the Air Force in 1951, and Bill Watkins would have to drop the managing duties for the home team to leave for Korea in 1952. A number of the Adams boys would also join the service because of the conflict on the Asian peninsula.

The Season

For the boys still in high school, a war on the other side of the globe was barely an afterthought. It was not like World War II, when everything, including baseball for rural high schools, was put on hold. And it was the boys at Angier High School who carried the baseball banner for the town in 1950. The Bulldogs had been knocking at the state playoff door for the past three seasons and finally tore it down in the spring of 1950. This year they would drive all the way to the state finals. With their 14-10 win over Gatesville for the school's first ever Class B Eastern title, Angier was one of the two best baseball teams in the state. Class B was the classification with the smallest schools, but this did not make such a feat any less challenging, since North Carolina was still a state of hundreds of small high schools. Harnett County itself had ten high school's.

Coach Joe Langley had Butch and Elbert Adams, Ben Price, Joe Partin, Fred Hockaday, and a young star who would suit up for Pea Ridge in coming years, Jimmie Odell Matthews. The team carried a 14-3 record into the best-of-three state title series against Clemmons, a team that had won the title in three of the past four years. Clemmons swept the series by 5-4 and 5-1 scores.

With such promise on the high school diamond, prospects for a summer-league team would have been good. But the Cape Fear League did not organize for the summer of 1950, and the towns and communities that been members of the league had to join another league in the area or be left with pickup games. That was how it turned out in Angier. With no league to play in, some of the players managed to organize a few games on weekends. But that was it.

There were other nearby leagues for players to seek out. The Twin County, Wake-Harnett, and Central Carolina leagues were all in the vicinity. Down the road, the Varina Sluggers team was heading for the state semipro tournament in Roxboro. But it was still a challenge for the teams of the abandoned Cape Fear League to find a non-league game to play that summer. Buies Creek, a member of the old league, promoted a July 4th game with Boone Trail in *The News & Observer* and pleaded that it was "seeking games with any semipro outfit within a 100-mile radius."[52]

Buies Creek and Angier had gotten up a game the week before, with Archie Lynch tossing a two-hitter to beat Angier, 5-3. And the Angier boys would find a few more games to play that summer. Elbert, Connie, Hayden, Gerald, and Raythell Adams played that year, and

178

Marshall Price, Kenneth Jackson, and Roscoe Flowers suited up. Jim Gardner and Bill Watkins shared the field management duties of the team, when it played.

Prison Time

None of them had any idea where the makeshift scheduling would take them from week to week. One weekend may have meant a stop in Raleigh, where they would take on a team from Cameron Village; the next might be out in the country against the Twin Oaks boys. But it was in 1950 that the local team found an opponent that would prove to have at least one open date every year. Semipro teams often needed non-league dates to fill, and this is probably how officials in the state prison system hatched the idea of letting their best inmate ballplayers test their talents against outside teams.

It had become fairly common throughout the years for baseball teams on practically all levels to venture inside prison walls or fences to play games against inmates. Among the most famous series of games was one in the early 1940s when Connie Mack's Philadelphia Athletics, spring training in California, played a series of exhibitions at San Quentin State Prison.

Closer to home, a team from Fuquay Springs played the Camp Polk prison team as early as 1934. In the 1940s there were newspaper references to segregated black and white baseball teams in the state prison system, and one gained some notoriety when the Central Prison team ventured into predominantly black Chavis Park in Raleigh to play the all-black Raleigh Grays. The state prison system even had playoff series in the 1950s. It was not unlike any other situation where a group of men were together. Just like a military unit, a mill, or any other industry, when men gathered, a baseball game was often in the making.

But a date in 1950 was the first for the young men from Angier to schedule a game at Central Prison, and they knew they were in for serious business when their tour of the complex took them to the execution chamber. It was sort of a reality check for the boys to see how things worked on the other side, which is probably why their memories don't necessarily involve the results of the games. They do recall the competition being well worth of their best efforts, though. "At least one of them was usually a former professional," said Marshall Price.

It was probably the only time actually winning or losing meant little to them in comparison to the experience itself. The prison games were not accounted for in any records, clippings, or standings. They do remember things like purchasing handmade items such as billfolds from the inmates or learning to play a ball off of a tall left field wall. One prisoner jokingly offered to fetch a home run ball, because, as Angier player Harold Ellen put it, "When the ball was hit over the wall, it was, well, out."

"I went in in relief up there once," said Jim Gardner. "They had all right-handed batters, I remember. And a very short [in distance] wall, shorter than the one in Boston, I imagine. But it was pretty high. Had to be."

180

After a few years, when the Angier-Central Prison series had been established, the prison system actually let the doors swing the other way on a few occasions. The Pea Ridge field became the venue. Seeing baseball players, some who hadn't been outside of the prison walls in months or years, was a natural curiosity in Angier, and a few Sundays brought the largest crowds the Pea Ridge ballpark ever had.

"They finally came down on a Sunday afternoon," recalled Harold Ellen. "We had standing room only all the way down the sides. They had to rope off so that they'd stay away from the fans. They roped it off and had a couple of guards. But they knew those guys wouldn't run, because if he runs, the whole deal is off; they don't get to go out again. They said everybody would be on perfect behavior, no argument or anything."

"I always know where my players are, and they are not going anywhere," a prison guard told Marshall Price.

Just like much of the semipro baseball phenomenon, the prison games would fade as the 1950s progressed. It was another case of boys raised on baseball, doing what they had learned as kids and what players before them had done: going wherever there was a place to play and another group who wanted to play. Whether it was an Army team, a mill team, a town team down the road, or a prison team — league or non-league — the Adams, Price, Ellen, and Gardner boys would play baseball. They had entered a new decade and a new era, with new things going on in their lives and in the world around them. But that would not make them put down their gloves ... not just yet.

Webster Lupton

Chapter 12 - Assembling a Winner

Pea Ridge Grows into a Power

It was the second week of June 1951, and Clyde Adams again had enough cousins to round up a summer baseball team. But after the previous season's blight of league baseball, Clyde didn't want to have a team without a league to play in. The boys in Angier didn't appear to be organizing anything, so Clyde took it upon himself to put something together. This was the beginning of a process that would repeat itself each year until it became almost routine to Clyde. He would recruit players, suit them up, make sure they were in some sort of league, and direct his kin to get the little Pea Ridge field in shape. Clyde put word out that he was heading up the organization of a new league and invited the interested parties to a meeting at the country store across the road from the field. His Pea Ridge boys had been warming up with the spring weather, and he needed to give them a regular schedule.

So on a Monday night in the little country store, plans were hatched for a new league with an old name. The original plans for the newest version of the Cape Fear League were to include six teams. But as the next few days passed and as Lillington and the community of McGee's Crossroads dropped out for various reasons, the league was reduced to four teams: Pea Ridge, Buies Creek, the Wake County community of Auburn, and a team sponsored by Wall's Store in Johnston County. Clyde set down some basic ground rules (which of course meant little), set a weekend schedule, and planned a post-season playoff format.

He did not know it at the time, but this was the meager beginning to something that would actually endure longer than any of the previous Angier baseball endeavors. His Pea Ridge team would play league ball for seven straight seasons. It would not be the fast semipro league of the past, with the price of playing often at the forefront, but it would be competitive league ball, and it would be Clyde's team, Pea Ridge's team, and, whether folks in town liked it or not, it would be Angier's team. These would be years in which Clyde Adams would consistently be reminded of how informal this brand of baseball was. Players would come and go, and so would teams and leagues. But Clyde would always be on top of things, making sure that his little Pea Ridge team had the right men at the time. He was on his way to building a consistent winner.

The 1951 league season was an interesting one if for no other reason than that the Buies Creek roster included a hitter of almost legendary proportions in North Carolina: Hargrove "Hoggie" Davis. The Wilmington native had just completed a minor league career in which he posted plus-.300 batting averages in each of his six seasons, mostly in the Tobacco State League. That included a remarkable .408 average during the 1949 campaign for Wilmington, a season in which he drove in 106 runs. The only thing that had kept Davis from moving to the majors was his speed in the field; a motorcycle accident had left him with a slight limp. Davis had been assistant baseball coach at Campbell College since 1947 under another minor league veteran, Earl Smith. Both manned the Buies Creek team in the 1951 Cape Fear League.

1951 - Meck, Runyon

The 1951 season was the season in which Clyde Adams, out of necessity, would learn the advantages of scouting and recruiting. He wouldn't ship players all the way from Louisiana and pay them regular salaries as had the 1938 and '39 Angier Bulls. That is probably why the team had had the staying power it did. But Clyde would find a way, in his wheeling-and-dealing, "Tell you what I'll do" style. He would pick up players here and there, always with his ear to the ground for the best players in the area. For little or nothing, he would make those players think there really was something at this little park in the middle of nowhere. This is how Pea Ridge consistently came up with a winner for the next seven summers and how town ball stayed alive in Angier.

Clyde's first pipeline of talent came from Fort Bragg. With Frank Gardner in the Air Force, Jim soon on the way, and Elbert Adams headed for the Marines, the town's baseball strength was becoming slightly diluted. So Clyde, with the help of his right-hand man, Bill Watkins, decided to use the military to his advantage. Watkins, a career soldier, was from Angier and was stationed at Bragg, now one of the largest Army installations in the nation and, to Clyde, a source of baseball manpower. Watkins was the connection the town needed for baseball players. For the next two summers, before he himself got orders to Korea, Watkins shipped in reinforcements from Bragg to fill in when needed. Both Ernest Meck, a pitcher from Pennsylvania, and Bill Runyon, an infielder from West Virginia, were among the troops that were instrumental in a successful 1951 season.

Raythell, Rexwell, Pete, Elbert, and Connie Adams were all on the team. Marshall Price was becoming another veteran player, and Bobby Gardner made contributions. Another hometown boy, Roy Earp, put on an amazing single-game hitting show on a Saturday in June that year. In a wild 19-10 victory over Buies Creek, Earp went six-for-six with a home run and two doubles. [53] This was also the year that Bill Bowden stepped to the mound for the Pea Ridge squad. A left-hander, Bowden struck out sixteen batters in a mid-August 7-3 win over Buies Creek that helped Pea Ridge to the finals of the league playoffs.

The team drove to a league finals series with Wall's Store. Pea Ridge took the opener, 10-5, with Meck pitching the win and helping himself with a double and a triple at the plate. Wall's Store took the next game, 6-3, as Bowden shouldered the loss. In the rubber match at Pea Ridge, the hometown bats cracked out a 15-6 win. Rexwell Adams went two-for-three at the plate, and Watkins was the winner on the mound.

Despite some roster shuffling, Pea Ridge had brought home Angier's first league title of any sort since the 1946 minor league team. It was not near as meritorious or noteworthy as winning a minor league title or a title the likes of which the semipro team had won in 1938. But it was something for Clyde Adams to build on, and he would make sure the town would not have to wait another five seasons for another title.

Clyde was learning the advantages of finding new talent. Even when his brothers and cousins weren't available to play — and their numbers would dwindle over the next few years — Clyde would still manage to have a winning team at the place folks called Pea Ridge.

1952 - Matthews, Faucett, Chapel, Kosakowich

To build this consistent winner, Clyde had to constantly find new leagues to play in and had to introduce new talent to the little park in the country. Each spring, new leagues — or new teams in old leagues — seemed to sprout up everywhere. There was not any sort of community commitment or organizational intent in all of this. The teams and leagues were driven solely by the number of people who wanted to play baseball. Each year the creation or renewal of another league came down to how many players in the community were still willing to put in playing time on summer weekends.

The Tri-County League was like a number of leagues in the region in 1952, and it was the league that Pea Ridge joined. The Johnston County, Neuse River, Strawberry, and Tobacco Belt leagues

187

were all playing the same sort of get-up-a-gang-and-go weekend ball in the area.

Clyde Adams lined his team up with Fuquay, Jones Sausage (Garner), Farrington, Vance, New Hill, Cary, and a team from the Wake County community of Millbrook called Falls of the Neuse, all small-town and crossroads community teams. The league actually began the season in late May with ten teams, but Lillington and Wake Forest, which had 2-7 and 1-8 starts, withdrew in June. That was how it went with town ball. If a team was having a losing season or if its players otherwise lost interest, they simply dropped out of the league standings, and the players either went to another team or played pick-up games for the rest of the summer.

In the new league, Pea Ridge was playing more and more outside of the Harnett County area and was gaining more exposure. The team, largely because the Adams boys had been playing together for years, was beginning to play as a unit. The core of Adamses and other Angier locals made the team work. But Clyde was supplementing his roster each time one of the regulars had to drop out for work, military service, family, or age. More new names appeared in the Pea Ridge lineup. Field manager Bill Watkins, in his last summer before going to Korea, had Bobby Chapel on the mound, and fielders Jack Faucett and Mike Kosakowich would supply some hitting strength for the team. Bill Bowden was back in '52 as were Adams regulars, Raythell and Hayden. Elbert Adams was away in the Marines, but Connie would hold down the left side of the infield, either at third or short. Wayron "Pete" Adams and Gerald

"Butch" Adams were occasionally called on in relief, and Ray McLeod and Marshall Price were back on the roster. Strangely enough, a Gardner was not in the lineup; Frank and Jim were both in the Air Force now.

This was also the first summer at Pea Ridge for high school player Jimmie Odell Matthews, who would be a fixture in Angier town ball for years. Jimmie Odell, as his teammates came to call him, was a high school junior and only seventeen years old, but it soon became clear that he could play with the men. He had already proven himself in the high school ranks by starring in football, basketball, and baseball. Angier High School didn't have a track and field team, but he would enter the 1953 state meet in Chapel Hill anyway. Without any training, he placed first in the broad jump and second in the 220-yard dash, losing only to the state record holder. [54]

In any sport, any game, any place, a person would want the muscled five feet, eleven inches, 180-pound Matthews on their team. The folks at Angier and Pea Ridge were lucky in that respect, because it seemed Jimmie Odell never wanted to play anywhere else. He loved home, and there was nothing — not even college scholarships or professional baseball offers — that could drag him from the little town of Angier. He was a star there and nowhere else. But he made people wonder: "What if …?"

Jimmie Odell Matthews' impact on the Pea Ridge team was almost immediate. He went three-for-four in a game in the first week in June, had three hits including a two-run homer the next week, and smacked a game-winning three-run home run the next. And this was only the start. With Matthews, Price, and Ray McLeod in the outfield and at the top part of the batting order, the Pea Ridge team now had a combination of speed and power that would produce a winner. An experienced crack infield filled with Adams boys and a pitching rotation led by Bowden supported that notion.

Their play on the field proved it. The team rolled to a 25-3 league season, finishing four games ahead of the Chatham County community of Farrington. This was a year in which, for any number of reasons, the playoffs were not recorded or reported. Pea Ridge went on to sweep Jones Sausage in the first round of the playoffs, with Bill Bowden pitching a 2-0 shutout in the clincher. But that series wrapped up on September 7, and between the new college and high school year and the height of the tobacco barning and market season, the teams might simply have run out of players. Though baseball was a dearly loved game, nothing — not even baseball — could supersede the necessity of getting the tobacco crop in the barn, cured, and to the market. This is, after all, why these were weekend leagues. Tobacco was the lifeblood of the community, and a man's family was, more often than not, also his farming workforce. Another factor might have been particularly pertinent that year. As Pea Ridge was closing out its playoff series, Angier's high school coach of six years, Joe Langley, died. It was a shock to the small town, and playing more baseball might have seemed out of order.

Nevertheless, Pea Ridge had won the regular season championship of the Tri-County League, posting a blistering 27-3 record, including the playoff wins. The successful season had proven that with leadership, a good nucleus, and adequate renewal of players, a tiny community could still produce a winning baseball team. Clyde Adams had watched his core of players become a team, had worked the pipeline of talent in the region, and had come out a winner. Adams had learned that the continual renewal of talent could pay off, and his philosophy of always being on the lookout for available players carried on for the next four seasons.

1953 - Ellen, Mangum, Wall

The following summer brought a new league, a new title run, and Clyde Adams typically on the prowl for new talent. The rest of his administrative duties were beginning to take care of themselves. Scraping up money was not as big of a problem. The team's success was bringing a few sponsors from in town to help offset costs of uniforms and equipment. Clyde was no longer having to call around to find a league. League organizers were calling him. That left the issue of gathering up enough players for a roster for the coming year, and even that was becoming easier. Word had gotten out that there was a small dynasty being developed in the middle of the country east of Angier, and college and semipro players were less hesitant to get on board with a winner.

Clyde, like any good baseball boss, was not going to let his little Pea Ridge bunch sit on their laurels. And a good pitcher was always welcome. Bill Watkins was now in Korea, and with him and Jim Gardner out of the picture, Clyde also needed an on-field manager. He would see that things worked out perfectly. He had seen Don Wall and pitcher Carlton Mangum play with the Jones Sausage team from Garner the year before. In Mangum, Clyde saw an exceptional pitcher. He knew that if he could lure Mangum, a successful veteran of the minor leagues, he would have a winner on the mound. Mangum was Wall's brother-in-law, so Clyde went through Don. In a "deal" that would have an effect on Pea Ridge for the next four years, Clyde promised Wall the field management of the team if he could bring Mangum along.

Carlton Mangum: Journeyman Pitcher

Carlton Mangum was one of those guys who made sure he had a full tank of gas in his car on a Saturday morning. There was a lot of traveling to do on the weekends, pitching in two or three different towns sometimes. A lot of time on the road. A lot of time to think. Nowadays he wondered what it could have been like if he had grabbed up his young family, packed his bags, and headed for Omaha, Nebraska, in 1951. Maybe he actually could have made a good living playing baseball. After all, he had won twenty games and led the Coastal Plain League in strikeouts just four years ago, and he still had a lot of good pitches left. But they wanted him to go all the way out there just to be a relief pitcher.

"Back then, I thought a relief pitcher barely put on a uniform," Mangum said. "It wasn't enough work for me. So I stayed in Winston-

Salem until finally they didn't give me that option. They just sent my contract to Omaha. And that guy I was talking to in St. Louis on the phone said 'You're not gonna give up baseball. You're gonna wind up out there.' I said, 'You think I won't.' I was back in Raleigh the next day. They sent me one contract right after the other to go out to Omaha, and I never would sign it."

Carlton Mangum went over this scenario for mile after mile. All water under the bridge, now. Have to get to a game — Roxboro, Garner, Asheboro, or wherever.

Mangum was a guy who never played a game of high school baseball. Those years were the war years, and he had to turn elsewhere to learn the ropes of the game. They were the years he got on with the Robertson Chemical team, a league team from Garner that played in the Raleigh area. With Robertson, Mangum got to play with James Stevens, Ford Jordan, and Billy West, all future professionals who were developing their games and all of whom would find their ways to Pea Ridge. He also got to watch some good college pitchers work.

"You could tell the ones that had good coaching, and I picked up a lot that I saw them doing. I was fortunate, too. We had by far the best team in the league with Ford and James and all those guys. I didn't lose a game in two years — and played every weekend."

With pro scouts everywhere after the war, Carlton Mangum was sure to get a good look. He was nineteen years old when K.D. Barnes and Jim Mills came calling with a professional contract. Barnes was the owner of the Concord club in the Class D North Carolina State League;

193

Mills was the manager. Mangum said, "I had gotten out of high school and was working for the state, making about $150 a month. They came by offering me a contract for a pretty good amount of money. I said, 'Where do you want me to sign?' I signed right there on the job."

Concord was a good baseball town, with a rich tradition of semipro ball from the 1930s. But their pro team floundered, posting a 44-62 record. Mangum won just six games, but he showed promise in striking out almost one batter per inning he pitched. He moved to the Coastal Plain League the next season where he helped the Goldsboro Goldbugs by appearing in forty-seven games, posting a 20-14 record and striking out a league-leading 248 batters.

He learned things along the way. One was that being a hot commodity in the minor leagues wasn't all it was hatched up to be. He was sent from Goldsboro to Wilson and finally to Class B Winston-Salem in the course of two seasons. It was during his term in Winston-Salem that the whole deal with the move to Omaha came up. The other thing that Mangum learned, the thing that would make his services more valuable, was a knuckleball. The fact that he was mastering the art of the dancing, diving, dodging pitch meant that he could get batters out and go inning after inning after inning. A knuckleball is a slow but effective pitch that requires talent to learn. It does not spin as it approaches the plate, and because it does not spin, the wind resistance meets the rise along the stitches of the baseball and causes it to make unpredictable moves as it heads for the batter. If it is thrown correctly, the "knuckler" results in pure frustration for the best of batters and sometimes for the

194

best of catchers, because when it leaves the pitcher's hand, no one knows quite where it will end up. The fact that the slow-moving knuckleball causes less wear on a pitcher's arm also makes a good knuckleball pitcher a valuable commodity.

That is why Carlton Mangum could toss nine innings on Saturday and come right back on Sunday with another full game. That is why his tank was full of gas on Saturday morning. His car and his durable right arm could take him to places that offered good money. Almost everywhere Carlton Mangum pitched, he was getting better than $20 a game and, in some places, a whopping $100.

Now he was carpooling with his brother-in-law to little Pea Ridge, where nobody was getting paid. He knew if he didn't go, he'd hear about it: There was no reason he couldn't go down there if Don was going, and it wouldn't hurt him a bit to play a couple of games for Don. Carlton Mangum would find out if the Pea Ridge trip was worthwhile.

Harold Ellen: A Good Learner

Clyde Adams didn't have to go far to find another player who would prove valuable for the next few seasons. For Harold Ellen, the two years prior to 1953 must have seemed like one long winter. You couldn't play baseball on a destroyer escort off the coast of Korea, and Ellen was a guy who liked being around a baseball diamond. He was another one whose father taught him how to handle a bat, watch a ball into the small glove, and follow through on a throw. He was too young to actually remember his dad breaking his arm throwing a curveball in a town-ball game in the 1930s. He had heard the stories growing up, though: "Somebody once told me it sounded like somebody shot a rifle. One guy even ran, thought Daddy had been shot."

But Harold did not shy away from baseball. His memories of the game would be much fonder. During his playing days in high school, the Angier High teams were good ones, though the team of his senior season had just missed the state playoffs. The next season was Angier High's state finals year, and by that time Harold was in the Navy and headed for the coast of Korea.

Now that he was back, he was ready to play baseball. He had his sights set on getting a college diploma, and would be making tracks to Campbell and Elon colleges over the next few years. Harold thought he could be a teacher and a coach, and for a young baseball player, teaching was a perfect "day job." The calendar was pretty much laid out: school in the winter, baseball in the summer. A lot of semipro and even professional players had followed such a schedule, and it was one that he would follow for years to come.

In Harold Ellen, Clyde Adams had the good fortune of picking up a player who could perform with almost equal ability as catcher, pitcher, and in the outfield. For the next few years, Harold would play spring ball at Campbell and Elon before his summers at Pea Ridge. At Campbell, he would hone his skills under Earl Smith and Hoggie Davis and learn the value of a solid battery by catching Jim Perry, who he termed "the best control pitcher I ever caught." Perry was on his way to a seventeen-year major league career. Harold Ellen himself credited much of his learning to "line shots and experience."

There was little doubt then that when Harold Ellen took the field, he knew what he was doing. "Haroldteen" was his nickname then. It was a nickname he had picked up in his high school days at Angier. "My middle initial was T., so somehow that nickname evolved. I know, though, that wherever I went in the world, if somebody called out, 'Haroldteen,' I knew they were from Angier." Haroldteen's proven skill and knowledge of the game would make their marks on the Pea Ridge team.

"He could play any position," Frank Gardner said. "He had a good head on him, and he loved to play the game. You enjoyed playing with Harold, because you knew Harold was playing to win."

The Season

With the new acquisitions on board and many of the old-timers back, Clyde Adams and his team embarked on a new season in the new league. It was the Central State League in 1953, but many names of old foes were again in the standings. Fuquay, Farrington, Sanford, Mamers, and Moncure were all on the league roster at the start of the season. Of course, the drop-add, natural selection of teams would take place during the season, but the six-team format survived the year.

Clyde Adams and Don Wall had a number of players to work with as the season went forward, with four Adams cousins, Marshall

"Pug" Price, Ray McLeod, and the new boys all lined up. Mangum, Ellen, and Bill Bowden carried much of the pitching, with Butch Adams being used on occasion. Jimmie Odell Matthews, who had batted over .600 in his senior year for the high school team, was in the lineup, and everyone thought it could be his last season in town, considering the scouts that were showing up for nearly every game.

Pea Ridge rolled off a 7-2 record before the end of May and, after a June slump, picked up the pace behind Connie Adams' strong bat. Connie got twelve hits in four games to help catapult the team into the league lead, which it kept for the duration.

Adams and company then shortened a five-game series in the first round of the league playoffs by eliminating Moncure three games to one. Then came the finals and Farrington, a series that would be partially washed out. The series opened in Farrington, and the first game was called just after Pea Ridge made a come-from-behind rally to take a 4-1 lead in the sixth. A trickle of September rain had gotten progressively worse, and after Farrington failed to score in the bottom of the sixth, the game was called. Rain was in the forecast for the next day, which is probably the reason why only four Farrington players showed up for the second game of the series. Pea Ridge was awarded a 9-0 forfeit and took a 2-0 lead in the series.

After Billy Powell tossed a five-hitter to stump Pea Ridge 2-1 the next Saturday, Pea Ridge clinched the playoff crown at home that Sunday with a 14-4 clubbing of the visitors. The winning battery of Carlton Mangum and Raythell Adams helped themselves by collecting six hits between them on the offensive side. The minor controversy that emerged over the rain game and the next day's forfeit would be bitter for a Farrington team that was used to winning, and it would be fodder for a new rivalry that would carry into the next season.

1954 - Honeycutt, Powell

With a few league titles on the record — however informal the record was — Pea Ridge had now become a team with a reputation for winning. It brought Clyde Adams a few headaches. He was running short of uniforms, for instance. At least seventeen players had put in time with his Pea Ridge team during the 1953 season, and with so many players coming and going over the seasons, it seemed uniforms were slipping out of the door. Clyde, with the help of some businesses in town, had bought two sets of uniforms for the team, both white with red trim, one with PEA RIDGE across the shirt front and another with PR on the left breast. But getting twelve or fifteen men into the same set was becoming next to impossible. The rule from here on would be that some of the players took the field in the PEA RIDGE set and others in the PR set, maintaining the same color scheme with red and white outer stirrup socks. Everyone had the standard black shoes with steel cleats, and most of the boys showed up with red unmarked caps, though it wasn't unusual for a player to don his old college or high school cap. This was just fine at Pea Ridge. These were not leagues of players with bright, new, perfectly uniform outfits on hand. These were teams that played with whoever showed up on

Saturday willing to play.

To Clyde, it didn't matter how many uniforms walked out the door, as long as good players were walking in. He added two more players that summer, "borrowing" from Fuquay Springs to help make his team still stronger, particularly up the middle. The ranks of the Adams players had thinned over the past few seasons, both because Clyde showed little familial favoritism when it came to putting the best players he could find on the field and also because many of the cousins were now taking on more family and business responsibilities ... and were simply getting older.

Clyde was fortunate enough to have Elbert Adams back from the Marines and ready for baseball duty. His solid glove and bullwhip arm were made for third base, and he was as effective at the plate. He and first baseman Hayden Adams, who likely put in more games in a Pea Ridge uniform than anyone else, would be fixtures at the corners for the next few seasons.

However, the other Adamses were fading from the team picture. Claybourne, Odell, and Rexwell were no longer regulars. Wayron and Butch were getting less and less pitching time thanks largely to the younger, better pitchers Clyde had picked up. Butch was also about to spend four years of service with the Air Force. He would not pitch again for an Angier team. Connie's time at short and third base was dwindling. For the first time since the team had gotten its legs, Clyde could see a future without a good catcher. Raythell Adams injured his arm in June, and the injury wasn't one that would heal for the summer. Harold Ellen could do some time behind the plate, but his services were needed elsewhere, particularly as pitcher.

Clyde again went hunting. Roger Honeycutt and Glenn Powell were just high school kids, but they had played well for the Fuquay league team the summer before and had been stars at Fuquay Springs High. Honeycutt was an agile shortstop who was a year away from college ball at UNC and four years from a stint in the minors. Tom Segroves, in his sports column in *The Independent*, had dubbed Honeycutt "Mr. Shortstop of the Central State League" in 1953. [55] Though he was still only eighteen years old, Honeycutt actually had a history with Clyde and the Pea Ridge team. He had played a few games with the team as early as 1951, though he was too young then to become a regular.

Honeycutt agreed to join the team and was willing to help recruit Powell, a good catcher with a homerun swing. "There was a semipro team in Raleigh I was thinking about playing with," Powell said. "And then one night, Elbert, Roger Honeycutt, and Harold Ellen came to my house and asked me to come play at Pea Ridge." The visit paid off for the Pea Ridge squad. Powell was on his way to becoming a prospect for the Phillies. His father's veto would send him to Campbell College and Wake Forest. Later, injuries would keep him from realizing his dream of becoming a pro player. Honeycutt and Powell were players Clyde could use during the summers before the pros came stalking, and with their addition, another winner took shape.

The Season

The team rolled into the 1954 season in a league with a new name but full of teams that had become familiar foes over the past two seasons. The six-team Mid-State League contained Pea Ridge and its ever-competitive rival, Fuquay. Farrington had proven a perennial power, and Moncure had former pros Doug Payne and Cecil Cotton, not to mention the leadership of a manager whom Angier old-timers knew well — Zeb Harrington. Harrington had become kind of a grand old man of baseball around Sanford, having played for or managed practically every semipro and pro team the town had produced. Mamers and a new team called Neuse rounded out the league.

The latest combination of talent produced predictable results for Pea Ridge. They again sailed through league play, posting a 24-6 mark at the end of the regular season. Moncure was two games back at 22-8. But Pea Ridge would not get to secure a playoff championship that year because of controversy, again involving the newfound league rival from Farrington. Farrington and Pea Ridge were matched in the first round of the four-team playoffs in September. Pea Ridge won the first game, 8-2, but Farrington took the next two, the last by a whopping 17-0 score. Pea Ridge had never been beaten so badly.

The details of the dispute are unclear, but five days after the 17-0 game, *The News & Observer* reported simply that Farrington was disqualified and that Pea Ridge and Moncure would play in the finals of the Mid-State League playoffs. "Pea Ridge advanced to the finals when its semifinal opponent, Farrington, was disqualified," the story stated. "Farrington was leading the series, two games to one, but league president Sam Howard upheld a protest by Pea Ridge claiming Farrington was using ineligible players." [56] Apparently the Farrington team had gone out and gotten some ringers.

The league ruling did not set well with people from Chatham County, and the title series was never played. A week later, Farrington and Moncure played a two-game series. Meanwhile, Pea Ridge and Wendell hooked up for a best-of-three series the newspaper described as "a series between the winners of the Central Carolina and Mid-State semipro leagues." [57] Wendell won the series in straight games. Pea Ridge would never play in the same league again with Farrington or Moncure.

In July of that season, the Moncure team went to the National Baseball Congress state tournament that had been held in Roxboro for the past three years. It was a tournament that allowed teams to test their skills against the best semipro teams in the state. The winner would go to the nationals in Wichita, Kansas. This was a tournament the Pea Ridge boys had been hearing about since they were kids. Byrne and Scarborough had gone to Roanoke Rapids in 1939 because the Owls had won the state title. Smithfield had been in the tournament, and so had Sanford, one year deciding to play in the national in Wichita rather than stay home and win the Tobacco State League.

The Pea Ridge boys figured that it was about time a baseball town like Angier might have an entry, and if Moncure could qualify for such a competition, they certainly should. They would check into qualifying next season, and that would open new roads for little Pea Ridge.

"I didn't have that many fastballs ...
I had to nibble here and nibble there."

- Harold Ellen

Carlton Mangum

Carlton Mangum won 20 games and led the Coastal Plain League in strikeouts in 1949, playing for Goldsboro. His knuckle ball made him a durable and effective pitcher for a number of professional and semipro teams for years.

(Photo courtesy of Carlton Mangum)

Chapter 13 - Covering New Ground

The Best in the State?

Frank Gardner had not let his baseball days pass him by. During his years at Travis Air Force Base in California, he had found a base commander who loved the game and a base team that needed his infield skills. He found town ball to be as tough as it had been in the East and had found that folks on the West Coast were just as avid about the game as they were at home. California was big-time minor league baseball country. Stockton, Modesto, and San Jose were California League teams in the neighborhood. Pacific Coast League teams were in the nearby cities of Oakland, San Francisco, and Sacramento. Major league baseball was just a few years away from taking the big step of locating in California and making big-time baseball a coast-to-coast game. Just as the other boys from Angier had learned when they traveled with the military service, Frank found that baseball was pretty much a common denominator among men from most anywhere in America. He had fallen in with the town-ball scene in the Bay area, and he liked it enough to keep his talents honed during the summers there.

But the Frank Gardner who played in the Appalachian League in 1950 was not the same Frank Gardner who took the field with Pea Ridge for the 1955 season. Baseball had tossed Frank a bit of a curve during his days with the Travis team. One of the team's stops was in the town of Winters, about an hour north of the base. It was there that a school principal's attractive, young daughter caught Frank's eye. Dee Dee Snow's brother played with the town team in Winters, and she was on hand for most of the games. That's how Frank and Dee Dee met in 1953. Their courtship lasted the summer; they were married that fall; and by the time Frank left the service in 1954, they had a child.

Frank was no longer a kid who could play out his dreams of baseball with the flexibility of a single man. He was a husband and a father who had the responsibilities of finishing his education, finding work, and being a family man. He brought his family home to Angier, went to school at Campbell, and after a short two weeks of semipro ball in Mullins, South Carolina, he realized there was no way he could make a good living playing baseball. He came back home, got a job with Jack Barnes, an electrician in Angier, and began settling down.

The Pea Ridge baseball team Frank Gardner returned to was not the same as the one he had left. The team was now stocked with new talent. It was a well-honed winner with strong bats such as Jimmie Odell Matthews, Marshall Price, Glenn Powell, and Elbert and Hayden Adams. With a veteran like Frank to help at the top of the diamond with young

Roger Honeycutt, this team could be even stronger on defense. Carlton Mangum had been the pitcher of choice for 1954, but since he was sometimes over in the piedmont industrial leagues pitching in the "money" games, Harold Ellen in 1955 would be a good starter when Mangum wasn't available. Pitcher Tommy Bradley had come over from Fuquay Springs with Powell and Honeycutt. The team had indeed grown, and with its growth came popularity. Nowadays it was hard to find a parking place around the PR field on weekends of all-star games or when the prison team visited.

Roxboro

With the team and its popularity growing, Clyde Adams was beginning to believe that his four-year process of stocking and restocking talent and stretching the playing schedule into new leagues was actually going somewhere. By the mid-1950s, Pea Ridge's dominance in league play had Clyde and his players beginning to realize the team's talents could be proven on a higher level. That proverbial bigger fish would be fried in the town of Roxboro.

For years of popular recreational and semipro baseball, the idea of a town-ball team competing outside of its own backyard had been only a dream, simply because there were few fast modes of transportation. Even the major league teams could compete no farther west than St. Louis until airplane travel helped open the West Coast to big-time baseball in the 1950s. Semipro teams had to settle with winning their own leagues and hanging up their gloves until next spring.

The National Baseball Congress changed that notion in 1935 when it answered the call of communities with strong semipro baseball teams that wanted to prove their worth. The NBC organized a series of regional and state non-professional tournaments that led up to a huge national tournament. The national winner would even represent the western hemisphere in a world tournament. At the beginning of a year, teams could apply to the NBC and pay a $10 fee for a chance at qualifying for these tournaments. By mid-July, if the applying team measured up to standards set by a regional office; it could compete for a state or district tournament title. [58]

North Carolina was a charter member of the NBC tournament. The state sent the Shelby-Cleveland Mills team to the nationals in Wichita in 1935 and had offered a representative almost every year since. The Shelby team qualified by invitation that year and went on to place third in the nationals. Over the years, Angier's league rivals from Fuquay, Sanford, and Smithfield had competed in NBC state tournament play, some earning the right to travel to Wichita for the big tournament. In the 1930s and '40s, when town semipro rivalries were at their fiercest, some of the teams that won the North Carolina tournament actually chose not to make the long trip to Wichita, both because of the time and expense spent on travel and because of the timing of the national event. In August, the best semipro team in the state was usually more interested in settling one of those backyard scores. The state tournament of course didn't actually settle the issue of who was the best non-pro team in the state. There were plenty of good teams that chose not to register with the NBC, opting to win their local skirmishes or one of the invitational tournaments that were held in the state. But for non-pro baseball teams, the state NBC event was the closest thing to an official state championship that anyone had devised, and it was a goal for many teams to set their sights on; a chance to test their skills against others in the state. That, and the fact that the tournament was a gathering place for pro scouts, made it attractive.

State NBC tournaments had been played in Greensboro, Raleigh, High Point, and Asheboro before coming to the small mill town of Roxboro, located north of Durham near the Virginia border. Roxboro had built a new baseball park and began hosting the event in 1950. [59] Roxboro was itself a hotbed of baseball, home to one of North Carolina's baseball greats, Enos Slaughter, the long-time major leaguer with the Cardinals and Yankees. The town always had a strong home team in the tournament. The Roxboro Blues, with the help of future major leaguer Dick Groat, had won the tournament in 1950.

The annual tournament became a source of pride — and financial gain — for the little town, and plenty of events were planned around it. A beauty pageant, fireworks for the opening ceremony, and a gathering of town fathers all greeted the sixteen teams who visited for the double-elimination play. The tournament was usually sponsored by the town Exchange Club, and businesses from the Durham and Roxboro areas packed the official program with ads.

In 1954, Pea Ridge had one of its best seasons on record, posting a 24-6 record in the Mid-State League and winning the first round of the league playoffs before being waylaid by controversy. Moncure, which had placed second in the Mid-State League pennant race, qualified for the state NBC tournament and was eliminated by the eventual runner-up, Smithfield. The Marine team from Cherry Point won the tournament for the second straight year.

The 1955 season would be different. Clyde Adams's team became an officially sanctioned National Baseball Congress club and set its sights on July and the state tournament. With the latest assemblage of players, Clyde certainly believed his team had a good shot at being one of the sixteen teams to qualify for the tournament. As the first weeks of the season played out, it was clear that Pea Ridge would make the grade. The team rolled off ten straight wins to start the league season, before losing in mid June, 8-2, to Fuquay. The league all-star game in early July indicated how Pea Ridge, now nicknamed the Panthers by *The Independent,* dominated the circuit's talent. [60] The Panthers, as the top team in the league, played against the best players from the other five teams in the league. The result: a 9-0 victory for Pea Ridge, with Mangum pitching a two-hitter.

By late July, Pea Ridge had posted a 15-2 record in the Central Carolina League, four games better than Garner. The other teams in the league were Fuquay, Wendell, Knightdale, and Sanford. It wasn't until the second week in July that Pea Ridge lost its first home game in league play, 10-9, to Wendell.

The state tournament opened in late July, and it was stocked with teams from larger towns and cities and with sponsorship from industries or other businesses. Durham was represented, as were Burlington, Kinston, and Roanoke Rapids. For Kinston and Roanoke Rapids, reputable baseball cities that were left high and dry when the Coastal Plain League dissolved in 1952, semipro was all the baseball that was left. It was another sign that while baseball was losing followers in smaller cities, there were still players willing to carry the town baseball banner.

The local tournament favorites were the Roxboro Colts, an all-black team, and Cavel, a team from a mill community near Roxboro. Cavel's team was sponsored by the area's big industry, the Collins & Aikman textile mill. Conspicuously absent from the tournament in 1955 was a representative from the Marine Corps. Marines had won the previous three state tournaments with a team from Camp Lejeune in '52 and teams from Cherry Point the next two years. But, according to the Roxboro *Courier-Times*, a new Pentagon requirement had restricted the service teams to playing intra-service tournaments for the right to attend the nationals in Wichita. The service teams had been good for attendance in the tournament, *The Courier-Times* noted, stating that the lack of the military teams in 1955 resulted in smaller gates.

But there was plenty of talent lined up for the tournament, as the Pea Ridge boys would discover. Roanoke Rapids, a past champion which was considered the tournament favorite, heralded a 19-2 record going into the event. Before teams could enter the state tournament, they had to submit a sixteen-member roster of eligible players, which they were required to stick with throughout the tournament. The players had to be certified for eligibility to prevent a team from slipping in someone who was under professional contract. Some roster shuffling was necessary for teams such as Pea Ridge, but not because they had ineligible players. They simply had some players who could not attend all of the games. The tournament sessions ran from Thursday through Sunday and began at six on weekday evenings, which meant that some players simply couldn't make it for the start of a weekday game. Many of the players were, of course, in the middle of the tobacco harvest season, which could be a day-and-night job.

So there was some recruiting before the tournament roster was submitted. Clyde Adams and Don Wall made pitching depth their top priority, since a double-elimination tournament format might require three or four games in three days. Pea Ridge cashed in by picking up a couple of college players. Boyce Haigler came over from Campbell College's team, and lefthander Lowell Davis, who had pitched for Wake Forest's national championship team, agreed to play. With those two, and the usually durable Carlton Mangum, Pea Ridge could have a good pitcher on hand in case they had to play games on straight days.

As it turned out, the Angier/Pea Ridge boys would need all the pitching strength they could get, and then some. Pitching would be the highlight of each game. The pitching help looked good through the first two games, both victories for Pea Ridge. Haigler took the mound in the first game, against Kinston, and tossed a four-hit shutout. He struck out eight and walked two as Pea Ridge took a 6-0 victory. He pitched with the lead for the entire contest, because Elbert Adams and Harold Ellen drove in three runs in the first inning.

While the scheduling of a double-elimination tournament usually punishes teams in the loser's bracket, it favors teams that stay in the winner's bracket. Pea Ridge didn't have another game until a week later. The pitching staff delivered another strong performance in that game against a team called Helena. Mangum went out and got another shutout, and his team blew across ten runs to keep him comfortable. Marshall Price slammed a hit into left-center field to send Frank Gardner and Jimmie Matthews across the plate to spark one of Pea Ridge's big rallies in that game. Mangum ended up stumping the hitters, allowing only four hits and striking out eight.

But advancing in the winner's bracket is the precursor to facing the toughest competition. Pea Ridge's pitching mastery ran headlong into stern competition in the person of a pitcher named James Hambrick. Hambrick had carried his Gibsonville team through the tournament, posting two wins. The team from the town just west of Burlington counted on him again. Haigler went to work for Pea Ridge and had a 1-0 lead going into the fourth inning. But Gibsonville's Jack Mitchell tripled to set up the game-tying run in the fourth. That was when Mangum took over in relief. He would surrender another run in the sixth, and that was all that was needed as Hambrick allowed only five hits in the 2-1 victory, a defensive gem that included only one error. Elbert Adams had two of Pea Ridge's hits.

This put Pea Ridge into the loser's bracket of the tournament, but they were fortunate enough in the scheduling to rest for nearly a week before the next game. They would play two games in two days the next weekend. Pea Ridge struggled back on the strength of the pitching of Davis, the Wake Forest star, who faced off against a college rival, University of North Carolina pitcher Ken Keller. Keller, who was better known as a star football halfback at UNC, took the mound for a team from Carrboro. But Davis bested his rival, allowing just three hits, striking out twelve, and walking none. Price banged a homer in the top of the ninth to give Angier the go-ahead run in a 3-1 victory. The next night, Angier would be entangled in another tight game—and another pitcher's duel. The Roxboro Colts, the all-black team, were the foes, and the Angier batters faced another sterling pitching performance.

The All-Black Team

All-black teams were still common on the semipro level in the 1950s in the South. Although integration of teams in the South was almost unheard of, there were a few instances — even close to home — in which blacks and whites were on the same teams. In Fuquay, Moody "Big Train" Cozart had played enough for *The Independent's* Tom Segroves to consider him the best pitcher on his Mid-State League all-star team. Cozart had played with the Negro League Newark Eagles in the 1940s before settling on a farm near Fuquay. At six feet, four inches and 240 pounds, Big Train became somewhat of a legend around Fuquay for his ability to hit the long ball.

Pea Ridge's Roger Honeycutt had spent some Sundays during two summers as one of two white players on the predominantly black Durham Rams semipro team. The crowds of 4,000-5,000 were the biggest he had ever played before. "That was one of the most rewarding and interesting experiences of my life. ... They treated us very special and that meant a lot to me."

Jackie Robinson had broken into the majors in 1947, and the old all-black professional leagues had since diminished. Though minor league teams in the South were still struggling with the issue, some teams had at least experimented with African American players in the early 1950s. By the mid-'50s black players were showing up on minor league rosters in North Carolina. In 1955, outfielder Dan Morejon of High Point-Thomasville was named the Carolina League's most valuable player.

But for the most part, non-professional black players were still playing on all-black teams that barnstormed or played in "Negro" semipro leagues. In the South, the black semipro teams held a separate Dixie championship, the winner advancing to the National Baseball Congress nationals in Wichita. The NBC had always welcomed black teams, since it was pitching great Satchel Paige who had helped the national tournament get started.

For the Pea Ridge players that day, there was the issue of beating another team and advancing in the tournament. Besides the normal chatter of a baseball game, there was little different about this one. The Roxboro team was not one of just hometown players, either. At least two of their players, Henry Cameron and Ulysses Payton, were former minor leaguers, members of the Salem, Virginia, Rebels, one of the first integrated minor league clubs in the Appalachian League. [61] Cameron would drive in a run that night, and Payton would pitch a masterful game.

The teams played through a closely contested pitchers' standoff. Mangum came through with a four-hit game, striking out six. But all of the hits Mangum allowed were for extra bases, and Roxboro's Payton surrendered just three Pea Ridge hits. The result: Roxboro 2, Pea Ridge 1. Pea Ridge was sent home.

The ever-improving Pea Ridge team had advanced its horizons and had run into a bit of tough luck. In five games, the team had scored twenty-one runs and allowed five, hardly a performance worthy of elimination. It was an example of how fickle the game of baseball can be. Just a few plays, a few pitches, can leave a team soaring or tumbling. The magical line between the highs and the lows can easily and quickly be crossed, twisted, or erased.

Pea Ridge had played well but lost in its first try at tournament play. But the team had proven itself to be a formidable foe in the state tournament arena. Teams across the state, as well as throughout the region, were beginning to discover that Pea Ridge players brought something. Little Pea Ridge, the informal community that couldn't be found on a geographical map, was now on the state's baseball map.

While Roanoke Rapids would win the state tournament and go on to reach the third round of the national tournament in Wichita, Pea Ridge would return to the little field in Harnett County and march toward its own title. They played into October that year, winning the series over Wendell and Garner to claim the Central Carolina League playoff title.

Bradley and Mangum were responsible for most of the victories in the playoff drive. Elbert Adams swatted a grand-slam home run in the eighth inning of the second game of the Wendell series, to lead the team to a 12-9 win. Harold Ellen tossed a three-hit shutout over Garner in the second game of Pea Ridge's three-game sweep. And manager-player Don Wall drove in the winning run in the title-clinching game.

It is interesting to note that Game 2 of the championship series was played on September 24, but Game 3 was not played until October 9, more than two weeks later. Why the delay? There was another series taking place at the time, which had captivated the state as well as the nation. Rookie Roger Craig's Brooklyn Dodgers were facing veteran Tommy Byrne's New York Yankees in the World Series. Craig was a Durham boy who had come up after World War II, playing American Legion ball against some of the Angier boys. Byrne, of course, was the lefthander who had become somewhat of a legend during his Wake Forest and Angier years. He was in the twilight of his professional career but was still valuable enough to take the mound and earn a victory in the Subway Series.

Back in Angier, and in much of North Carolina, baseball folks were captivated by this drama being played out in New York. It was an indication of the grip that baseball still had on the attention of Americans. It seemed that when World Series time rolled around, things were put on hold. Kids sneaked time out from their school work; farmers, buyers, and auctioneers gathered around televisions and radios at tobacco warehouses; stores closed. And, of course, a couple of country baseball teams with their own playoff to settle, would just have to wait.

So Pea Ridge's Central Carolina League championship was conquered and celebrated after the issue of the Subway Series had been settled. It laid the groundwork for 1956, another state tournament bid, and a "subway series" of their own.

1955 Pea Ridge state semipro tournament team

In their first foray into state tournament play, the Pea Ridge boys outscored their opponents, 21-5, but were sent home after five games. The bat boy in front is Melvin Hughes. Front row, left to right: Manager Don Wall, Tommy Bradley, Glenn Powell, Jimmie Odell Matthews, Pete Adams, and Boyce Haigler. Back Row: Roger Honeycutt, Connie Adams, Hayden Adams, Elbert Adams, Harold Ellen, Marshall Price, and Frank Gardner.

Chapter 14 - Town and Country Rivalry

Challenges at Home and on the Road

Angier baseball was back. Not since the successes of the 1950 high school team or the 1938 star-studded semipro team had so much interest been generated over the game in town. The Pea Ridge team, with five league titles in five years, was getting bigger than its proverbial britches. Almost overnight it seemed, the little field that had been built for a family to play pick-up games was now a weekend gathering place for much of the Angier community. There was no real area for parking, so on home Saturdays and Sundays, the gleaming, two-tone Fords, Chevys, and Buicks and the step-side pickup trucks lined both sides of the road near the Pea Ridge field. As many as 500 folks were showing up now for games when Fuquay or the prison team visited or when Pea Ridge hosted the league all-star game. It was nothing like the 1,000-2,000 that packed Angier's park when Byrne and company were mowing down opponents in 1938, but it was certainly burgeoning for a Pea Ridge field that had bleachers for fifty or so people. On those summer Sundays, there was little time between the last prayer at church and the first pitch of the game, so some of the players had to make a quick change and hustle out to the park. The fans didn't bother to change. People showed up in their Sunday best, risking ruination of their nicest shoes just to get a good place to view the game. It had become as much of a social gathering for the women as it was a sporting event for the men. Wives of players, some now with an infant in one arm and their hubby's old glove or favorite bat in the other, would show up early with the players. Girlfriends of the single players arranged to get a ride to the game, leaving open the option for the ride home and creating a scene of flirtation and gossip as certain as the scene of competition. The young kids, who would never again see baseball quite like this, positioned themselves near the fences to scuffle for Price, Matthews, or Adams home runs as they headed for the pond past right-center. And the little store nearby did a booming business.

With spring's arrival, folks around town were thinking baseball again. Who would play? Who would manage? Who would be in the league, and what league would they be in? And with all of this renewed popularity, came another question: Was it time for baseball to move back into town?

For a while, folks who lived in town had harbored the notion that the Pea Ridge ball team had sort of hijacked Angier's baseball identity. Here was little field in the middle of nowhere that had worked its way into becoming the home of a semipro powerhouse, and the town itself didn't even have a team — at least not one called Angier. The folks who remembered that it was Angier that had won the semipro league title in '38, Angier that had captured the minor league playoffs in '46, and Angier that had sent its high school team to the state finals in 1950, were watching this Pea Ridge team capture all of the glory. Though some of the good players in town had never played for Clyde Adams's team, they would get another shot. Town ball was about to come back to town.

"Most of the time Pea Ridge was out there playing ball, some of us in town just kinda decided we'd like to have a team here in town," Ben Price said. "Tommy Gilbert and a few others came to me and said 'Ben, lets get up a ball club,' and asked me to play."

Tommy "Screw" Gilbert was a salesman with savvy not unlike that of Clyde Adams. He made it difficult for the folks he approached to scoff at the prospect of having a new baseball team in Angier. And he had a few things going to make his argument. The Pea Ridge team had evolved into a team of players from Fuquay and Garner. The team's home field was hardly a suitable place for a real crowd. Angier's high school field would be more suitable. And the Angier High School field could soon have lights.

If Gilbert could get the high school field, arrange for financial backing to pay for the team equipment, and round up enough players, Angier could again have a baseball team. Gilbert had actually gathered up a group of players and picked up some games during the summer of 1955. For 1956, he would enter Angier in the same league as Pea Ridge, and the early spring was filled with talk of who would play for whom and when the first Angier-Pea Ridge game would actually come off.

Gilbert had created a sort of mini-mini-version of a Yankees-Dodgers rivalry, and it would keep interest stirred in the community for two summers. It was cause for divided loyalties among the townsfolk, particularly the ones who had spent many weekends following the progress of Clyde Adams's team down the road. An Angier fan's choice of teams usually came down to a player who was a neighbor, friend, or family member. Even that got confusing for fans who saw some of the players, such as Elbert Adams and Tom Zachary Jr., actually move from one team to the other during the course of the season. And Ben Price played for Angier, while brother Marshall played for Pea Ridge.

Gilbert soon proved he could be as persuasive as his Pea Ridge counterpart when it came to luring in players. He would gather up some of the old high school crowd, link up with a few college players, and even traipse onto Clyde Adams's territory to find personnel for the new Angier team.

Clyde Adams did his usual coaxing to get his regulars back and had his right-hand man, Bill Watkins, back from his overseas military duty to resume his post as manager. Raythell Adams was called into regular service again, because Glenn Powell had been lured to Fuquay. Raythell also got support in the person of Billy West, a former minor league catcher who had played with Fuquay. Hayden, Connie, and Wayron "Pete" Adams were all on the Pea Ridge squad. Jimmie Odell Matthews, Frank Gardner, and Marshall Price were other town boys who stayed out at Pea Ridge. Jackie Revis, an outfielder and former high school player at Angier, was also at Pea Ridge. Mangum, Bradley, and Honeycutt made up the out-of-town contingent.

But Gilbert did some recruiting of his own. Harold Ellen, who was attending Campbell College at the time, recalls the agreement that took him and Campbell teammate, catcher Marion Hargrove, to play in Angier: "I was going back to Pea Ridge to play, but the motor in my old car had gone bad. I was the only one amongst our group at school who had a car. Screw Gilbert came down and wanted us to play in Angier. He said, 'If you two will come and play in Angier — both of you — I'll put a motor in your car.' I looked at Marion, and he said 'that looks like what we're gonna do. That's our transportation.' "

Tom Zachary Jr., a teacher in town, played for both teams during the season. Zachary had led UNC in batting in 1955 with a .380 average. His father, Tom Sr., had played a colorful eighteen-year major league career, but he would go down as a footnote in baseball history. He pitched Babe Ruth's sixtieth home run in 1927.

Gilbert also had Ben Price and Kenneth Jackson as well as catcher Hargrove from Campbell College. Gordon Matthews of Angier and two college pitchers, N.C. State's Lou Dickman and UNC's Johnny Johnson, also made appearances for Angier.

The fact that Fuquay and Coats were in the same league made the scramble for ballplayers even tougher that year. This put four teams within about a twenty-mile radius all trying to keep their own players at home, while trying to lure players from other towns and colleges. Mamers, Neuse, Garner, and Knightdale made up the rest of the Central

223

Carolina League. With the teams chosen and the twenty-three-game league schedule set, Angier and Pea Ridge played their early-season games with one big date in mind. As Jim Gardner put it: "Angier was just waiting to play against Pea Ridge, so they could show them what they had."

In late May, the wait ended. In a Saturday game at Pea Ridge, Carlton Mangum took the mound against Harold Ellen. Pea Ridge jumped on Ellen with five runs in the fourth inning, and Angier never recovered. The final was Pea Ridge 7, Angier 1. Kenneth Jackson's home run accounted for Angier's only run. Pea Ridge made it a sweep the next day in Angier. Marshall Price and Jimmie Matthews thumped their town pals in the chin with three hits each as Pea Ridge triumphed, 11-6. This league-ball rivalry continued with no indication that Angier would get the upper hand until 1957, when another big personnel shift would help give Angier its first win over Pea Ridge.

Ben Price recalls an Angier victory: "Pat Williford — who couldn't break a window — pitched for us one game against Pea Ridge, and I still kid those boys about it out there, because they had a much better ball club than we did here in town. But we just had a good day, and Pat shut 'em out that day nine to nothing. You know, they always had good talent, even when they didn't have but nine Adamses out there."

The head-to-head contests aside, each team kept an eye on the other as they competed through June, each team showing signs of the type of offensive brilliance that kept folks around Angier interested. In an early June game at Knightdale, Jimmie Odell Matthews hit a tape-measure home run that got the attention of the Fuquay newspaper columnist. Tom Segroves ball-parked the shot at 450 feet and quoted Hayden Adams saying, "It was the longest hit I ever saw, and I've been around baseball all my life." [62] Two weeks later, Kenneth Jackson, Ben Price, and Harold Ellen hit consecutive home runs in Angier's 15-9 triumph over Garner.

Pea Ridge's dominance in league play was not as evident as in years past, but they clearly were more consistent than their rivals in town. By mid-June, Pea Ridge was tied with Knightdale in the tight league standings, with a 10-4 record. Fuquay was half a game back, and Garner was one game behind. Coats was at 7-7, and Angier was at 6-8. Mamers (3-11) and Falls of the Neuse (1-12) rounded out the standings.

The next big date was the league all-star game, and Pea Ridge, which had walloped the rest of the league in the previous year's event, was about to get another indication that talent around the league was closing in fast. Holding a one-game lead in the league standings, Pea Ridge had again earned the right to host the game and to be the team the rest of the stars played. The all-stars lined up a team of notable talent, sprinkled with a few players of professional caliber. Kenneth Jackson, James Stevens of Fuquay, Charles Jones of Knightdale, and a few others had either played professionally or were being scouted.

The game was played on Sunday, July 1, and had the added attraction of the crowning of a league beauty queen. About 500 fans showed up to see Pea Ridge take its most stern whipping in years. Starter

225

Carlton Mangum didn't make it through the fourth inning, and reliever Tommy Bradley had similar luck. The all-stars piled up twenty-two hits, including three homers, and claimed a wild 17-9 victory. Marshall Price was the only Pea Ridge player to hit a home run.

Back to Roxboro

Just like the closeness of the early Central Carolina League race, the all-star whipping had reminded the Pea Ridge boys that their team was not quite invincible, and it would be a good reminder for the challenge ahead. That challenge awaited them in Roxboro, where the team would make its second try at a National Baseball Congress state title. With the state tournament about three weeks off, Clyde Adams began scraping together another set of names to fill the official tournament roster. Again, some of his regulars would not be able to make the trip because of various obligations, so the Pea Ridge squad had a different look.

Mangum was still a pillar of the pitching staff, and the team added Jack Craig, a lanky former minor leaguer from Durham and a cousin of major leaguer Roger Craig. Ellen and Bradley could fill in on the mound. Three new players were in the up-the-middle positions, turning defensive strengths into offensive ones. Billy West, who had a knack for catching the knuckler, having played in previous years with Mangum, was the latest in the line of catchers. Ford Jordan, a solid infielder who had batted .277 in four Class A and B minor league seasons, was new at shortstop. West and Jordan had played most of the regular season for Garner. Jim "Bull" Hinton was now sharing duties at second with Gardner. Better bats at short and second would make a difference. Price was still the left fielder of choice for Pea Ridge, but James Stevens of Garner was the best and fastest threat that could be put into right. Matthews in center and Hayden and Connie Adams at the corners rounded out the tournament lineup. Others on the tournament roster, according to *The Independent*, were Elbert and Wayron Adams, Jackie Revis, Doug Payne, and Millie Joe Johnson.

The Garner Boys

For West, Jordan, Stevens, and Mangum, it was a reunion of sorts. They had all played together as teens on the Robertson Chemical team in Garner in the 1940s. Together they had made that team an exceptional one before they parted ways to pursue the professional game. Two of them — Stevens and Mangum — had reached Class B, the next-to-highest rung on the minor league ladder at the time, and each brought a valuable set of talents. Jordan, who by all accounts could have been a star on anyone's team, made it all the way to the Class A Eastern League.

Stevens was another example of a player who had experienced some disillusionment with the minor league game. His exceptional speed in the outfield and on the base paths had made him the object of professional scouting lists as he was leaving high school. He signed up and spent most of 1950 with the Raleigh Caps, a team floundering in the bottom of the Class B Carolina League standings. Like Mangum, Stevens knew he could still make money in semipro baseball, as he had done in previous years. And like Mangum, he would find out that contractual obligations of professional baseball left him with little control.

Stevens recalled: "Long about the last of August, I was getting on the bus ... and Skip called me, said 'Stevie, come here. You're not going.' I said, 'What you mean I'm not going?' He said 'You've been traded. Rudy traded you last night.' Then he said he wanted me to come down to his office. I said: 'No use in me going to his office. I'm not going anywhere'. He said, 'If you don't, he's gonna blackball you.' I said 'I don't care. I told him to start with.... I made a deal.' He said, 'But you signed that piece of paper.' "

That piece of paper meant everything in professional baseball. It was a part of baseball that didn't set well with guys like Mangum and Stevens. They simply wanted to play ball, make a little money, and realize a dream of a shot at the majors. The contract with its reserve clause just didn't figure into all of that. [63] Stevens said, "I was offered contracts to play in B and C ball later, but I got so ill and disgusted with that crowd I was playing with that I never wanted any part of professional baseball again."

Stevens was almost exclusively a tournament player for Pea Ridge. He had played in a number of semipro leagues before and since his sour experience with the minors. "But, at Pea Ridge I played for nothing, because it was fun. Baseball was a whole lot of fun to me until somebody started throwing money at me. Then it was more like a job."

It was not as if Stevens refused money to play. He had seen experience in the paying semipro leagues in the eastern part of the state, and he knew what it took to make a trip from Wake County to Carteret County profitable. He played in the little town of Smyrna. He said, "They didn't pay us that much in the Tidewater League, but all you had to do was get a hit to win a ball game or make a good catch in the outfield. And some us learned after a while how to make some of those routine catches look hard, 'cause they were gonna pass the hat. And they would really pay. You would wait to the late inning or something and make good catch in the outfield, and they'd pass that hat."

Stevens's ability to bunt, steal bases, and cover a lot of ground in the outfield made him a valuable player in any lineup. The network of baseball in the state had James Stevens's name. "I played in a lot of towns in this state," he said. "You'd be surprised at the number of places that would call me from out of the blue to get me to play. How in the world they knew about me is more than I know."

Ford Jordan had been as close to the majors as anyone who would ever play for Pea Ridge. A shortstop with superb ability, he had turned down offers by coaches Bunn Hearn of UNC and Chick Doak at N.C. State to play college ball, choosing to sign a minor league contract. After batting .333 with Warsaw of the Tobacco State League in 1947, he was moved up to Raleigh, where he batted .283 and drove in ninety-one runs. That got him real travel time. He signed with the Braves and spent three seasons in the minors in Hartford and Hagerstown. But he could do no better at the plate than .251, and with Johnny Logan and Eddie Mathews holding down the left side of the Braves' big-league infield, Jordan figured the big move would be next to impossible. He returned home to his father's tobacco farm and the semipro teams that awaited. With a little more strength at the plate, the Pea Ridge boys hoped that opposing pitching wouldn't keep them at bay again.

The Roxboro tournament featured another sixteen-team field, including teams from Durham, Greensboro, and Winston-Salem. Fuquay was in, and the military had loosened its restrictions on tournament play again, allowing the always-competitive Marines to send up a team, this one from Camp Lejeune. Cavel, with former professionals Sam and Ernest Shotwell and Bob Slaughter, was one of the local favorites. One of their pitchers was a man the Pea Ridge players had seen before, though in a different uniform: James Hambrick.

Pea Ridge took the field for its first tournament game on Saturday, July 21 and easily handled Woodland, 9-1. The game ended in the seventh inning because of an eight-run rule intended to speed up tournament play. Hayden Adams (two-for-three) and Jimmie Matthews (three-for-four with a triple) were stars at the plate. Mangum posted the victory. A week later, Mangum pitched himself out of a jam, and Pea Ridge survived a 6-4 decision against Yanceyville. Elbert Adams provided the heroics at the plate. His two-run single to right in the ninth inning broke a 4-4 tie.

The following Thursday, Greensboro's Binswanger Glass Company team engaged in a back-and-forth battle with the Pea Ridge gang. The game was tied, 6-6, in the eighth inning, when the clouds opened. With the game tied and rain pouring down, the two groups played the game from the start on Sunday. It appeared that Pea Ridge's tournament luck had changed, because the team didn't allow the game to be close when they faced off against Greensboro again. Mangum put together a five-hitter, and the latest additions to the team began to pay off. James Stevens went three-for-four with a triple, and Ford Jordan went two-for-three. The final score: Pea Ridge 11, Greensboro 2, in eight innings.

Meanwhile, Pea Ridge managed to keep its league pace intact back at home. The Central Carolina League standings in the first week of August showed Pea Ridge with an 18-4 record, three and one-half games ahead of Knightdale and four up on Fuquay. Their rivals in Angier were in the lower half of the standings, with a 7-14 record.

With three straight wins in the state tournament, the Pea Ridge team had once again piqued the interest of folks in the Angier area. Segroves noted in the August 7 edition of *The Independent* that one Angier business had reported that half of its calls were inquiries about the progress of the team. [64]

August 9 marked the start of the last weekend of the tournament, and four games over the next five days would test Pea Ridge's pitching depth. During that time span, the team would send Mangum and Craig to the mound, with Craig pitching two straight days. Their nemesis: the home favorite, Cavel, and its pitcher, James Hambrick. Hambrick, a former star at Elon College, had confounded the Pea Ridge batters in the tournament the year before in a 2-1 victory for Gibsonville. On Thursday, August 9, Cavel sent Pea Ridge to the loser's bracket. Despite a home run by Ford Jordan and a three-for-five hitting effort by James Stevens, Cavel and Hambrick claimed a 7-2 victory. Mangum was the loser of record.

On Friday, Craig took the mound, and Pea Ridge sent the Durham Bees home with a 13-2 pounding. This left Pea Ridge and Cavel standing and Pea Ridge a loss away from elimination. Pea Ridge would have to sweep Cavel over the next two games to win the state title.

On Saturday, Pea Ridge was up to the challenge, and the battery of Craig and West was sterling on offense and defense. Craig claimed the mound victory, went two-for-two at the plate with a home run and two RBIs, while West had three hits. Pea Ridge took a 14-3 victory, Cavel's first loss of the tournament.

This set up a championship game Monday and another face-off between Hambrick and Mangum. Hambrick homered in the third inning to give the home favorite the lead, 1-0. But the Pea Ridge boys battled back with single runs in the fifth and sixth innings, Jimmie Odell Matthews in the thick of the action. Matthews tripled in the fifth and was driven in by Ford Jordan. He reached on a single in the sixth and was eventually driven in by Hayden Adams to give Pea Ridge the 2-1 lead. But that was all the scoring for Pea Ridge, as Hambrick managed to scatter the eight hits he surrendered among eleven strikeouts. And Cavel strung enough hits together in the eighth inning to take the lead, starting with E.L. Taylor's triple. Taylor scored on Ernest Shotwell's single, and

R.B. Tingen followed up with a run-scoring double. Hambrick held Pea Ridge at bay in the top of the ninth, and Cavel preserved a 3-2 win and claimed the state crown.

An all-state team was named after the tournament, and Pea Ridge had four players on it: West, catcher; Jordan, shortstop; Stevens, right field; and Matthews, center field. Pea Ridge had fallen short of the state title once again but had come within a couple of hits of victory. And, as it turned out, the consolation prize would be a big one. Cavel had too many players either on the mill payroll or farming in the height of the tobacco-barning season. And there was a question of being able to raise the money for the trip to Wichita, Kansas, and the National Baseball Congress nationals. The Cavel team simply couldn't put together enough players or money for the trip. The state turned to little Pea Ridge.

Webster Lupton

"At Pea Ridge I played for nothing, because it was fun."

- James Stevens

1956 Pea Ridge state semipro tournament team

The 1956 Pea Ridge team entered the tournament as Angier. They lost in the finals of the tournament in Roxboro to Cavel. Cavel could not represent the state in the National Baseball Congress tournament in Wichita, so Angier went. They were eliminated in two games. At front is Rex Matthews with sign. Front row left to right are Jimmie Odell Matthews, Jackie Revis, Marshall Price, Pete Adams, and Frank Gardner. Second Row: Carlton Mangum, Billy West, Hayden Adams, James Stevens, and Connie Adams. Back row: Clyde Adams, Jimmy Hinton, Ford Jordan, Elbert Adams, and manager Bill Watkins.

(Photo courtesy of Cherry Adams Franks)

Chapter 15 - No Place Like Home

A Long Trip is Cut Short

When news reached Clyde Adams that Cavel couldn't make the trip to Wichita, he told officials to go ahead and pencil in North Carolina's place in the bracket. If his Pea Ridge team was eligible, he'd find a way to get together a lineup and make the trip. The way he figured it, he could round up enough players to give most any team a run for their money.

In typical Clyde Adams fashion, the roll-call of players who could actually make the 1,300-mile trip to Wichita came up extremely strong. The team would miss valuable outfielder Marshall Price, who couldn't break from his job with the Fort Bragg Fire Department, and Elbert Adams, who suffered an arm injury before the trip. Injury had plagued Elbert Adams all year. He had taken his shot at professional ball that spring, traveling to the Braves training site in Waycross, Georgia, but had injured his shoulder and returned home without ever seeing his first minor league pitch. It would be his only try at professional ball. He had managed to keep a spot on the Pea Ridge and Angier lineups because of his reliable hitting.

Price had hit at a torrid pace, too, particularly in July and particularly in the small confines of the Pea Ridge park. His three-run shot had been the only home run the Pea Ridge team could manage in the all-star game in early July. Two weeks later, just hours after his wife, Mattie, had given birth to their first child, Marshall kissed them both, left the hospital and headed to the ball field where he posted a two-homer game. "I left the hospital that day, and she knew I was going to play ball." Typical baseball-obsessed Marshall Price. But leaving the wife AND new baby AND work to travel halfway across the continent — that was another thing.

Elbert Adams and Marshall Price left big shoes to fill, but a good portion of the state tournament roster made the trip. The Angier contingent of Hayden and Connie Adams, Matthews, Gardner, and Ellen, who had played together for most of the last two years, came along. Then there was the Fuquay Springs-Garner connection, some of whom had played with Pea Ridge from the start of the season. James Stevens, Billy West, Carlton Mangum, Jack Craig, Bull Hinton, and Jackie Revis all were in for the long ride.

Clyde may have been trying to fill the numbers on the official roster because he knew that he couldn't take the time away himself. Nor could his field manager, Bill Watkins. They would turn to the only other person on the team who had good enough baseball sense to make everyone feel the team was in good hands: Frank Gardner. Most folks, both family members and employers, understood the importance of baseball to these players. Jimmie Odell Matthews got days off from his supervisor at the Westinghouse plant, and Harold Ellen got the nod from his job at Fort Bragg.

They carpooled in groups of three and four, making the trek almost non-stop. "We drove all night, because I know I picked it up in Little Rock, Arkansas," Harold Ellen said. "We ate supper in Little Rock and I drove from then until the next morning about six o'clock. Then we were about 150 miles from Wichita." The long drive would labor the players with at least some mental wear before the first pitch was tossed. And how serious these men were about actually winning baseball games was another question.

For most of these guys, the trip to Kansas was more than a simple baseball foray. It was a chance to get far away from home, wives, girlfriends, and the daily grind. This trip gave the boys the opportunity to steal away from all of that and visit a new town. For some of these farm boys, it was about the only trip out of state in which they weren't in a military uniform or minor league uniform. This, in fact, was a real road game.

Wichita

What was waiting for them was a baseball event unlike any they had seen before. Wichita, Kansas, had been born as a booming cow town of the post-Civil War era, rejuvenated as an oil town of the 1920s and '30s, and it had now grown into a center of the aviation industry.

Folks were as crazy about baseball there as they were most anywhere else. Minor leagues and semipro leagues had garnered huge popularity over the years in Kansas, Oklahoma, Nebraska, Iowa, and other states of America's heartland. St. Louis was one of original major league cities; Kansas City and Wichita had been in the prestigious American Association of the minor leagues; and there were six minor leagues covering the region in the 1950s. [65] The competition in the semipros was fierce, and by the 1950s some semipro teams were backed by big money. In the late '40s and early '50s, semipro teams in the most competitive leagues offered their best players more than $300 a month, which was comparable to a minor league salary. [66]

Barnstorming also was a popular attraction in towns and cities of the Midwest, and one of the most famous barnstormers of all helped establish the NBC national semipro tournament in 1935. With the promise of $1,000 from tournament organizer Hap Dumont of Wichita, Satchel Paige brought his touring team from Bismark, North Dakota, to compete in the first NBC World Series. Paige got what was considered a huge check back then, and he earned it. He struck out sixty batters in four games and led his Corwin Churchill team to the title. Equally important, Paige's performances drew a big enough gate to firmly establish the tournament. It had grown ever since. [67]

The *Official Baseball Annual* the NBC published each year was more than 300 pages of rules, photos, statistics, boxes, and summaries of state and district tournaments and profiles of teams in the national and international tournaments.

North Carolina teams, though never winning the national title, had represented the state each year, and well. The most successful of the state's representatives had come from the Piedmont mill country, where semipro baseball was a way of life. Paige's team had eliminated the Shelby-Cleveland Mills team, which eventually placed third. North Carolina teams would go on to place third in two of the national events, and the Elkin-Chatham Blanketeers posted the best North Carolina finish by making it to the finals of the 1948 tournament, losing to the Fort Wayne, Indiana, General Electric team. 68

In 1956, the city people were ready to put on another good show for the thirty-two teams, 512 players, and thousands of fans who would see the competition in Wichita's Lawrence Stadium. A fireworks display honoring past champions, marching drills, and a pitching contest offering $10,000 in prize money were among the spectacles for fans on the opening night, Friday, August 17. As a special attraction, Kansas's famed mile runner Wes Santee would be honored as the state's top athlete. Santee would run against a relay team as part of the activities that Sunday ... and win. Radio's Mutual Broadcasting System, which had more than 500 affiliates, would air a game of the day.

It was wall-to-wall baseball, with games starting in the morning and ending at night for the three weeks it would take to settle the issue. The competition was more than formidable. Many of the teams were big semipro operations that played fifty-plus-game schedules, traveled on team buses, and performed in real stadiums with lights and dressing rooms. They recruited players not only from surrounding communities but from other states. Some even flew in players to compete in the tournament. Roughly half of the teams were financed by big industries or by backing from big-city chambers of commerce or civic clubs. The NBC acknowledged this by awarding a separate trophy to the nation's best "town" team, a team from a smaller community that didn't have the benefit of big industry support. Town teams were at a considerable disadvantage.

Plenty of baseball talent was on hand. The Alpine, Texas, Cowboys boasted three former major leaguers in their lineup, making them one of the tournament favorites. John Sanford, a former pitcher with the Phillies, was one of the Cowboy players, and their catcher, Clyde McCullough, had played for the Chicago Cubs. World Series hero Johnny Podres, a star for the Brooklyn Dodgers before entering the service, had been certified to enter the tournament just a day before Alpine's first game, *The Wichita Eagle* reported. The Sinton Plymouth Oilers, also from Texas, had the services of former New York Giant Clint Hartung. The Oilers had defeated Alpine in the Texas state championship, making them another favorite. The top seed was Fort Wayne, Indiana, a four-time national champion. The hometown Boeing Bombers were the defending champions. Also in the tournament field was an all-black team, the Jasper, Texas, Steers, a barnstorming team that had won the Dixie World Series to qualify for the event.

The annual tournament was a huge deal for this city, with big crowds showing up each day, special tickets offers, and contests going on a week before. It had become a tradition. And here came the boys from North Carolina, looking for a few days off work and away from home. The scene must have hit them like a brick wall. "We didn't quite have the ball club, and the ones we did have, well, they got away from home and wanted to have some fun," Carlton Mangum said.

The long haul put the Angier troupe at a distinct disadvantage to the veteran teams who were returning to the tournament for their second, third, or fourth trips, familiar with the town, the travel routine, and the level of competition. The finicky weather seemed uncooperative for Angier, too. There was no rain, but the night game was unusually cold, and the day game was steaming hot. "I thought I would freeze to death," Mangum said of the opening game for Pea Ridge, which started at eight in the evening. "I was so glad to finish an inning and get back and put my warm-up jacket back on."

"The guys got out there and tried to go around the bars and eat and play and didn't get their rest," James Stevens said. "Then we got out there and didn't feel like playing ball at twelve noon in 118-degree temperature, which is what it was on the field."

Taking all this into account, the result was predictable. They didn't stay in town long enough to even establish an identity with the local press, who saw them listed as Angier in the bracket, then saw the uniforms and somehow came up with Angier-Pearidge or Angier (N.C.) Pearidgers in the few references to the team. The North Carolina team barely made an impression.

Pea Ridge was matched against the Casa Grande, Arizona, Cotton Kings for the eight o'clock opening game, the feature game of day. Casa Grande was a perennial tournament entry, having won seven straight Arizona state tournaments. The Cotton Kings had placed as high as fourth in the national tournament and in the top ten two more times. They had a mixture of former pros and college players on their team.

Pea Ridge sent Mangum to the mound, and the Cotton Kings tagged him for a run in the first inning. Then in the fourth, Ted Lasovich, a player on University of Arizona's national runner-up team in the spring, swatted a grand-slam home run to give Casa Grande a 5-0 advantage. Pea Ridge scrambled back when Jimmie Matthews delivered a three-run home run in the fifth, and Harold Ellen added two more with a bases-loaded single in sixth. The score was tied at 6-6 at the end of nine chilly innings, but Mangum and reliever Jack Craig had a troublesome tenth inning. The Cotton Kings scored a run on three walks and a single and a sacrifice fly. Casa Grande took the win, 8-6.

On Wednesday, Pea Ridge took the field at noon against the Evanston, Illinois, Erickson Boosters, another team with a number of former professionals and the survivors of a tough Illinois state tournament. The Evanston team wore down Pea Ridge in a 4-3 decision. Former minor leaguer Doug Davidson's solo home run in the eighth inning provided the winner.

The boys from Pea Ridge packed what little they had unpacked and headed home. They returned home to find the Central Carolina League playoffs underway. Choosing to make the trip to Wichita had kept Pea Ridge out of the league playoffs. Knightdale took the league crown that year, sweeping Angier and beating Coats in the final series, three games to two.

In September, *The Independent*'s Segroves published his all-league team. Here's how he listed the four Pea Ridge players and manager, including his comments:

1B - Hayden Adams - "like Old Man River, he just keeps rolling on."

LF - Marshall Price - "good hitter, better than average fielder."

CF - Jimmie Matthews - "good speed, good arm, long ball hitter."

P - Carlton Mangum - "good in tough spots."

Mgr. - Bill Watkins - "quick thinker, knows when to pull pitcher."

Jordan and West made the team from Garner, and no one from Angier's town team was on the Segroves team. [69]

The tough league races, local rivalries, scrambling for players, and running up thousands of extra miles on their cars hadn't yielded much. But the boys who had grown up on baseball would most certainly do it all again.

Webster Lupton

Chapter 16 – Twilight at a Country Field

Day Games Pass with the Times

Success had cut both ways for the baseball team at Pea Ridge. The little team had certainly come a long way since the Adams boys drew their baseball diamond in the country a decade earlier. But despite all of those wins and league titles, it had become clear by 1957 that the future of the country team was a bit precarious. With the re-emergence of a team in Angier, the constant renovation of personnel, and the always-nagging question of how a quality team could continue on a shoestring budget, Clyde Adams's little hobby was beginning to fade. Pea Ridge had certainly served its purpose; it kept the notion of a town baseball team alive and popular in the Angier community, and it gave the men and boys who wanted to play competitive baseball a place to play on weekends.

But maintaining a team out in the country was like fighting

progress. Night baseball was about to return to Angier. The town had started a fundraising drive to get lights at the high school field, and by mid-summer, Angier High School would host its first night baseball game. Much of the summer would be spent promoting and playing exhibition games to help pay for the lights in time for the school's football season, the primary reason for the lights.

Of course, night baseball was nothing new, having been around since the 1930s. But night baseball was now the rule rather than the exception, a natural progression for a game that was beginning to struggle to keep its popularity. The lighting systems were more reliable and sophisticated than they had been in the 1930s and '40s, and the convenience and comfort of the night game held a distinct advantage. Even little Angier had latched on to the night game when the pro team was in town in 1946. The implications were clear for country parks such as Pea Ridge, where the notion of having a lighted field was simply out of the question. The cost and logistics of lighting the little field made it so Pea Ridge and day baseball were behind the times.

These growing pains were not unlike the ones the game of baseball itself had to endure everywhere. Baseball was struggling to maintain the moniker of America's pastime, because it was leaving a big portion of America behind. In North Carolina, smaller towns were out of the minor league game altogether. By 1957, Charlotte and the Carolina League cities of Kinston, Greensboro, Durham, Winston-Salem, and High Point were the only minor league teams in the state. [70]

The game was dwindling at the semipro level, too. The fast leagues of the 1930s had been virtually supplanted by the surge in minor leagues after World War II, and when the minors faded in the early 1950s, many towns simply quit fielding teams. There even a movement afoot in the old Coastal Plain League towns to start an all-college amateur league, just to keep college players in the state during the summer. Many of the college players in the state and in Atlantic Coast Conference schools were traveling as far away as North Dakota or Nova Scotia to find good summer leagues. [71] North Carolina's semipro leagues, which had once been good training grounds for college players from all over, couldn't find rosters for all of their players.

Then there was basketball. Atlantic Coast Conference basketball was sweeping the state on the coattails of N.C. State's venerable coach, Everett Case. And Frank McGuire's University of North Carolina basketball team had just brought home an NCAA national championship. Now iron hoops and baskets were being nailed to barns and garages and trees and light poles everywhere in the state. The cleared areas where baseballs were once tossed now had poles poking up with backboards. Kids were taking time during their baseball summers to attend the new basketball camps like Case's in Raleigh and Fred McCall's and Bones McKinney's over at Campbell College. [72] Baseball was no longer every kid's favorite summer game in North Carolina. It was becoming more evident that baseball had to advance with time, even if it left behind beloved little parks like the one at Pea Ridge.

For the Adams, Prices, and Gardners, the spring of 1957 was the start of another season of their game. To them baseball was still the only game in town. There were enough men like these still around and still willing to put in a weekend on the road if it meant getting in a couple of games. And there were still a few townsfolk who recalled the heyday of semipro baseball. Baseball in many small towns was still something to do, but the phenomenon of the town team was in its late innings.

The Season

Only four teams enlisted for the new Mid-State League in the spring of 1957: Angier, Fuquay, Pea Ridge, and Coats. The balance of power in the league shifted when Jimmie Odell Matthews and Marshall Price both took their slugging talents to Angier. Getting Matthews alone would have been enough to tip the scales in any team's favor, but with both him and Price on board, Angier definitely became the new team to beat in the league. Harold Ellen was back at Angier that season, too. Frank Gardner, Roger Honeycutt, and some of the Adams boys were back at Pea Ridge. Jack Craig and Carlton Mangum had mound duties at Pea Ridge. The Pea Ridge team would use Angier's park for some of its home games in 1957, because of the lights. With more of the old Pea Ridge players taking their talents into town, the league standings changed. Though the win-loss records were not published, *The Independent* of Fuquay reported on July 11 that Angier had a "fat lead" in the Mid-State standings, with Pea Ridge and Fuquay battling for second. [73]

Angier had turned the tide on Pea Ridge, an example being a late June meeting between the rivals. Angier made the short trip to the country field and put lefty Ben Baker on the mound. Baker, who was from Zebulon and had played Legion ball in Raleigh and semipro in Fuquay, tossed a four-hitter, and the Angier boys pelted Jack Craig with four runs in the first inning. Harold Ellen's home run led the scoring rally. Ben Price ended up with three hits in the game. Angier won, 4-1.

Roxboro

However, the league season was no longer the end-all for Pea Ridge baseball. Tougher competition awaited in state tournament play. Though Pea Ridge had not had as good a season, the state tournament allowed the team an automatic bid by virtue of its runner-up finish the previous year and its willingness to travel to Wichita.

When mid-July arrived and it was time to head for Roxboro, Pea Ridge assembled a team much like that of the 1956 tournament team, with a few exceptions. One exception was the fact that Pea Ridge actually submitted lineups in some games without an Adams. Hayden and Elbert were able to make only some of the state tournament games, and Connie and Clyde were subs. It was a first for Pea Ridge and another indication of how much the team had changed. Matthews, Ellen, and Frank Gardner would be registered to play for Pea Ridge in the state tournament. Billy West, Ford Jordan, James Stevens, and Jack Craig were all now-familiar names at Pea Ridge. Cecil Fuquay, a catcher and outfielder from Coats, was a new name in the Pea Ridge order, and Haywood Kelley from Garner would play some first base for the team.

This Pea Ridge tournament team proved to be unquestionably its best. But it shaped up, as usual, through some dealing. Frank Gardner had managed the team during the regular season, but he would have to surrender the post in order to get the best players available. "Frank selected the rosters, and he wanted Jim Stevens along," Harold Ellen said. "But in order to get him, Ford and Billy West would have to come. Stevens was made manager in order to bring Ford and the others in." Stevens, West, and Jordan would play crucial roles in the tournament.

The goals of this experienced tournament team were loftier than they had been in years past, and it was reflected throughout the event. Pea Ridge rolled through it with hardly a contested game. They were undefeated in five games, outscoring opponents by a whopping 37-3. One close game Pea Ridge played was a ten-inning 6-2 victory over Roanoke Rapids, the third win of the tournament. Successive hits by West, Matthews, and Jordan brought in the tenth-inning runs Pea Ridge needed to win the game. But it was a play by Stevens in the outfield that Segroves of *The Independent* described as the "turning point" of the tournament for the team. With two down and the score tied, 2-2, Stevens fielded a single and threw to West at the plate to put out a runner trying to score from second base.

It was the first tournament loss for Roanoke Rapids, the champions in 1955, and Pea Ridge would have to deal with the team again. In the meantime, Pea Ridge got a three-run double from Jordan to take a 3-0 victory over Burlington in the tournament semifinals.

In the title game, Pea Ridge put together thirteen hits, and Harold Ellen threw a five-hitter to defeat Roanoke Rapids, 10-0. Ellen, who was considered a utility man, was clearly learning the craft of pitching. His description of how he went about shutting down the powerful Roanoke Rapids team could be a tutorial on pitching: "I used the change-up a lot: Knock him back with fastballs, give him a curve, and change up on him, but don't give him a hit; throw a change-up, because good hitters don't want to hit it. … I still say it's the best pitch in baseball, and Glavine and them have shown it. I may have four or five good fastballs, but that was it. … They used to call it 'old junky mess.' You do that for a period of time, and hitters in the late innings come up and they're looking for it. So you save those fastballs - until you got them to the nitty gritty and they know you're going to come with it, and now you give him the fastball. Heck, I had to do that, because I didn't have that many fastballs. … I had to nibble here and nibble there." But it was Jack Craig and Carlton Mangum who each had two pitching wins in the tournament. Matthews batted .529 in the five games.

Pea Ridge had a state championship in earnest, and if baseball at the little field in the country was on its way out, its baseball team would try to make sure Pea Ridge went out with a bang. For the Pea Ridge gang, the next stop was Wichita.

1957 Pea Ridge tournament team

Pea Ridge went undefeated in state tournament play in 1957, the last year of league baseball at Pea Ridge. The team would place fifth in the nation in Wichita and be named the nation's top "town" team. Front row, left to right: Hayden Adams, Harold Ellen, Jackie Revis, Jimmie Odell Matthews, Frank Gardner, and Connie Adams. Back Row: Ford Jordan, James Stevens, Larry Moore, Jack Craig, Jimmy Hinton, Billy West, and Carlton Mangum.

(Photo courtesy of Cherry Adams Franks)

Chapter 17 - A Last Stand

Wichita Discovers Pea Ridge

The 1957 state tournament ended on August 10, and the nationals were to begin six days later in Wichita. Pea Ridge was scheduled to play on August 20. Again the team had to gather up enough players to commit to making the long trip and submit a roster to the National Baseball Congress. Most of the key players would be able to make the trip, including the Angier-area boys, Matthews, Gardner, Ellen, and Hayden Adams. The Pea Ridge team would also have the services of one of Angier's baseball "fathers," Kenneth Jackson, who had made a name during the semipro years of the late '30s and by playing professionally during the 1940s. In his late thirties by this time, Jackson would be the old man of the team, but he still had enough prowess at the plate to make him at least an effective pinch hitter.

Then there were the Fuquay and Garner-based players who had proven Clyde Adams's recruiting machinations to be nothing short of pure genius. Mangum, Stevens, Jordan, Honeycutt, Craig, and West went on the trip. New players for the nationals included another Garner boy, Haywood Kelley, who would share first base duties with Hayden Adams; catcher Bob Kennel of New Bern and N.C. State; and two left-handed pitchers, Gene Summerlin and Bob Cruze, both former journeyman minor leaguers. Summerlin had played professionally for seven years, reaching as high as the Class B level. Cruze had reached the AA level and had earned All-Carolina League honors as a pitcher with Durham in 1954.

The team had not had the services of Ford Jordan for its trip to Wichita the year before. Jordan's father needed him at home for the tobacco harvest. But Clyde Adams, this time, would find a way.

"I told them, here we are in the middle of tobacco barning season, and that there was no way I was going to be able to get away and go way out there to play," recalled Jordan. "So, Clyde Adams told me, said, 'I'll tell you what. If I bring a boy over to help in your place, will you go with us? I got a nice boy who is a good worker and will come over and work in your place if you'll feed him and put him up.' So, that's what he did. That boy came over and stayed in our house and worked with my daddy."

James Stevens was Pea Ridge's field manager for the Wichita trip. Stevens's influence as manager would pay off. The Garner player's association with Pea Ridge over two seasons gave him a determined commitment to winning — for the players and the Angier community.

He recalls the talk he gave to his players before their tournament play began: "When we got out there, I got the boys together and said, 'Look, I'm one of you. I just happen to be listed as manager. You know how the people around Angier and Pea Ridge kicked in their own money to send us out here. We haven't had to spend our own money to come out here and play. I think we owe it to the people at home who raised the money to send us out here to play baseball and represent that neighborhood. I want for us to get in bed by eleven o'clock and behave ourselves and be ready to take the field and play ball and be able to play ball like we are capable of playing and to represent the community the best we can as baseball players.' I told them, 'I'm not trying to tell you what to do. I'm just giving you something to think about.' "

Stevens was by no means a tyrant as manager. The Pea Ridge boys would have their fun. They would chase a jackrabbit at the Wichita airport, go on a roller coaster ride that made Clyde Adams turn green, and, as baseball players are prone to do, they would play pranks. "We came in after one game," Ellen recalled, "and Gene (Summerlin) turned on the hot water in our bathroom and said 'Kenneth (Jackson), jump in, the hot water's about to give out.' So Kenneth jumps in, and the water is scalding hot. ... We had a bed that folded up into the wall, and so later, when Gene was sleeping, Kenneth slammed that bed up into the wall, propped a chair under it and said, 'You pick on me, buddy, and you're gonna stay 'til tomorrow.' "

The Tournament

The 1957 National Baseball Congress non-pro tournament opened on August 16 with much the same fanfare of years past. The thirty-two teams that would face double-elimination format included a number of favorites that were familiar names from previous years. The Fort Wayne, Indiana, Dairymen were the defending champions, having defeated Alpine, Texas, in the title match the year before. The Dairymen were riding a twenty-two-game winning streak. The Sinton, Texas Plymouth Oilers, had Hartung, the former New York Giants pitcher and outfielder. Wichita's own Boeing Bombers were also among the teams predicted to be among the contenders. The Oilers and the Bombers had both won the national title before.

A $10,000 prize awaited the tournament winner, and cash prizes were divided among the other top teams. Twenty team trophies and twenty-five individual trophies would be awarded for various tributes and not just according to competition. There was a trophy for the best-dressed team and one for the most popular player. There was also a trophy for the best "town" team, the group of small-town teams of which Pea Ridge was a member. There were also a few military or "service" clubs and a few that were backed by unions. [74] The tournament included a mixture of players at various talent levels. The Perry, Oklahoma, Oilers were mostly ex-professional players, while the Florence, Missouri, Centrals had a majority of college players.

Pea Ridge was just looking for the right name to go by. The team was officially entered as Pea Ridge this time, but there was a new hitch. The team had never adopted a nickname that stuck, and their uniforms were not exactly uniform. Some of the shirts had "Pea Ridge" on the front, and others had "PR." A couple of players even had the "A" for Angier on the fronts. In the August 14 edition of *The Wichita Eagle*, Pea Ridge was introduced as the Tobacco Pickers. As the event progressed, the paper would refer to Pea Ridge simply as the Pickers. But the team would sharpen its play during the tournament, and Clyde Adams was determined to sharpen its look. Before they left Wichita, they would round up some new uniforms with a big "E" emblazoned on the front. They became the Pea Ridge Eagles. [75]

The team had enough of a following to justify $600 in contributions from the community for the trip, and a radio broadcast from one of the stations back home, WFVG of Fuquay Springs. [76] The broadcasts would not be live; recordings were shipped by air from Wichita back home for airing the next day. Though the news of the day's score might reach homes first, probably via *The News & Observer*, plenty of folks got details of the games from these broadcasts.

The Pea Ridge gang roared into town on August 19 and suited up for play the next day, a bit road weary, but ready to go. The first opponent, Columbia, Missouri VFW, went down quickly, 12-1 in seven innings. Whether it was because of a radio broadcast, word of mouth, or

257

an alert politician from back home, North Carolina Gov. Luther Hodges got wind of the victory and wired congratulations to his state's baseball representatives:

```
CLYDE ADAMS, BUSINESS MANAGER=
PEA RIDGE BASEBALL CLUB NATIONAL BASEBALL
CONGRESS WICHITA KANS=
    CONGRATULATIONS ON WINNING YOUR FIRST GAME
12 TO 1 LAST NIGHT IN THIS NATIONAL SEMI-PRO
TOURNAMENT. WE ARE PROUD OF YOUR ACCOMPLISHMENTS
AND SEND YOU BEST WISHES FOR YOUR OTHER GAMES=
    LUTHER H HODGES GOVERNOR OF NORTH CAROLINA
```
[77]

A superstitious baseball player would not want any further correspondence from the governor because of the next outing's results. Victory over Columbia matched Pea Ridge against the Sinton Plymouth Oilers and the boatload of talent and reputation that the Oilers sported. The Plymouth Oil Company of Sinton, Texas, had developed a strong and reputable semipro organization in its nine years. Sinton was one of the teams that recruited players from everywhere. They had the former Giant, Hartung, and a number of other former pros, including Earl York, who was just out of the Texas League and had batted .324 for Oklahoma City during the 1956 season. They also had Matt Sczesny, a four-year minor league veteran who was currently riding a six-game hitting streak.

The Oilers had won the NBC national crown once and had placed third twice.

The game offered little Pea Ridge a chance to shine against a big-time semipro outfit. But instead of shining, Pea Ridge was shelled. The Oilers seemed to hit the ball everywhere, picking up a run in the first inning and then bleeding Gene Summerlin for six runs in the second. At one point, Summerlin tried to fool Hartung with a curve, but the pitch seemed to stall in midair. The six feet, five inches 220-pound "Hondo Hurricane," who was just two seasons out of pro ball, swatted a steamer down the third-base line.

"(Ford) Jordan was playing third base and just held his glove up," Harold Ellen recalled. "It tore the webbing out of the glove and went to the left field fence. He (Jordan) says, 'You crazy damned left-hander. You throw another pitch like that, and what I'm gonna do is … you take my glove and you play third base and I'll pitch to him.' "

As the base paths were getting worn with Sinton runners, Ellen was finally called on in relief, and had his own best pitches whacked. But Ellen would finally stop Hartung — with considerable work. "He was high-strung. 'Throw that damned ball,' he said. And I did. I threw him high inside, then I knocked him back twice. Then came a 3-2 pitch, and I got him with curve ball."

Meanwhile, the Pea Ridge boys couldn't seem to get the bats off of their shoulders. Sinton pitcher Paul Temple confounded Pea Ridge's powerful lineup to the tune of just two hits. They struck out eight times. The one-sided disaster finished in seven innings on the ten-run tournament rule, 11-0. The North Carolina representatives already had their backs to the wall. The team had not played that poorly, committing only one error in the array of balls that went into play. But they had run into a whale of a pitcher and a hornets' nest of hitting.

Pea Ridge took a day's rest and went to bat again on Saturday, August 24. The results would be better but not without another round of fireworks. Craig took the mound and scattered seven hits in a 4-1 victory over the Linden, Iowa, Merchants. But the team needed a clutch hit from one of its newcomers to clinch the victory. Haywood Kelley's two-run double provided the winner.

Stealing First Base

The real fireworks came in the form of a freak base-running incident that prompted an argument, a consultation with the rule book, and considerable embarrassment for catcher Bob Kennel. Kennel, a three-sport athlete and "A" student at N.C. State, who was a year away from signing with the Orioles, refers to the incident as the only time he ever heard of anyone "stealing first base."

"The game was tied and I reached first base on a walk. Frank put on a sacrifice. Well, I saw the bunt and at the crack of the bat I took off and slid in to second. When the dust cleared, I got up and saw the pitcher with the ball in foul territory and the batter walking back to the plate. I walked back toward first, thinking it was a foul ball. Then the pitcher got all excited and the first baseman started getting excited and they go to throw back to first. Then I got excited and slid back into first under the tag. The umpire called me safe, then said, 'No, you can't do that; you're out!' Then there was this huge argument."

The ball had been bunted and the batter was actually walking to the dugout after having been tagged out. But Kennel did not hear the call.

James Stevens, who was in the coach's box at first base, recalled the argument: "He called him safe and then out. I said, 'What you mean he's out?' Then he said the rule says a runner can't run the bases backward. I knew the rule, and we both said some things you wouldn't want to repeat. He walked out to right field, and I just followed him out there and argued. I asked him if he would consult the home plate umpire, and he said no. ... So I did, and I said 'Do you want to overrule him?' and the plate ump said no. Then I said, 'Well, you might as well not even plan on playing the rest of this game, because I'm not going anywhere.' That's when they stopped the game and got a ruling. The reason I fought so hard was just to show them that we meant business." During the extended debate, a red-faced Kennel just eased into the dugout.

"In those tournaments they had to rule right away," Kennel said. "So, to settle the argument, the commissioner came out on the field and got on the loudspeaker and said that the rule book says that a player may not run the bases in reverse order in an attempt to confuse the opposition. He said, 'I have overruled the umpire and ruled that the runner may be placed back at first, because he wasn't confusing the opposition. He was

261

just confused himself.' After he said that, everyone laughed, and there must have been 2,000 people there. So, I had to come back out of the dugout and stand on first."

As if Kennel hadn't suffered enough, "That night after the game, they made me listen to the twenty minutes of that from the radio broadcast."

"We called him rookie from then on," Carlton Mangum said.

Extended Stay

Pea Ridge was winning, but its success was coming at a price. The win over the Iowa team meant that Pea Ridge would stay at least a full week in Kansas, and the $600 that Clyde Adams had managed to scrounge up with an exhibition game and a brief fund drive had just about been depleted.

"You got $100 each time you won a ball game," Ellen said. "We had raised money to go; went around and begged it, actually. Well, we'd win and then try to get enough to stay, because the paycheck would come a little later. So Clyde was calling back home to raise us some more to last us to the next game."

This was when Carson Gregory, Red Williams, and other baseball backers in town recruited the Angier Chamber of Commerce to keep a sort of running fund drive going to keep the boys fed and sheltered in Wichita. A couple of stories in *The News & Observer* helped the cause, and the Angier team back home would play three exhibitions in the next few days. The home folks would get their money's worth.

Pea Ridge went to work the following Tuesday with the hometown Boeing Bombers in their path. Wichita had earned a reputation for baseball, and Boeing — the aircraft plant and its baseball team — was the city's pride and joy. The Boeing company provided considerable financial backing to the baseball team, not to mention the money the team earned through the Kansas state tournament. A story in *The Wichita Eagle* noted that the top teams in the state tournament shared more than $10,000 in "cash awards and allowances." The Bombers received $1,100 for winning their district tournament and $5,000 for winning the state title. [78]

Wichita teams had won three of the national tournaments, Boeing taking the 1954 and '55 titles. As in the games against Sinton, and Casa Grande the year before, little Pea Ridge was going up against a Goliath of a semipro outfit, and on that team's home turf. Few in Wichita were pulling for Pea Ridge.

Like Pea Ridge, Boeing was playing in the loser's bracket of the tournament, desperate to survive. That was why Pea Ridge and pitcher Carlton Mangum would have to excel in the feature game of the day. It would be the performance of Mangum and the Pea Ridge team that night that earned the respect of scouts, fans, and newspapers in the baseball-savvy city of Wichita.

Wichita Eagle Sports Editor Bill Hodge described a "soft, sinking curve ball" that stumped the home team in clutch situations that night. [79] Harold Ellen called it a knuckleball. Whatever the pitch, it dropped out of sight as far as the Boeing Bombers were concerned.

"The Bombers were supposed to eliminate us, but Carlton fooled them with that knuckler, and we whipped them," Ellen said.

Mangum struck out seven batters and managed to get outs when the Wichita team was in position to score. The Bombers left fifteen runners on base.

"Out in Wichita, I guess fifty percent of my pitches were knuckleballs," Mangum said. "It was slower. Then I'd come back with a fastball - and spot it - be careful, though, to make sure I didn't throw it down the middle of the plate, because my fastball won't that fast."

Meanwhile, Jimmie Matthews had three runs-batted-in to lead a ten-hit Pea Ridge attack as the team stunned the heavily favored Bombers, 6-2. Ford Jordan had a double and two RBIs.

"I think they thought they would beat us," Mangum recalled. "But I had pitched against some good hitters in pro ball, and at that point, we felt we could play against any of them."

The victory was the third of the tournament for Pea Ridge and put them clearly among the class semipro teams in the nation. It also brought Mangum some instant attention from professional scouts, despite the fact that his best pitching days were behind him. After all, it was way back in 1949 when Mangum had led the Coastal Plain League in strikeouts. When the scouts discovered that the small, slender right-hander was thirty-two years old and had already had his best season in the minors nine years earlier, they shook their heads in awe of his endurance. However, they couldn't see the point in making an investment.

"They were broadcasting the games and had a radio booth up there," Mangum said. "After I had won the first game and was going pretty good in the second game, the Yankee scouts went up to the booth and wanted some information on me. After they found out how old I was, they like to have tore the door down getting out of there. They were interested in signing me until they found out how old I was. I certainly was not a prospect."

Two nights later, Pea Ridge was on the board for a game against the Macon, Georgia, Crawfords, still battling their way through the loser's bracket of the tournament. This time, the heroics would come from the plate. With Pea Ridge locked in a 3-3 tie in the seventh inning, Billy West, the veteran outfielder-catcher, knocked a high fastball out of Lawrence Stadium, drove in three runs, and sent Pea Ridge on to its fourth win, by a 7-3 score. Summerlin got the pitching victory, scattering eight hits and striking out six.

The local paper was dubbing the country boys from North Carolina the Cinderella team of the tournament and the most aggressive team. In the tournament notes column of the next day's *Wichita Eagle*, the writer pronounced: "... Pea Ridge players showed the most hustle in bumping off both the Boeing Bombers and Macon in their last two games. ..." [80]

In that Sunday's *News & Observer,* Jack Briebart wrote of Pea Ridge's success. The story, about fifteen column inches long and at the top of an inside page, was more press than the team had ever received. [81] And Gov. Hodges sent another telegram to Stevens and the team. "If the

Eagles win tonight, my staff and I will be attending the remaining games," Stevens recalled it saying. For the superstitious, that may have been the last straw.

The Last Stand

The Pea Ridge boys had played nothing short of brilliant baseball in winning four of their first five tournament games. They had beaten a fourth seed and sixth seed in the thirty-two-team tournament and now were among only five teams left. The other teams were big-time semipro operations with reputations in the national tournament: Sinton, a former champion; the Milwaukee Falks, which scouts at the tournament considered the most talented in the field; the Jasper Steers, the barnstorming Texas team that had won the all-black Dixie World Series; and the defending champion Fort Wayne Dairymen from Indiana.

Friday night's victory over Macon had put Pea Ridge into the semifinals of the tournament and into a Saturday night showdown against the powerful Dairymen. The Dairymen were poised to repeat the previous year's success and to represent a city that had a tradition of good semipro teams. Former professional player John Braden had managed five national tournament champions from Fort Wayne.

The Dairymen had been tripped in their previous outing, but they had won twenty-four straight games before that, including their regional and league play in Indiana. The Dairymen, like Pea Ridge, had a mixture of former professionals and college players on their roster. They had pitcher Walt Wherry, a former minor leaguer who had won a tournament-record five games for them in the event the previous year. Five other players on their roster were former professionals or on their way up. They also had one of the heaviest hitters the national tournament had ever seen. Wilmer Fields, who was always referred to in the Wichita paper as "Big Wilmer Fields" was a utility player for the Dairymen. He had been an ace pitcher for the vaunted Homestead Grays of the Negro League before World War II and had batted .291 as a minor leaguer for Toronto of the International League in 1952. The year after the tournament, Fields would bat a whopping .375 in the Mexican League. But what he was noted for in Wichita — and what he had done to perk the attention of tournament fans — was hit four home runs in the four tourney games. The tournament record was six. He had hit three homers in the title drive in the previous season's event.

Despite the reputation of the Fort Wayne team, little Pea Ridge seemed to measure up, at least if one were to judge the caliber of players the way pro scouts saw things. After all, Jordan, Honeycutt, Mangum, Craig, Summerlin, Cruze, Stevens, Gardner, Kennel, and Jackson had either been in the professional ranks or soon would be.

Craig had the unenviable position of being the man to have to face the Dairymen and Fields. He was up to the task for the most part, allowing just five hits in nine innings. Two of those hits were a single and a triple that helped Fort Wayne to a 2-0 lead in the fourth inning. But Honeycutt doubled, and Kennel singled in the fifth to make it 2-1. Craig yielded two singles and a walk in the seventh to spot the Dairymen a 3-1 advantage, before Pea Ridge mounted an eighth-inning rally that tied the game. The aggressiveness on the base paths would put them in position to win, but it would foil their chances as well.

The rally started when James Stevens singled and moved to second on Kennel's walk. One out later and with Jimmie Odell Mathews up, Stevens became antsy. Though Matthews was a reliable hitter, the young center fielder was hitless thus far in the game. Stevens figured it was time for a gamble, and he set his sights on third. The Fort Wayne infield appeared to be reading his mind, and their catcher tossed to the shortstop to try to catch Stevens hanging off of second. It put Stevens in a rundown. But luck was in Pea Ridge's favor. Shortstop Jim Higgins's wild throw went past third and sent Stevens and Kennel off to the races. When the dust cleared, Stevens had scored, and Kennel wound up on third base with the tying run.

Then Matthews put his own speed and hitting to work. He creased a long drive and wheeled all the way around to third, sending Kennel in to score and putting the go-ahead run just 90 feet away. But the base-running prowess went a step too far down that third base line. With a rally going and the Fort Wayne infield off kilter, putting the infielders to the test again may have been just the right strategy. But what transpired — *The Wichita Eagle* described it as a squeeze play, and Jim Gardner recalled the radio announcer describing a pitchout — proved to be a gamble gone wrong. [82]

"Ford Jordan would have been at the plate, and Ford was a good bunter; he was a good ball player, could do just about anything," Frank

Gardner said.

"I think we had tried bunting, so they called a pitchout; they knew something was up," Ellen recalled.

Matthews, the team's last and best chance at pushing across the go-ahead run, was caught heading home and was tagged for the inning's second out. The sting was enflamed, because Jordan ended up getting a hit, the one that would have put Pea Ridge in the lead. Kenneth Jackson then pinch hit for Haywood Kelley and grounded out. The wild inning was over. The Pea Ridge boys had made one of their few mistakes of the tournament. But another mistake, which would be even more costly, was on the way.

The game went to the bottom of the tenth inning. Leading off the inning for Fort Wayne was Wilmer Fields. Stevens recalled the situation: "I had called time out. I was playing in right field and noticed the pitcher (Craig) kept shaking him (the signal) off. He turned and looked at me, and I walked all the way in from right to talk with the pitcher (Craig) and catcher (Kennel). I said, 'What is the problem?' He said, 'I've signaled for everything he's got except the curve ball.' Every scout that was there and had seen him said don't curve that man. I had seen him hit some out. Every time you threw him one with just a little wrinkle, it was gone. The score was tied; we were in the tenth inning; and we had walked him the last time we faced him in the same situation. I told Jack, 'Don't curve that guy under any circumstances, unless it's walking in the winning run or something.' So, finally I thought I had him aware of the situation, and I walked back into right. I had told Mangum on the way in to get ready, and I started to put him in, but I knew he wasn't completely loose."

But, as pitchers often do, Jack Craig figured he knew better. His curve ball careened off of big Wilmer Fields's bat like it had been launched. "I was in left and Jimmie Odell Matthews was in center," Harold Ellen recalled. "I took about two steps and said, 'No use, Jim. Ho, ho. It was still climbing when it left the park. Just slowly, like an old B-36 taking off - getting higher and higher. There is no telling how hard and far he hit that one."

"The last time I saw it, it looked like a BB going over the left field wall," Stevens said. The Pea Ridge players were watching their last hurrah sail over the Midwest horizon. The party was over.

"It just broke my heart for us to lose that game," Roger Honeycutt said, "because we had played so well in that game and in the tournament."

It could be said that Craig's curve was not the defining play in Pea Ridge's elimination loss. They had gambled — and lost — on the base paths in the eighth when they tried to push in the winning run and Matthews was picked off. And Craig himself had performed brilliantly in Pea Ridge's state and national tournament drives. Pea Ridge had literally come from nowhere to make an impression on the national tournament. They left as the tournament darlings and earned the award as the best town team in America. They had gone about as far as a carpooling, roughshod mixture of small-town players could.

"You know, I don't know of a one of those guys that didn't heed what I told them and behave themselves perfectly that year," Stevens said. "And we went out and played some baseball."

In addition to placing among the top five semipro teams in the nation that year and winning the town-team trophy, Pea Ridge placed Stevens and Mangum on the first team of the tournament's All-American list. Roger Honeycutt was on the second team.

The Sinton Plymouth Oilers and the Fort Wayne Dairymen, the two teams that had eliminated Pea Ridge, reached the finals of the NBC national tournament that year. Sinton, the team that had clubbed Pea Ridge in seven innings, claimed the title with a 6-4 victory over Fort Wayne. Wilmer Fields was named the tournament's most valuable player. The Sinton team disbanded the next season, and Fort Wayne, which had brought home six national titles, would never again have a national champion.

A week after their return home from Wichita, the Pea Ridge boys played their final game as a team, appropriately against the rival Angier squad. And appropriately, proceeds from the admission charges went toward paying for the lights at the Angier High School field. About 800 fans went to the park and saw Gene Summerlin and Jack Craig square off against Ben Baker and Owen Wright, each team allowing just three hits. Pea Ridge won, 2-0. It was the only event that marked the end of an era of baseball in the Angier community.

PEA RIDGE. N.C.	AB	R	H	BOEING BOMBERS	AB	R	H
Stevens rf	4	1	2	Scott 3b	5	0	1
Ellen lf	2	1	1	Mitchell 2b	4	0	1
West 2b	3	2	2	Layton cf	5	2	2
Matthews cf	4	1	2	Packard 1b	5	0	1
Jordan 3b	4	1	2	Wells lf	4	0	1
Kennell c	4	0	0	Ippolito rf	5	0	0
Kelly 1b	4	0	1	Rogers ss	4	0	2
Honeycutt ss	4	0	0	Carson c	4	0	0
Mangum p	4	0	0	Galey p	1	0	0
				Smith p (3)	1	0	0
				Upchurch p (7)	0	0	0
				Good (8)	1	0	1
				Morris (8)	0	0	0
				Drake (9)	1	0	0
Totals	33	6	10	Totals	40	2	9

Good singled for Upchurch in 8th.
Drake forced Rogers in 9th.

Boeing .... 000 000 101—2
Pea Ridge. N.C. .... 012 000 30x—6

E—Scott 2, Carson, Honeycutt, Jordan, 2, 3 RBI—Packard. Wells, Honeycutt. Matthews 3. Jordan 2. 2B—Jordan 2. Layton. Rogers. 3B—Wells, SB—West. S—Ellen. 2. DP—West to Kelly. Left—Boeing 15. Pea Ridge, N.C. 7. BB—Mangum 5. SO—Smith 4. Morris 2. Mangum 7. HO—Galey 5 in 2⅔ innings; Smith 4 in 3⅔ innings; Upchurch 1 in ⅔ inning; Morris 0 in 1 inning. HBP—West (Smith). WP—Smith PB—Kennel. W. — Mangum. L—Galey. U—Brill and Monty.

Full box of the Boeing Bombers game in Wichita in 1957.

(From the Wichita Eagle)

Going the Cycle

Webster Lupton

Chapter 18 - Clinging to the Game

Reunions of a 'Fast' League

The 1957 season would turn out to be the last for the baseball team called Pea Ridge. But the folks who had been raised on the baseball of Doc Smith, Tommy Byrne, and Kenneth Jackson were not ready to give up the game in their small town. In fact, Pea Ridge's long drive to prominence, topped off by the draw of the benefit game at the end of the season, had fueled the notion that town ball was still very much alive in Angier. It was just time for a new version.

It had become more difficult as the seasons progressed to lure the best teams and the best players to the little field in the Pea Ridge community. Since 1956, Angier had established its own baseball team and had turned the tables on the rivals at Pea Ridge. There were still plenty of baseball fans in the community and certainly plenty of skilled players still young enough to put in a few more seasons. All of this would spur the town's baseball leaders into the notion of rekindling the community's association with two old friends: Tommy Byrne and the Tobacco State League.

In mid-September of 1957 a *News & Observer* story noted discussions of reviving the Tobacco State League as a semipro league. Ben Price was leading the effort, and the early word was that folks in Angier, Fuquay Springs, Erwin, Smithfield, Clinton, Benson, and Lumberton had all shown interest in forming the league. Two weeks later, an organizational meeting of the new league was held, and little was decided, other than the election of league officers. There would be discussions throughout the winter.

It was not coincidence that the rebirth of the Tobacco State League came during the same winter that the notion of another new league fizzled. The movement to get a college summer league started in the cities of the old Coastal Plain League had begun in the summer of 1957 but had gone nowhere. [83] If it had, the TSL idea would probably have been dropped; two semipro leagues competing for college players in the same region could not have worked as well as it had in the old days.

Early in 1958, plans for the new Tobacco State League were finally announced, and something akin to the league of twenty years earlier began to take shape. It would be a fast semipro league, seeking some of the best college and "class" baseball players available, class players being those with some previous professional experience. There would be four games per week and a fifty-game schedule; admission would be charged, usually fifty cents for adults, and twenty-five cents for students. Some of the players would be paid, an average salary being $20 to $40 a game for those who were paid. ₈₄ Many of the players would be recycled performers from the old semipro and pro leagues. Most of the games would be night games.

In Angier, a number of businessmen huddled to form ownership of the team, promising up-front money to get the team started. They knew full well that as all baseball enterprises had gone in Angier — or in any small town for that matter — this would be a roll of the dice. There were no guarantees that they could have a competitive team or, even if it was competitive, that they could draw enough people to games to pay for players, equipment, or even the lights. And the sticky issue of salaries would again raise its ugly head. It was an old story.

The one advantage the league had was lack of competition from other leagues. This Tobacco State League was the only one of its type in eastern North Carolina, the idea of the fast semipro league having faded over the years. For college players and prospective pros, it was one of the few summer options to minor league ball in the region, and the league took advantage of its proximity to the major colleges. The supply of players was consistent. And there were still a number of towns in eastern North Carolina where interest in baseball was still strong — towns that had lost minor league teams during the curtailment of the 1950s.

But the league was an anachronism of sorts. It was a throwback to the days when a town's baseball team was a source of pride, a sentiment that had faded since World War II. The new league would have to revive that sentiment with good players, strong rivalries, and a competitive league race. The town and the league needed one good boost to give the new idea a jump-start.

Enter Tommy Byrne

Since Tommy Byrne had last pitched in Angier in 1939, he had taken his talents about as far as a wild lefthander could. He had signed for a huge $10,000 bonus in 1940, worked his way through the minors, posted seventeen wins one season in Newark, and made it all the way to the dugout of the New York Yankees. He continued to be a pitcher with an unpredictable pitch that folks in Angier had become familiar with. He led the league in hit batsmen five times and the American League in walks three times. But his hard-to-follow pitch got him three seasons with fifteen or more wins, two World Series victories, and eighty-five major league victories. His hitting had also earned him a reputation as a valuable member of any batting order. He hit fourteen home runs as a major leaguer and was called on to pinch hit eighty times. He had spent the 1940s with the Yankees, except for two years of the war; the early 1950s with the Browns, White Sox, and Senators; and had landed back at Yankee Stadium in 1954.

Despite the war, the ups and downs, the trades, and battles with his control, the nearly twenty years in the majors had been good ones for Byrne. He had played with some of the great teams and players, had made a good — though not extravagant — living for his growing family, and had even got to pal around with his idol. The aging, sometimes ailing, Babe Ruth still visited the Yankee dugout from time to time during the 1940s, and those moments were highlights for the other lefty from Baltimore.

"He came to the dugout one day, just to play catch with some of us and asked around for a glove. Someone said 'Byrne over there has three or four gloves.' And he came over and said, 'Hey, Baltimore,' 'cause everybody — the newspapers and all — called me the Baltimore Babe. He asked if he could borrow a glove, and I said, 'Sir, you can have everything in my locker.' "

Through it all, the fans in Angier who remembered Tommy Byrne's playing days there had followed him every step of the way. And through it all, Elmo Fish had remained a familiar face from those days. The Fuquay Springs boy who had been the first baseman and a friend on Byrne's teams in Angier had remained in touch. He was often at the gates or the clubhouse doors of parks in Washington, New York, or Philadelphia to greet Byrne with encouragement, news from Fuquay and Angier, and usually some sort of entrepreneurial proposition for Byrne to weigh.

It was the last of those propositions that Byrne seriously considered when he ended his professional baseball career at the end of the 1957 season, a season in which he had fewer starts than at any time since the early '40s. Byrne said, "They used me in relief, and I could see that I wasn't going to make much more money. I had a number of business things going at the time, and my wife and I had children."

The forward-thinking fellow who had opted to attend college rather than sign out of high school had also seen his career's end coming. He had invested in all sorts of enterprises from trucking to poultry farming to oil, and he was beginning to see his investments actually becoming more lucrative than baseball. He was still making $18,000 to $20,000 a year playing — good money at the time, no doubt. But he knew baseball couldn't last forever, and Elmo Fish's offer to put him in the clothing business in Angier was another opportunity. It was the binding factor that brought Tommy Byrne back to Angier.

Though he resided in the town of Wake Forest, as far as the Angier baseball trust was concerned, Tommy Byrne was back in town. He could still toss a ball and swing a bat well enough to be a star in this new semipro league, or certainly make an impression. The name of an accomplished major leaguer like Byrne was in itself worth a lot.

On May 15, Byrne signed to play eight games with the Angier Braves, one of six teams in the Tobacco State League. The *News & Observer* story the next day quoted Byrne saying, "I pitched down here twenty years ago, and those fellows were good to me. They treated me fine. I decided to help them. ... Each team is allowed one class player. I guess you could call me a class player." [85]

Tommy Byrne had come full circle. Some of his most memorable experiences as a youth were spent in an Angier uniform. And here he was, twenty years later, in business in Angier and playing in the fast semipro Tobacco State League. He would play a limited number of games, but those few games would give him the chance to again be the big man in the dugout, "in the middle of the activity" as he had been in the old days.

It was also the completion of a sort of cycle for the men who had grown up worshipping the heroes of the 1930s and '40s and who were now playing with one. The "youngsters" would relish getting a hit past Byrne the pitcher or, even more, getting an out against Byrne the batter. They were bitter-sweet victories for the local boys, almost as if they watched as a star became a mortal man, as if they had beaten their father at arm wrestling for the first time.

For the Angier team and the Tobacco State League, Byrne's signing was a shot in the arm, as demonstrated a week after the deal was completed. "Tommy Byrne Day" in Angier brought out almost 1,400 fans, a crowd the likes of which Angier hadn't seen since 1946, the town's minor league season. In a small ceremony, Byrne received a plaque and a trophy from the welcoming fans, who still considered the Baltimore boy their own. He started and pitched three innings of the exhibition against Smithfield-Selma, allowing one hit and striking out three. An unearned run made him the losing pitcher of record as Smithfield and former minor league pitcher Ray Sugg came away with a 6-0 win. However, Byrne's presence had given the new league the jump start needed for what would be a challenging season.

New Stars

For the Angier boys who had been raised on baseball in the

1930s, going the cycle did not only mean reuniting with a hero of the past. They were also seeing the future of baseball, running into players who were ten years younger, bigger, stronger, and faster. As surely as they had seen a phenom the likes of Tommy Byrne twenty years earlier, the boys from Angier were now about to discover a young player who would make an even bigger impact on the majors.

A tall, hard-throwing nineteen-year-old from Williamston had shown his superiority in high school baseball over the past three years, and major league scouts were paying attention. He had pitched a few innings with Smithfield-Selma's Tobacco State League team, but the scouts wanted to see him play against some other veteran hitters. It was natural they would turn to nearby Angier to find the right lineup.

"Sam Allen called me wanted to know if I could get a ball club together, go see how good this boy is," Frank Gardner said. So on a chilly night, just two days after Tommy Byrne Day in Angier, Frank lined up a group of players to travel to Smithfield and face the powerful right arm of young Gaylord Perry. Perry had earned his reputation as a fastballing whiz kid during his junior year in high school, a year in which he had pitched five no-hitters and had not allowed a single earned run until the state finals. [86] For part of the summer of 1957, Perry was the only high school player on the Alpine Cowboys, a perennial power in the Texas semipro circuit and in National Baseball Congress tournaments in Wichita. His senior year had not been so imposing; he finished with a 7-2 record. The area's professional scouts who weren't making a path to the doorstep of the state's other young star, Tony Cloninger, were tailing the six feet, five inches, 210-pound Perry. [87]

Frank Gardner rounded up his brother Jim, Marshall and Ben Price, Kenneth Jackson, Jimmie Odell Matthews, and some others. Carlton Mangum went along, but Jack Craig pitched. A player from Coats named Kenneth O'Neal joined the crew and would be the only player to get a hit off of Perry. The site was a field in Smithfield. The lights at the park were dim, and Perry's fastball was blurring.

"We got up a scrub team and went down there to play them in those softball lights," Marshall Price recalled. "I went to bat four times and struck out four times. I told somebody I didn't see it; I heard it. I'd liked to have faced him in the daytime, but he was still the fastest thing I ever went up against."

"It was like playing by candlelight," Mangum remembered. "When he turned the ball loose — he threw hard anyway — and sitting over there on the bench, I could hardly see the ball go from him to home plate."

"I don't remember that well, but I'm sure he struck me out three times," Frank Gardner said. "It was a poorly-lit field, but Gaylord didn't need any help."

A newspaper account noted that nine major league scouts were on hand for the game. The Angier team hit one ball into fair play during the first six innings, a grounder to second base, according to *The Independent* of Fuquay Springs. In eight innings, Perry struck out nineteen batters and gave up one hit and walked two before leaving in the eighth. Angier scored an unearned run in the first inning to actually take the lead, and Craig held off Smithfield until a rally in the fifth put the Leafs in the lead. Perry did the rest. Smithfield won, 6-1.

Ben Price recalls O'Neal's hit: "He took a check swing in the sixth or seventh inning, and that ball hit his bat and went over the shortstop's head just like he had swung that thing from the bottom of his heart. … It made Gaylord so mad that night for Kenneth to get that hit, 'cause he wanted to pitch a no-hitter."

Perry signed with the Giants in less than a week, an unprecedented contract for which some of the Angier players took credit. "I've always said Gaylord owes us some money for that game in front of all those scouts," Frank Gardner said.

The Angier players had seen another experience that helped complete their own cycle of baseball. As kids they had watched Tommy Byrne's dancing pitch confound batters, then witnessed the elder first hand; and now they had seen — though barely — the pitch of a new star. They had lived, and played, through an era in baseball that saw dramatic change financially: In 1940, two years after the Angier Bulls' sterling season the young Angier boys had witnessed, Tommy Byrne signed with the New York Yankees for $10,000, a huge sum that would give him the moniker of Baltimore Bonus Babe. In 1958, as those same Angier boys played out their final days of town ball, Gaylord Perry signed with the San Francisco Giants for $73,000, the most the Giants had ever paid a rookie. The state's other big prospect, Cloninger, signed for $100,000. [88] The boys had seen big-city, big-time baseball become a bigger business than ever. The new breed of players, these Perrys and Cloningers, were stepping into an age of salaries that were much more than a good living for a family of four. They were embarking on an age when young players could become downright rich.

But the world those young stars were headed for might as well have been a million miles from where the boys from Angier headed for that summer of 1958. Sure, big time baseball had become top-heavy and left small towns behind. But for the Gardners, Prices, Adamses, and Harold Ellen, baseball was still a game; a pastime.

Webster Lupton

Chapter 19 - Titles in Pairs

The Braves Battle on Two Fronts

The exhibitions featuring Byrne and Perry were among several the Angier boys played that year, as they assembled a team to start the new Tobacco State League season in June. The new team was nicknamed the Braves, possibly because old Braves uniforms were the cheapest outfits they could acquire. It was managed by Frank Gardner and included other Angier players such as Kenneth Jackson, Harold Ellen, Hayden Adams, and Jimmie Odell Matthews. The team also had new faces that would make up the contingent of paid players. They went out and got future professional Joe Wooten and former minor leaguers, first baseman Arnold Wallis and pitcher John Dennis. They also had the services of Bruce Shelley, a pitcher from Mullins, South Carolina, and Campbell College. Former Pea Ridge player Jack Craig and Johnny Johnson, a young pitcher from the University of North Carolina, would be the team's top starters.

Many of the other old Pea Ridge and Angier players were spread throughout the league. Carlton Mangum, Billy West, Roger Honeycutt, and James Stevens were over at Fuquay; Gene Summerlin was pitching at home in Goldsboro; and Marion Hargrove was in Dunn-Erwin. Smithfield-Selma and Fayetteville were other members of the league. All of the towns except Goldsboro had had representatives in the old semipro Tobacco State League of the 1930s.

The Angier team proved to be by far the best in the league. With 1,000 fans on hand, the Braves opened the Tobacco State League season to an 8-5 loss to Fuquay, despite Jim Brown's grand slam home run. It was the first of what would be a number of memorable confrontations between Angier and Fuquay for the next three seasons. Angier cruised through the regular season. By July 28, the Braves were 25-9, seven games up on second-place Smithfield. In the all-star game the week before, Angier took on the best from the rest of the league and roared to a 12-3 victory behind the pitching of Johnson and Craig and the hitting of Wooten, Matthews, and Brown.

Wooten was a true semipro slugger. Though only stories, rather than statistics, still remain to verify his feats, he was apparently good enough for Byrne to make a personal effort to see that Wooten got a professional tryout. The result was a ten-year pro career that took him as far as the Southern Association and the Pacific Coast League, two of the top minor leagues of the day. In the 1959 season, Wooten would hit twenty-two home runs for Winston-Salem. Wooten and Matthews helped form a sort of murderer's row for Angier. Wooten's reputation for long drives would soon match Matthews's.

"Joe Wooten probably hit the longest ball I've ever seen hit," recalled Ben Price. "He hit one down in Smithfield one night. We were playing [in] that park area where you don't even see the fence — if you hit the ball over the man's head, and if you could run at all, you had a homerun. Joe like to have gotten out coming home 'cause he couldn't run that well. But if a ball ever went 500 foot, he hit one that night. They had to relay the ball three times to get it back in the infield."

Roxboro Again

When mid-July arrived and the state NBC tournament in Roxboro started, Angier had a place in that, too. But it left Angier manager Frank Gardner and the ownership in an old dilemma. They wanted to send a team to the state tournament and even to the nationals — but without losing any ground in their league. The state tournament in Roxboro was to begin in the third week of July, so Angier had to try to maintain a hold on its league lead at the same time it was competing in the NBC state tournament. Despite burning a lot of gas for the next three weeks, Angier was able to field what was essentially two teams. The Braves recruited their old Pea Ridge pals Carlton Mangum, Billy West, Gene Summerlin, and Ford Jordan to go along with them to Roxboro, hoping to duplicate the winning combination of the previous year. The players would return to their league teams for their regular games, some of them having to play two games a day.

The juggling act worked — at least for the time being. Angier rolled up a 36-13 record in the TSL campaign, with Smithfield-Selma placing second at 29-20. Fuquay-Varina had a 28-22 record, and Goldsboro finished at 27-23. The top-heavy success of the league had forced the other two teams, Dunn-Erwin and Fayetteville, out of the league altogether. [89]

The Braves also went to Roxboro and went undefeated to the finals and a showdown with the Marine team from Camp Lejeune. The Marines won the first game on a Saturday night, but a quirk of fate similar to the 1956 tournament with Cavel allowed Angier to advance to the nationals again. The Lejeune team was scheduled to leave the next day to play in the Marine national tournament in San Diego and was unable to play what would have been the title game against Angier. The Braves were awarded the state title by forfeit and were eligible for the Wichita trip.

This brought a new head-scratching problem. Since the Tobacco State League playoffs and the NBC national tournament in Wichita were held at the same time, there would have to be a week in mid-August when Angier had to play for titles 1,300 miles apart. In the old days, it had been an either/or situation: play for the title at home or play for the one in Wichita. There was no way that a town could have two teams. Or could they?

The success of the Pea Ridge team the year before had made players and fans around town think that Angier could in fact bring home a national title. But this Tobacco State League team was one of the town's best, and it would have been hard to surrender an almost sure thing on the chance that maybe the team could win the national event.

Somehow, though, the folks in Angier found a way. It meant more shuffling and recruiting for Angier to be able to fill an official roster for the trip, but they did it. The Braves in Wichita ended up with pitchers Bruce Shelley, Wilson Carruthers, and Larry Crayton, and fielders Billy West, Arnold Wallis, Marion Hargrove, Ford Jordan, Bobby Tart, Jimmie Matthews, Ray Mozingo, and Joe Wooten. The team that stayed home for the TSL playoffs had pitchers Jack Craig, Don Bagdonovich, Johnny Johnson, and Owen Wright, and Angier regulars, Buck Jackson, Frank Gardner, Kenneth Jackson, and Ben Price among others.

However, the long trip to Wichita would yield results similar to those in '56. The Braves were eliminated in Wichita in two games. Crayton, a year away from being an All-North State Conference star with East Carolina, took the mound on August 19 and suffered through two innings as Angier went on to lose to Glenville, Illinois, 8-2. The next day, Shelley was the starter against Midland, Pennsylvania's, Ed Smrekar, a six-year minor league veteran. Shelley pitched five innings of hitless ball, and West drove in a run to give Angier a 1-0 lead. But Shelley was tagged for a run in the sixth, and a three-run rally in the eighth took Midland to a 4-1 win.

Back home, Angier had won the first two games of its first-round Tobacco State League series against Fuquay. The first of those was a 4-3 win in which Tommy Byrne scored the winning run on a double steal.

291

But the Fuquay team clung to life in the best-of-five series with a 5-1 victory the same night that Angier's Wichita team was eliminated. Wooten, Matthews, Shelley, Wallis, and company hustled home to help the TSL team eliminate Fuquay and advance to the playoff finals. The Braves would not have such success against Smithfield-Selma in the finals.

Smithfield, who had former minor league pitchers Amby Foote and Ray Sugg, as well as slugger Bob Whaley, surprised the Braves in five games, winning the clincher, 12-1, in Angier.

Despite the playoff-title loss, Angier, with the help of night baseball, a retired major leaguer, and enough talent for a winning season, had new confidence in its baseball prowess. And despite the dimming popularity of hometown baseball, there were still a few pockets in rural America where fans came out to see the town team. The new TSL was just successful enough to make another go of it.

1958 Angier Braves - North Carolina semipro tournament team

This is the Angier team that won the state tournament Roxboro in July of 1958. The team won the title game by virtue of a forfeit by the Camp Lejeune Marine team, which could not play the final game because of a scheduling conflict. Angier would represent the state in the National Baseball Congress tournament in Wichita, Kansas, but the Braves would be eliminated in two games. Front row, left to right, are Frank Gardner, Harold Ellen, Johnny Johnson, Carlton Mangum, and Jimmie Matthews. Second row: Billy West, Bruce Shelley, James Stevens, Gene Summerlin, and Arnold Wallis. Back row: batboy W.C. Ashworth, Ford Jordan, Jim Brown, Joe Wooten, John Dennis, and Jack Craig.

(Photo courtesy of Harold Ellen)

Chapter 20 - Too Close to Call

A Tight Race Keeps the League Alive

The town baseball game had changed once again. The new semipro Tobacco State League had brought a bigger schedule by conforming to night games, ticket takers at the gate, and salaried ball players. Other elements — the revival of the old league rivalries, the entrance of a former major league player, and a playoff that proved more competitive than the regular season — had also helped the league get its new start.

However, the boys who had lived baseball in Angier — the older players named Adams, Gardner, and Price, who had been the nucleus of the Pea Ridge team in its early years — were fading. In 1959, Angier would field a team without an Adams or a Price for much of the year. The chief reason was the fact that the single, carefree boys of summer who had started the Pea Ridge team, had watched the game in town distance itself from them. They were weekend players, family men, farmers, and businessmen who couldn't break away forty or fifty times a summer to play ball. The other reason was simply time. It was catching up with their arms, legs, and eyes, and they knew they had to step aside for the younger, college-aged boys who were struggling with the same dreams their elders once had.

Frank Gardner was the exception, but even his time was running out. He had become the local postal carrier and would be sharing the team's management duties with Bob Cruze. Frank would not be available for some games. Jimmie Odell Matthews, who was still only twenty-three years old and still a player of exceptional caliber, was another of the old gang that played.

The league itself was more revenue-driven now than it had been, and as a business, the ever-present questions of salaries had to be faced. Who would be paid and how much? Like the semipro leagues of the past, the local players who might be willing to play for nothing were overlooked in favor of the more recent professionals and promising young college players that were brought in from out of town.

For the most part, the league had been a success. About the only thing it had lacked in 1958 was a close regular-season race. Angier had been the top dog during the 1958 season, leading for most of the year, dominating the all-star game, and finishing five games in front. The Braves had slipped only in the title series, when many of the players were road-worn from NBC tournament play.

All of that would change in 1959. Angier, Fuquay, and Smithfield would engage in a league race so close that the whole regular season would come down to one last desperate weekend to decide the pennant. The playoff title series would go down to a seventh game. The closeness of the Tobacco State League race that year would also veto the notion of another team for the NBC state tournament in Roxboro. No one would be willing to lend players out for tournament games when every game at home was crucial. Besides, two of the three trips to Wichita had been duds, and the community might not be as willing to send another team on a cross-country trip. Goldsboro was the other team in the league that year and stayed in the league only as a sort of spoiler to the rest. The team started out 2-13 and was never in the race the rest of the way.

The other three teams all started the season figuring to be in the race in August. Angier had Cruze, Jack Craig, and Bruce Shelley anchoring its pitching staff, while fielders Ray Mozingo, Marion Hargrove, Arnold Wallis, and Frank Gardner would be in the lineup for most of the year. Tommy Byrne was again a featured player but again played only a few games, and Jimmie Odell Matthews would start in Angier but would be playing in Fuquay before the end of the year. A number of players would be in and out as the team moved personnel.

In Fuquay Springs, Chester Holland's Twins had Carlton Mangum, another minor league veteran Harry Nicholas, and East Carolina pitcher Johnny Ellen to use on the mound. Former Pea Ridge stars Ford Jordan and James Stevens, along with ex-pro Jesse Haswell, were also in Fuquay. [90]

Smithfield-Selma was managed by Ray Hardee, who had been one of Angier's best during the 1946 professional season, and Virgil

Payne, who had managed and played in the Coastal Plain and Tobacco State minor leagues for years. They banked their pitching on college stars Ben Hammett of UNC, and Joel Gibson of Wilmington College, along with veterans Amby Foote and Ray Sugg. Raeford Fulghum and Harold Moore were other seasoned players who had helped them to the 1958 playoff crown.

The stage was set for a fierce race for the 1959 Tobacco State League crown, and the teams would not disappoint. Fuquay darted out to the early-season lead, winning its first seven games, including close victories over Angier. A wild 8-7 game in Fuquay in which the lead changed five times would be the last win in the Twins' string. Angier would return home to take a 3-1 win over the Twins the next night on the strength of Cruze's three-hit pitching performance and a bases-loaded single by Byrne. By the last week in June, Fuquay was sitting pretty at 13-4, with Smithfield 9-8 and Angier 8-9. Goldsboro stood at 2-13.

Controversy perked fan interest that week when Byrne drew a three-game suspension for using profanity in contesting an umpire's call. The suspension itself wasn't that crucial to Byrne or the Braves because of Byrne's limited playing agreement. But, like the old days, it gave the league another plug in the newspaper and was certainly no penalty to attendance. In fact, the league had no shortage of that type of fire, though few of the incidents grabbed the press that Byrne's did. Harold Ellen was tossed from an Angier-Fuquay game and suspended after being accused of hurling an insult at an umpire, only to be reinstated the next night at the behest of the league president who witnessed the row and knew the insult had in fact come from the bleachers.

Despite Fuquay's searing start, the Twins could not shake the other two contenders, and when they went down in a double-header in Smithfield in early August, the standings placed the top three teams within three and a half games. Angier and Fuquay would play no fewer than five one-run games against each other that year, and one of the most notable was an August 7 game, a pitcher's duel in which Bob Cruze and Johnny Ellen refused to surrender. Despite nineteen total hits, the game stretched into the bottom of the fifteenth inning scoreless. Jesse Haswell doubled in Ollie Wall to give the Twins the 1-0 victory. Both Cruze and Ellen pitched the entire game, Cruze striking out twelve and Ellen fifteen.

Angier returned home the next night and claimed a 4-3 victory over their rivals to tighten the race even more. At that point Fuquay had a 21-15 record; Smithfield was 20-15; and Angier was 20-16. It was during this close race that Fuquay made a deal that Twins fans figured would certainly clinch the title for them. Jimmie Odell Matthews left Angier and went to play for the Twins. What lured Matthews to leave the Braves is not clear. A fuss over playing time, pay, or even Matthews's battle with injuries that had arisen over the past few seasons were likely causes. He had suffered a broken collarbone, a thumb injury, and numerous leg injuries that had kept him from the minor leagues.

But by mid-August he was in a Twins uniform, and he began making a difference almost right away. As Fuquay, now a game behind Smithfield in the standings, hosted Goldsboro on August 20, Matthews unleashed a barrage of home runs that accounted for all of Fuquay's runs in an 8-5 win over the visitors. Matthews homered in his first four at-bats, all off of his old Pea Ridge teammate Gene Summerlin, to lead the team to the win and prove that despite the injuries, he could still swing a bat. But Fuquay was not out of the woods. On the last Sunday of the regular season, the Twins needed a win at Goldsboro and relied on their rivals from Angier to defeat Smithfield to create a tie for the league lead. That happened, and Smithfield and Fuquay finished the regular season tied for first. Angier ended up one game back.

An extra game was then needed to decide the regular-season pennant winner and determine the pairings for the playoffs. The winner not only earned the pennant but also got to play Goldsboro instead of Angier in the first round of the playoffs. Smithfield eked out a 3-2 win in the showdown game to set the stage for the playoff duels.

The air-tight regular-season race had indeed been a boom for a struggling little semipro league of 1959. But the first round of the best-of-five playoffs would be somewhat anti-climactic. While Smithfield did as expected in sweeping Goldsboro in the opening round, it was surprising that Angier did the same against Fuquay, the team that had held the league lead for most of the season and had consistently played close games with Angier. Fuquay went down in three straight games, by scores of 6-2, 3-0, and 13-6. Elbert Adams, who had joined Angier late in the year, provided much of the punch for Angier in the series, driving in two runs to lead a four-run rally in the third inning of the first game and picking up a home run and two triples in the final game. Jim Overby pitched the shutout in Game 2.

The title series would be different. Angier and Smithfield battled to a seventh and final game in the series, with almost all being close games. Joel Gibson, the Wilmington College standout, hurled a no-hitter with thirteen strikeouts to shut down Angier in the opening game of the seven-game series in Smithfield, 1-0. Angier bounced back with Fred Caviness hitting a homer in the tenth to give the home team a 2-1 win. In the third game, Smithfield jumped out to a big lead but had to put a halt to a five-run Angier rally in the ninth and survive by an 8-7 score and take a 2-1 lead in the series. Angier tied the series in another ten-inning thriller the next night in Angier when Ray Mozingo hit a bases-loaded single to give Angier a 3-2 win. The only wide-open match of the series came in Game 5 when Smithfield scored six runs in the fourth inning and piled on an 11-4 victory. But Angier didn't surrender. With their backs to the wall, the Braves had a four-run rally in one inning and relied on Bob Cruze to hold off Smithfield's bats to claim a 5-3 win and tie the series at three games each.

The teams traded the lead in the final game, too, with Angier taking a 3-1 lead on a home-run blow by Tommy Byrne in the seventh inning and Smithfield bounding back with a five-run rally charged by Gibson's bases-loaded double to regain the advantage. Then, in the eighth, future pro Mozingo smacked a three-run homer to lead a five-run Braves rally. Bob Cruze, who had taken the mound in the seventh, held off the Leafs the rest of the way. Angier won the game 8-6 and claimed the league title, avenging the 1958 series loss to Smithfield.

About 800 fans showed up for the climactic game of the 1959 league season, a Monday night game in Angier. That figure indicated that, despite the excitement caused by the closeness of the regular-season race, attendance was still relatively light. One cannot help but think that attendance for a Smithfield-Angier title game in the 1930s or '40s would have been at least twice that size. But the popularity of baseball in the TSL communities, though waning, was not low enough diminish the winter talk of yet another season. Angier and the league would cling to their own pastime.

1956 Campbell College battery

Left to right, pitcher Bruce Shelley, catcher Marion Hargrove, and Campbell head baseball coach Hargrove "Hoggie" Davis at the end of the 1956 junior college season. Shelley and Hargrove would play for Angier teams in the semipro Tobacco State League. Davis, who would coach baseball and golf at Campbell for years, was one of the best hitters in minor league baseball in North Carolina in the years after World War II.

(Photo courtesy of Rubell Shelley)

Chapter 21 - The Last Stars

'People Just Seemed to Lose Interest'

The thrilling show the Tobacco State League put on in 1959 would be a driving force for the coming year. The league would go out and recruit new players, even new teams, and would embark on a new season with new hope. The fact that it was a new decade seemed to mean little on a small-town baseball field. Baseball as a pastime had faded during the last decade, and it was as evident in North Carolina as anywhere else. There were still some recreational baseball leagues in the eastern part of the state, but they were almost exclusively amateur, much like the leagues Pea Ridge had competed in. The true semipro baseball leagues — leagues where scouts went to find new talent and former pros went to play out their last days — were almost nonexistent, at least in North Carolina. It was becoming more difficult to get people to spend a half dollar and a summer evening at the park. Even the professional Carolina League, whose five North Carolina teams were grooming stars such as Raleigh's Carl Yastrzemski, Durham's Jim Rice, and Greensboro's Jim Bouton, reported declining attendance. [91]

Baseball's attraction had indeed faded. People had other things to do; things they wouldn't have considered in, say, the 1930s, when baseball was still America's pastime. Things such as playing golf or tennis, recreations once reserved for the upper-class elite, were now becoming middle-class summer recreations. People were going to race tracks and drag-strips that dotted the landscape of the state. They were also playing slow-pitch softball, a recreation that was more and more the outdoor summer game for diamond fanatics. Church, town, and industrial softball leagues were taking over diamonds, and many of the men who once donned the woolen baseball uniforms were now in softball shorts and T-shirts.

"When I was getting on in years and facing some of those younger boys with their fast pitches, I tell you, I knew it was time for me to head out to the softball field and play there," Ben Price said.

The folks who maintained the Tobacco State League during the summer of 1959 were still trying to relive the 1930s and '40s and even the Pea Ridge '50s. Things had changed, though. Many of the players from the 1950s were still around, and even the stars from the 1930s and '40s still donned uniforms, though usually in managerial roles. Others had long since put away their gloves. Angier fans hardly ever saw an Adams or a Price in uniform anymore, and Frank Gardner, Harold Ellen, James Stevens, and the rest of the 1950s stars were just about at the end of their playing days. Tommy Byrne, who had helped jump start the league, did not play in 1960. His family and expanding business ventures kept him from spending much time in Angier, his adopted hometown. At age forty-one, he had played his last season.

The TSL was still a summer destination for up-and-coming talent. In fact, two young players who made the Angier roster that year would become the eighth and ninth Angier semipro players to go on to the major leagues. Calvin Koonce had been a high school star in Hope Mills near Fayetteville and was playing spring ball at Campbell College. He had been a star on the Cumberland County American Legion teams and had been named a junior college all-American at Campbell after a 1960 spring in which he struck out eighty-seven batters in seventy-three innings. He played outfield as well, and carried a .326 batting average. Koonce would don an Angier Braves uniform and be a guest at Frank Gardner's home on the nights he played for the Braves.

Before the season was over, a Raleigh high school and American Legion star named Jimmy Roland would be on the mound for the Braves. Koonce and Roland would have parallel careers in the majors: Koonce eventually signed with the Cubs and played from 1962 to 1972 with the Cubs and Mets; Roland signed the same year with the Twins and played with Minnesota and Oakland through the decade.

Koonce and durable Bob Cruze would be the one-two pitching punch for the Braves for most of the summer. But the early mound star would be Johnny Ellen, the East Carolina standout who had anchored Fuquay's staff in 1959. He struck out twenty-three batters in a 4-3 duel with Goldsboro on June 21, and his performance was an eye-opener for scouts. Three days later, he signed with the Orioles and headed for their Bluefield, West Virginia, team. The former Garner High School player was entering the first of four minor league seasons.

Cruze was now the sole manager of the Angier team, as Frank Gardner had to taper his baseball duties because of his job as the town mail carrier. Cruze would also have local boys Elbert Adams and Jimmie Odell Matthews to start the year, as well as returning players Ray Mozingo and Buck Jackson. Bob Kennel, who had spent one .259 batting season with the Orioles' Knoxville, Tennessee team, was back in town and was playing catcher for the Braves. Veteran players Bobby Tart and Jimmy Hubbard were also on the Angier team, as was short stop Gordon Welch.

The league actually expanded that season, though it was a troublesome expansion. Goldsboro did not finish the season, but two former Coastal Plain League cities stepped in. New Bern was in the standings at the start of the year, and Rocky Mount would replace Goldsboro at mid-season, agreeing to accept the record and some of the players for the mid-season start. The five-team league would still offer four playoff spots at the end of the year. Fuquay, with the old Pea Ridge tournament gang of Mangum, Jordan, Stevens, and Harold Ellen, returned to the league along with Virgil Payne's Smithfield team.

The league race was not the three-way sizzler it had been the previous season, but it was competitive. Fuquay and Angier traded places at the top of the standings for most of the campaign, with Smithfield hovering a few games back. New Bern was competitive enough to maintain fourth place, and Rocky Mount trailed the league. The vast majority of Fuquay's pitching strength was in the durable arm Carlton Mangum. By late July, Fuquay had eighteen wins, and thirteen of them were Mangum's. [92]

Probably the most noteworthy thing about the 1960 TSL season was Angier's amazing finish. With Koonce and Cruze on the mound and Roland down from Raleigh to join them after his American Legion season, Angier capped off the year with a fifteen-game winning streak, including post-season sweeps of New Bern and Fuquay. The Braves clinched the pennant in Fuquay on August 5, the last day of the season, with a 5-0 victory, Cruze crafting a four-hitter against Mangum. They then breezed through the two best-of-five playoff series without a nick. The title clincher came on September 7, Koonce again defeating Mangum, this time in a 9-1 game.

Angier had fielded one of its best teams since the "old days," but it would be the town's last, at least in league play. The Tobacco State League had run its course and would never re-form. Too many things had chipped away at the popularity of baseball for towns the size of Angier, Fuquay, or even Smithfield or Goldsboro, to continue to field a team.

"It's hard to say. People just seemed to lose interest," is the answer most of the people who recall that time give when asked why semipro ball ceased.

The immediate cause of the league's demise could be accounted to money. It had always been a struggle to keep a semipro team alive in

Angier, even during the 1930s. But now things were even tougher, both because players required more money and because there were fewer folks at the park to support that payroll. The issue of winning while making ends meet was still there.

Ben Price, one of the team's financial officers, recounted the familiar issue of paid and non-paid players. "I kind of looked after what little bit we had in the bank," he recalled. "I was writing the checks to those boys that you might say we hired to play. We had ballplayers here, and when you start paying out to some of the players … it got the boys around here to thinking, 'Why are you paying them when we have better ball players in Angier here that aren't getting paid?' It was a little bit of the problem."

It was a similar problem to the problems of years past in any semipro league in most any town. The drive for the best team money could buy invariably punished the folks who had to fork out the bucks. Toss in the lack of regulation — or enforcement of regulation — in semipro leagues, and the recipe for disaster is evident. Angier fans had seen it in the league of the 1930s and again twenty years later. Even the minor league team of 1946 — despite its more strict regulation of salaries — had, as Red Williams put it, "barely broke even" despite winning the playoffs in 1946. No matter how gratifying it was to field a team of winners, baseball financial backers in Angier always had to face the balance sheet at the end of the week, the month, or the year. Trouble was, in those "old days," big games brought out fans in droves. By 1960, if 500 showed up at the park, it was considered a good take.

As it turned out, the most consistent team Angier ever fielded was the Pea Ridge team that played on a tiny country field, charged no admission, and offered no official salaries to its players. Pea Ridge, with practically no budget at all, fielded a team for eight league seasons.

League baseball was over in Angier after that September game in 1960. It had been quite a run. Since the 1935 season, when Angier first ventured into semipro league baseball, an Angier team had captured fourteen titles of some sort, including one championship with the town's only all-professional team. Angier fans had cheered nine players on their way up to the major leagues, and at least thirty other future and past professionals.

Baseball had bounced back from the Depression and World War II. It had given folks in town something to look forward to when players began warming up on skin infields during the first days of spring. It had brought them glorious triumphs and stinging defeats. And it had given boys named Adams, Price, Ellen, and Gardner a chance to follow in the shoes of the heroes they had worshipped as kids. There was no ceremony or mourning on that last day Angier fielded a league team; there was no way to know it was the last league game. It was just a silent passing into the memories of the few people living today who had the privilege of experiencing league baseball in Angier.

Chapter 22 - A Final Fling

The 'Town Team' Fades into Memory

It's hard to keep an old baseball player down. The boys who had grown into men in the 1940s and '50s and still only knew just one game worth playing on a summer day would not give up that game easily. To them it was still "about the only thing to do" around town on a summer afternoon or evening. Since they still knew how to play it well, it would take a lot to keep them from the skin infields on a July weekend. It didn't mean much to them that folks weren't showing up to watch them play as much anymore. Baseball remained their beloved game.

That is why Angier's last TSL game was not its last game. The last Angier town team was formed in 1961, when James Stevens rounded up a group to go back to Roxboro and try and recapture for themselves and the community the glory that tournament competition had brought Pea Ridge. Getting the team together was reminiscent of the old days when teams gathered at Pea Ridge, or even the days when they were kids, just gathering players together for a neighborhood skirmish.

"By then, none of us were playing organized ball. We were all over the hill a little bit," Stevens said. "I stopped by Rae Fulghum's one day, and we got to talking about playing, and I talked with some others. So, we got together and played. ... We had a pretty good group, but that year I don't think we could have raised the money to go to Wichita."

Bob Cruze, Carlton Mangum, Ford Jordan, Buck Jackson, Jimmie Matthews, Rae Fulghum, R.B. Tingen, Jack Craig, Ray Mozingo, Sherrill Jones, and Marshall Long joined the team. Stevens also rounded up Harold Ellen and Jesse Haswell to help shore up the pitching. Ellen and Matthews were the only hometown Angier players. Angier had no league team that summer, not even one that would find pickup games here and there, like in the old days. So the last version of a baseball team in the little town organized in early July and played three exhibitions — winning all of them — before heading into the state tournament.

The Braves rolled through the tournament, tripped up only by a team from Greensboro, Rainey Shell. But that was enough. The Greensboro team topped Angier first in the semifinal round, 5-3, and again in the finals, 5-4. Former professional pitcher Dick Stewart was the winner of record in both games. The last game was a hard-fought battle in which the always-reliable Jimmie Odell Matthews was left on base as Angier battled back in the bottom of the ninth. It was the last game for an Angier semipro team.

Generations of players and fans had trotted the fields and stirred the stands of Angier baseball from the days when Doc Smith, Bill Holland, and Woodrow Upchurch gave a Depression-era town a reason to cheer, to the days when a clan of Adams boys roughed out a field of dreams in the middle of nowhere and made it somewhere, to the last gasp of the Tobacco State League. The town game had finally given up.

Today

The places where players once stirred a town's energy are barely recognizable now. A law office stands where Tommy Byrne's strike zone once was. The place where Spell scooped and fed Ryan who relayed to Fish for the double play is now a backyard. A pharmacy is on the corner that once was the destination for one of Kenneth Jackson's home run shots. The Pea Ridge field, which was kept up well enough to host a warm-up or pickup game from time to time until the 1980s, has now grown over. And the field behind the old high school, where Jimmie Matthews and Joe Wooten rattled the woods with their powerful swings, still manages to be an adequate, though run down, practice field.

They are all special places to the men who remember when baseball was played there. Frank Gardner could hardly forget them. After all, he passed by them almost daily for the thirty years that he carried the mail in the Angier community. They became a constant reminder to him of the days when he struggled through his .250 batting with the always-welcome return to the field to guard his beloved second base. Harold Ellen and Marshall Price made it a point to occasionally take their children, and later their grandchildren, out to the Pea Ridge field to show them where they had spent so many summers of fun. The kids may not have understood the exact significance of such trips, but through the years of recounted stories they had to understand the importance of baseball in their fathers' lives.

Despite the fact that the old men had told them they played baseball because "it was something to do" in a small town, they had to know that there was something more.

The Adams kids had to know because for the rest of the twentieth century, Ernest Meck and Bill Runyon, the West Virginia and Pennsylvania boys who were hauled in from Fort Bragg by Bill Watkins to help the Pea Ridge team in the early 1950s, made annual journeys to Angier to visit their pal, Raythell Adams. They had to know that the connection those men made on a diamond lasted for a lifetime.

The Stevens and Ellen kids had to know, because James Stevens still stayed in touch with Harold Ellen until Stevens's death in 2005. And on it goes: Elbert Adams and Jim and Frank Gardner still have coffee together in town; they all cross paths with the Price brothers, who maintain businesses in Angier.

The times these men experienced were times when a love of baseball carried whole communities and whole families. Harold Ellen's mother decided to proceed with open heart surgery at age seventy, reasoning that when the count was against her, she still had a chance to stay alive. Her doctor told Gladys Ellen that with her age and a diabetic condition, she had two strikes against her. Mrs. Ellen didn't flinch:

"Well, I come from a baseball family - I'll take a chance at a third strike." The count stayed alive for Mrs. Ellen for the next fifteen years.

Harold himself would become a lifetime baseball man. He would coach six years of high school ball, and 21 years of college ball, 18 of those at Pembroke State College (now UNC-Pembroke). He also umpired on the high school and college levels, and played a role in designing batter's helmets for college players. His name is in the UNC-Pembroke Athletics Hall of Fame and the National Association of Intercollegiate Athletics (NAIA) Hall of Fame. He died in 2007.

The kids would never approach the game quite the same way their fathers and grandfathers had. For them, baseball was little league, maybe high school, and maybe even college. To them it was never just something to do. They were bombarded with other things to do. Because of that, baseball is what it is today, a game of heroes and goats, played by kids in the towns and men in the cities. It is still a popular game, beloved by many, including my generation, the generation that heard the stories of the town teams but were too preoccupied to carry on such a tradition.

Today, when Angier plays Lillington or Smithfield plays Fuquay in a summer game, it is on the closely cropped, well-kept little league field, a field that most of the players of their grandfathers' generation never had. And when Grandpa says, "Go out and beat them Smithfield boys," the youngster has no idea what it once meant to the old man.

Their grandparents built these fields so that their young ones wouldn't have to go to the nearest clearing and scrape out a diamond for themselves. They offered the youngsters an opportunity to play organized ball, so that they could play the game before they reached the hectic age when time for recreation ran out. And maybe, just maybe, so they could pick it up and enjoy it as an adult. That's why little leagues, high schools, American Legion posts, and Babe Ruth leagues carry the baseball banner for neighborhoods and communities across the nation today. College players still have their spring seasons and summer leagues of competition. It is in those summer college leagues that a competition similar to the level of the old semipro leagues can be found. For players above college age, it is harder to find an amateur league team.

Many have managed. Amateur baseball for adults is still a big deal in much of the nation. From Alaska to the West Coast to Florida to Maine, college kids and even a few old pros still compete on summer evenings, maintaining their passion for the game. There are over-twenty, over-forty and over-fifty leagues spotted across the landscape. There are fantasy camps and old-timers championships. All are for players who are past high school or college years, who are not quite good enough for a professional team, or who just want to play around home.

The National Baseball Congress still hosts a state tournament in Roxboro and a national tournament in Wichita. Nowadays, the state tournament has to work hard to get eight teams to enter. The national tournament is still big, but teams such as the Sinton Oilers and the Fort Wayne Dairymen, fearsome powerhouses of the 1940s and '50s, have long since disbanded. The vast majority of the strongest teams come from west of the Mississippi. Teams from California are the dominant ones, and Alaska is now practically the center of the adult non-pro baseball world.

Folks in Angier are still within an hour's drive of a minor league game and within five hours of a major league contest. But it is a distant game. Most of the minor league players have little of the attachment to their cities that they once had.

The men still living who played on the Angier and Pea Ridge teams still follow the game. They grumble about the designated-hitter rule, high salaries, and pampered pitchers. That's because they remember a time when pitchers had to hit and hitters had to field, a time when major leaguers made something less than an extravagant salary and when glory was their only bonus, and a time when pitchers pitched for nine innings. They remember when baseball and its players touched small towns and communities.

The men who played for Pea Ridge and Angier and the folks who watched them were part of the last generation that could carry a baseball team on sheer love. It was the last generation of self sufficiency. It was the last generation to create its own recreation rather than just signing up; the last generation to build its own fields rather than just show up on time; the last generation to obtain its own uniforms rather than wonder how much uniforms would cost this year; and the last generation to learn bunt, steal, cut off, squeeze, and hit-and-run all on its own. It was the last generation of kids to witness great players in their own hometown and to go out and emulate them in later years. It was the last generation of people who actually went out and found a place to play.

Webster Lupton

The Players

This is an alphabetical list of players for each year Angier and Pea Ridge fielded teams, according to newspaper clippings, memories and the few official records that remain. The only team that left official records was the 1946 professional team.

* - league champion

1932 Angier Outlaws (independent)

Adams, p

Mason Bugg, p

Wales Blalock

Mike Crawford

Tally Dupree, if

Doc Smith, mgr.

1933 Angier (independent)

Charles Adams, p

Hugh Buchanan

Mason Bugg, p

Carroll

Collins

Mike Crawford

Mike Dupree

Nick Dupree, c

Tally Dupree

Bill Ferebee

Ham Ferebee

William Gardner, p

Harrington

Hockaday

Bill Holland, p

Johnson, c

Kennel, p

DeWitt Perry, p

Doc Smith, c

Woody Upchurch, p

Young, mgr.

1934 Angier (independent)

Charles Adams, of

Ball

Wales Blalock, of

Harry Buchanan

Leo Buchanan

Mason Bugg, p

Jimmy Collins, of

Mike Crawford

James Denning, 3b

Nick Dupree, c

Tally Dupree, if

William Gardner, p

Zeb Harrington

Elmo Hockaday

Douglas Johnson, p

Elmo Johnson

Knowles

Doc Smith, c

Larry Smith, c

Thompson

Woody Upchurch, p

Wall

Garland Adams, mgr.

D.W. Denning, mgr.

S.H. Gardner, mgr.

1935 Angier Bulls (Tobacco State League, exhibition)

Aderholt

Bailey

Bruce, p

Mason Bugg, p, of

Bennett Bullock, 1b

Celey, p

James "Chubby" Dean, p

Nick Dupree, c

Tally Dupree, ss

Elmo Fish

Gardner, p

Bill Holland, p

King

Kurdys, if

Tom Lanning, p

Ed Libby, if

Jimmy Maus

Frank Melton, p

Glenn Mullineaux, of

Mullins

Dick Newsome, p

Page, c

Perry, c

Ray Rex

Roberson, p, of
Howard Smith
Larry Smith, c
Leroy Spell, ss
Joe Talley, p
George Turbeville, p
Woody Upchurch, p
Wesley Upchurch

Tommy Williams, p

Wilbur Adams, mgr.
Walter Latham, mgr.
DeWitt Perry, p, mgr.
Porter Sheppard, c, mgr.
Doc Smith, mgr.

1936 Angier Bulls

Mason Bugg, of
Bennett Bullock
James Denning
Tally Dupree
James Gardner
William Gardner, p
Hockaday
Bill Holland, p

Elmo Johnson
Mickey O'Quinn, p
Reed
Larry Smith, c
Spainki, p
Alton Stephenson
Woody Upchurch, p

1937 Angier Bulls (Tobacco State League)

Ayers, c
Barton
Blalock, of
Jeff Bolden, of
Bennett Bullock, 1b
Cross, c
Tally Dupree, 3b, ss
Elmo Fish, 2b
Andy Fuller, p
Fuquay
James Gardner, p
Hoot Gibson, of
Harrington, p, c

Pee Wee Hight, p
Bill Holland, p
Emmett Johnson, 3b
King, p
Larnie, of, 2b
Lavine
McIntyre
Jim Satterthwaite, p
Howard Smith, of, 3b, ss
Larry Smith, c
Leroy Spell, ss, of, 3b
Spruill, p
Tommy Williams, p

319

Bennett Bullock, 1b, asst. mgr.   Woody Upchurch, p, mgr.

1938 Angier Bulls (Tobacco State League)*

Blalock

Jeff Bolden, of

Tommy Byrne, p

Jake Denning, p

Bob Dexheimer, c

Tally Dupree, 3b

Fred Eason, of

Hal Farley, p

Ferguson, p

Elmo Fish, 1b

Stuart Flythe, p

Andy Fuller, p

Gardner, p

Charlie Gilbert, of

Hoyle, ss

Ed Johnson, p

Charley Jordon

Al Jurisich, p

Connie Ryan, 2b

Leroy Spell, ss

Bill Sweel, c

John D. Wills, p

Mickey O'Quinn, p, mgr.

1939 Angier Bulls (Tobacco State League)

Oliver Grigsby, p

Marvin Black

Hal Bodney

Paul Brotherton

Tommy Byrne, p

Frank Chambers

John Clower, p

Cobb, p

Crawford

John Dirman, p

Renfro "Peanut" Doak

Tally Dupree, 3b

Elmo Fish

Pate Fish

Price Ferguson

Gardner, p

Glover, 1b

Skinny Hall, p

Bryan "Ace" Hammett, p

Hardin, p

Jack Holt

Adolph Honeycutt, of

Kenneth Jackson, c

Ed Johnson, p

Tom Jones

Maynard, c

Outen, c

Aubrey Pittman

Bob Reid, 1b

Connie Ryan, 2b

Ray Scarborough, p

Bill Senter

W.T. Taylor

Walters, c

Bob Dexheimer, c, mgr.
Mickey O'Quinn, p, mgr.

1943 Angier Bluebirds

Cadvill Adams, c
Lee Brown, p
Ellen

Wayron Gardner, p
Price

1946 Angier-Fuquay (Class D Tobacco State League)*

Aiken, p
Walter "Bud" Barbee, p
Neil Belcher, p
Warner Chinnis, p
Cloris Clinard, p
John Colclough, p
Art Crummie
Bill Daniels, p
Jack Eager
Ruie Eubanks
Everette, p
Pate Fish, p
Harry Fortune, p
Ernest Gallo, p
Gardner, p
Roscoe Gentry, 2b
Frank Grubbs, p
Ray Hardee, p
Bruce Hedrick, c
Art Heffner
Walt Hergent, p
Bob Holland, p
James House, p
Paul Hunt, ss

Randolph Ingle, p
Kenneth Jackson, of
Jones, p
Harry Landay
Neil Lefler, p
Marvin Lorenz, 1b
Bob Lynch, p
Bob Mann, of
Meador, p
Don Monterose, p
Joe Mills, 3b
Sally Newman, of
Dave Odum
John Privette, of
Bill Ratteree, c
Dan Ray, 1b
Gaither Riley
August Rogers, ss
Joe Santomauro, p
Dennis Saunders, 2b
Andy Scrabola, of
Sam Sellers, p
Otis Stephens, of
Jim Taylor, p

Garland Wilmer, 2b

John Wisecup, p

Ray Bomar, p, mgr.

Paul Dunlap, of, mgr

Doc Smith, mgr.

1947 Angier (Cape Fear League)

Gerald "Butch" Adams, p

Baker, c

Barber, c

Burch, p

Tally Dupree, if

Jim Gardner, p, if

Ray McLeod, of

David Price, p

R.C. Price, p

Harold Wells, c, p

C. Williams, c

Kenneth Williams

1948 Pea Ridge (Cape Fear League)

Clyde Adams

Gerald "Butch" Adams, p

Hayden Adams, if

Raythell Adams, c

Winfield Adams

Wayron "Pete" Adams

Currin, c

B. Gardner, c

Frank Gardner, 2b

Jim Gardner

Ray McLeod, of, c

David Price, p

Marshall Price, of

Wells, p

Bill Watkins, p, mgr.

1949 Angier (Cape Fear League)

Clyde Adams

Connie Adams, ss

Elbert Adams, 3b

Gerald "Butch" Adams, p

Hayden Adams, 1b

Raythell Adams, c

Winfield Adams

Davis, p

Denning

Tally Dupree

R. Flowers, p

Holland, p

Kenneth Jackson

Parker, p

David Price, p

Marshall Price

R.C. Price
Wells, p
Williams, c

Jim Gardner, p, mgr.
Bill Watkins, p, mgr.

1950 Angier

Connie Adams, ss
Elbert Adams, 3b
Gerald "Butch" Adams, p
Raythell Adams, c
Roscoe Flowers
Holland, p

Kenneth Jackson
Price, c
Marshall Price, of

Jim Gardner, p, mgr.
Bill Watkins, p, mgr.

1951 Pea Ridge (Cape Fear League)*

Clyde Adams
Connie Adams, 3b
Elbert Adams, ss
Hayden Adams, 1b
Raythell Adams, c
Rexwell Adams
Wayron "Pete" Adams
Bill Bowden, p
Roy Earp
Bobby Gardner

Jim Gardner
Gorman, c
Roger Honeycutt
Ernest Meck, p
Ed Moffett
Marshall Price
Bill Runyon, if
Williams, c

Bill Watkins, p, mgr.

1952 Pea Ridge (Tri-County League)*

Clyde Adams
Connie Adams, 3b
Gerald "Butch" Adams, p
Hayden Adams
Raythell Adams, c

Wayron "Pete" Adams, p
Bill Bowden, p
Bobby Chapel, p
Jack Faucett, p
Holland, p

Mike Kozakowich
Matthews, p
Jimmie Matthews, of
Marshall Price, of

Ray McLeod, of
Wilkins, p

Bill Watkins, p, mgr.

1953 Pea Ridge (Central State League)*

Clyde Adams
Connie Adams, 3b
Gerald "Butch" Adams, p
Hayden Adams
Raythell Adams, c
Bill Bowden, p
Harold Ellen, p, c, of
Kozakowich
Carlton Mangum, p

Matthews, p
Jimmie Matthews, of
Ray McLeod, of
Parker, p
Marshall Price, of
Rowland, p
Rhodes, p

Don Wall, p, mgr.

1954 Pea Ridge (Mid-State League)*

Connie Adams, ss
Elbert Adams, 3b
Hayden Adams, 1b
Raythell Adams, c
Harold Ellen, p, c, of
Roger Honeycutt, ss
Jones, c
Kozak

Carlton Mangum, p
Jimmie Matthews, of
Glenn Powell, c
Marshall Price, of
Rhodes, p

Don Wall, p, mgr.

1954 Angier (Twin-County League)

Adams, p
Young, p

Ogburn, c
Williford, p

1955 Pea Ridge (Central Carolina League, National Baseball Congress state tournament)*

Clyde Adams
Elbert Adams, 3b
Hayden Adams, 1b
Raythell Adams, c
Wayron "Pete" Adams, p
Tommy Bradley, p, ss
Lowell Davis, p
Harold Ellen, p, c, of
Frank Gardner, 2b
John Griffis, of

Boyce Haigler, p
Roger Honeycutt, ss
Carlton Mangum, p
Jimmie Matthews, of
Glenn Powell, c
Marshall Price, of
James Stevens, of

Don Wall, if, mgr.

1955 Angier (Twin-County League)

Tommy "Screw" Gilbert
Honeycutt, c

McLean, p

1956 Angier (Central Carolina League)

Elbert Adams
Bradley, p
Lou Dickman, p
Dupree, c
G. Ellen, c
Harold Ellen, c, p
Ellington, p
Bobby Gardner
Tommy "Screw" Gilbert
Marion Hargrove, c
Kenneth Jackson, of

Johnny Johnson, p
Gordon Matthews
C. Pate, p
Price, p
Ben Price
D. Stevenson, c, p
Wells, p
Williams, p
F. Woodfin, p
Tom Zachary, Jr.

1956 Pea Ridge (Central Carolina League, NBC state tournament, NBC national tournament)*

Clyde Adams, 3b
Connie Adams, 3b
Elbert Adams, 3b
Hayden Adams, 1b
Raythell Adams, c
Wayron "Pete" Adams
Tommy Bradley, p
Jack Craig, p
Frank Gardner, 2b
Jimmy Hinton, 2b
E. Holland, p
Roger Honeycutt, ss
B. Johnson, p

Millie Joe Johnson
Ford Jordan, ss
Carlton Mangum, p
Jimmie Matthews, of
Doug Payne, p
Marshall Price, of
Jackie Revis, of
James Stevens, of
Billy West, c
Tom Zachary Jr.

Bill Watkins, mgr.

1957 Angier Bulls (Mid-State League, exhibition)

Ben Baker, p
Collins, c
Dupree, c
Harold Ellen
Buck Jackson, c
Bob Kennel, c

Jimmie Matthews, of
Ben Price
Marshall Price, of
Bruce Shelley, p
Gene Summerlin, p
Owen Wright, p

1957 Pea Ridge (Mid-State League, NBC state tournament, NBC national tournament)*

Clyde Adams
Connie Adams
Elbert Adams, 3b
Hayden Adams, 1b
Jack Craig, p
Harold Ellen, of, p, c

Cecil Fuquay, c, of
Roger Honeycutt, ss
Kenneth Jackson, of
Ford Jordan, ss, 3b
Haywood Kelley, 1b
Bob Kennel, c

Carlton Mangum, p
Jimmie Matthews, of
Glenn Powell, c
Gene Summerlin, p

Billy West, c, 2b, ss

Frank Gardner, 2b, mgr.
James Stevens, of, mgr.

1958 Angier Braves (Tobacco State League, NBC state tournament, NBC national tournament, exhibition)*

Hayden Adams
George Allen
Ben Baker, p
Don Bagdonovich, p
Jim Brown, of
Tommy Byrne, p, 1b
Nel Cooper
Larry Crayton, p
Jack Craig, p
Wilson Carruthers, p
John Dennis, p
Harold Ellen, c
Cecil Fuquay, c
Marion Hargrove, c
Kenneth Jackson

Johnny Johnson, p
Ford Jordan, 3b
Carlton Mangum, p
Jimmie Matthews
Ray Mozingo, of
Kenneth O'Neal
Ben Price
Bruce Shelley, p
Bobby Tart, 2b
Arnold Wallis, 1b
Billy West
Owen Wright, p
Joe Wooten, ss

Frank Gardner, 2b, mgr.

1959 Angier Braves (Tobacco State League)*

Elbert Adams, 3b
Don Brown
Jim Brown
Tommy Byrne, p, 1b
Fred Caviness
Jack Craig, p
Wilson Carruthers, p
Dean, p
Neal Easom

Wayne Edwards, ss
Marion Hargrove, c
Holder, p
Buck Jackson, c
Sherrill Jones
Lovingood
Jimmie Matthews
Dick Miller
Ray Mozingo, c

Murphy, p
Jim Overby, p
Bruce Shelley
Arnold Wallis
Wilson, p

Harold Workman, ss

Bob Cruze, p, mgr.
Frank Gardner, 2b, mgr.

1960 Angier Braves (Tobacco State League)*

Elbert Adams, of
Sam Bishop, p
Fred Caviness, of
Johnny Ellen, p
Frank Gardner, 2b, 3b
Johnny Gomez, p
Jim Hubbard, ss
Buck Jackson, 2b, c
Bob Kennel, c
Calvin Koonce, p
Bernie Latusick, of

Joel Long
Jimmie Matthews, of
Ray Mozingo, c
Ray Perry, c
Jimmy Roland, p
Bobby Stephenson
Bobby Tart, 1b, 2b
Gordon Welch, ss

Bob Cruze, p, mgr.

1961 Angier (NBC state tournament, exhibition)

Jack Craig, p
Bob Cruze, p
Harold Ellen, of
Rae Fulghum, c
Bill Harrington
Jesse Haswell, c
Buck Jackson
Sherrill Jones
Ford Jordan, if

Marshall Long, p
Jimmie Matthews, of
Carlton Mangum, p
Ray Mozingo
R.B. Tingen

James Stevens, of, mgr.

Notes

The majority of facts from this book are derived from interviews and newspaper archives. Most of the standings and minor league player statistics are from newspaper archives and from Old Time Data, Inc.'s Professional Baseball Player Database.

The following notes are attributions to other facts of interest.

Chapter 1

1. Most attendance figures in the book are estimates from newspaper accounts. There were rarely any official ticket counts.

2. *Cumberland County 250, 1930-1954*, a supplement to *The Fayetteville Observer*, Copyright 2004.

3. The number of minor leagues in the nation dropped from 26 in 1929 to 13 by the end of 1932; R.G. (Hank) Utley and Scott Verner, *The Independent Carolina Baseball League, 1936-1938* (Jefferson NC: McFarland & Company, Inc., 1999) p. 27.

4. The majority of minor league statistics in the book are from Old-Time Data, a minor league statistics database

5. R.G. (Hank) Utley and Scott Verner, *The Independent Carolina*

Baseball League, 1936-1938 (Jefferson NC: McFarland & Company, Inc., 1999) pp. 6, 98-102

6.*The News & Observer* of Raleigh, "Angier's Big Day," May 9, 1933

7. R.G. (Hank) Utley and Scott Verner, *The Independent Carolina Baseball League, 1936-1938* (Jefferson NC: McFarland & Company, Inc., 1999) pp 39,40

Chapter 2

8. Leaksville-Draper-Spray, Mayodan and Mt. Airy were the North Carolina teams that opened the season in the Bi-State League in 1934, J. Chris Holaday, *Professional Baseball in North Carolina* (Jefferson, NC: McFarland & Company Inc., 1998) p. 4

9. *The News & Observer* of Raleigh, "Eight Clubs Now In Coastal Plain," June 3, 1935

10. R.G. (Hank) Utley and Scott Verner, *The Independent Carolina Baseball League, 1936-1938* (Jefferson NC: McFarland & Company, Inc., 1999) p. 44

11. Crowd estimates for the game ranged from 4,078 (official paid) to about 10,000. Ruth went 0-2 with two walks and no home runs in the game. The Braves won 6-2, but the game had to be stopped in the 7th inning when the teams ran out of baseballs, so many had been hit into the crowd and not returned. *The Fayetteville Observer*, "4,078 Paid Cash To See Ruth Play," April 6, 1935;

12. No official records of the league salary limits remains, and newspapers didn't report details of Tobacco State League meetings that year. The Coastal Plain League placed a $450 per team per week limit on its teams in 1935. It would be safe to say the Tobacco State League limit was slightly below that.

13. *The News & Observer* of Raleigh, "Sheppard Will Stick As Skipper At Angier," July 18, 1935

Chapter 3

14. Figures are based on interviews and newspaper stories which state a wide range of pay. Robert Gaunt's book, *We Would Have Played Forever, The Story of The Coastal Plain Baseball League,* notes that pay was as much as $25 per week plus room and board in 1935, p. 21. Official contractual agreements between players and teams then were rare, and salaries varied, according to player talents and gate receipts. According to the accounts of Byrne, Chester Holland and Crash Davis, who played with Sanford in 1939, a paid player received anywhere from $40 to $140 a month.

15. Robert Gaunt, *We Would Have Played Forever - The Story of The Coastal Plain Baseball League* (Durham NC: Baseball America, 1997), p. 24

16. From an interview with Jim Gardner

17. *The News & Observer* of Raleigh, "Still Trying," May 24, 1936

18. Chris Holaday, *Baseball In the Carolinas*, (McFarland, 1998), p. 56

Chapter 4

19. R.G. (Hank) Utley and Scott Verner, *The Independent Carolina Baseball League, 1936-1938* (Jefferson NC: McFarland & Company, Inc., 1999) pp. 98-102

20. The Big Five, not an official conference, was composed of Duke, UNC, N.C.State College, Wake Forest College and Davidson College.

21. *The Independent* of Fuquay Springs, "Four Teams In Tobacco League," May 21, 1937

22. R.G. (Hank) Utley and Scott Verner, *The Independent Carolina Baseball League, 1936-1938* (Jefferson NC: McFarland & Company,

Inc., 1999) pp. 60, 91

23. This was not the same Art Fowler who played in the Major Leagues in the 1950s and 1960s.

24. *The News & Observer* of Raleigh, "Angier Rallies in Eighth For 5-4 Victory at Erwin", Sept. 5, 1937

Chapter 5

25. Robert Gaunt, *We Would Have Played Forever - The Story of The Coastal Plain Baseball League* (Durham NC: Baseball America, 1997), p. 51, and from references in *The News & Observer* of Raleigh

26. *The News & Observer* of Raleigh, "Erwin Defeats Angier; Zebs Win Over Faytex," Aug. 15, 1938

27. R.G. (Hank) Utley and Scott Verner, *The Independent Carolina Baseball League, 1936-1938* (Jefferson NC: McFarland & Company, Inc., 1999) p. 55

28. Ibid, pp. 77-78, 106

29. Chris Holaday, *Baseball In the Carolinas*, (McFarland, 1998), p. 57

30. *The News & Observer* of Raleigh, "New Ruling Made In League Playoff," Aug. 25, 1938

31. *The News & Observer* of Raleigh, "Tom Byrne Strikes Out 18, But Sanford Gets Verdict," Sept. 9, 1938

Chapter 6

32. Mike McCann's Minor League Baseball Page, Internet

Chapter 7

33. R.G. (Hank) Utley and Scott Verner, *The Independent Carolina*

Baseball League, 1936-1938 (Jefferson NC: McFarland & Company, Inc., 1999), p. 34

34. *The News & Observer* of Raleigh, "Former Legion Stars In Tobacco State League; Several Members of Harnett Nine Now in New Class D Circuit," June 6, 1946

35. *The News & Observer* of Raleigh, "Wedding Proves Fine Attraction," Aug. 6, 1941

36. UNC Libraries website, Internet

37. *The News & Observer* of Raleigh, "DiMaggio Homers As Norfolk Beats Pre-Flight, 4-2, Here," July 15, 1943

Chapter 8

38. Mike McCann's Minor League Baseball Page, Internet

39. Chris Holaday, *Professional Baseball in North Carolina*, (McFarland, 1998), p. 5

40. *The News & Observer* of Raleigh, "Harnett County Census Is 44,231," July 7, 1940

41. The NAPBL classifications were AAA, AA, A, B, C, D and E, though no Class E leagues existed in 1946.

42. Robert Gaunt, *We Would Have Played Forever - The Story of The Coastal Plain Baseball League* (Durham NC: Baseball America, 1997), p. 177

43. $1,500 per team, per month was the salary limit for all Class D teams.

44. *The News & Observer* of Raleigh, "Angier-Fuquay 5, Sanford 1," Sept. 5, 1946

45. *The News & Observer* of Raleigh, " 'No Contest', " Sept. 10, 1946

46. Mike McCann's Minor League Baseball Page, Internet

Chapter 9

47 Calculations based on N.C. Dept. of Agriculture statistics for 1947.

48. Mike McCann's Minor League Baseball Page, Internet

Chapter 10

49. Robert Gaunt, *We Would Have Played Forever, The Story of The Coastal Plain Baseball League* (Baseball America, 1997), p 210.

Chapter 11

50. William Neal Reynolds Coliseum was completed in 1949.

51. Chris Holaday, *Professional Baseball in North Carolina,* (McFarland, 1998), p. 6

52. *The News & Observer* of Raleigh, "Buies Creek To Play Boone Trail Tonight," July 3, 1950

Chapter 12

53. *The News & Observer* of Raleigh, "Pea Ridge 19, Buies Creek 10," June 17, 1951

54. *The News & Observer* of Raleigh, "Big League Scouts Seeking Signature of Angier Youth," June 4, 1953

55. *The Independent* of Fuquay, "Game With Prison Boys Turns Into Rout For Rebels," April 16, 1953

56. *The News & Observer* of Raleigh, "Moncure, Pea Ridge In Mid-State Finals," Sept. 4, 1954

57.*The News & Observer* of Raleigh, "Wendell Is Winner In Playoff Series," Sept. 13, 1954

Chapter 13

58. National Baseball Congress Official Baseball Annual, 1957; and from interviews with Arnold Ashley of Roxboro and Harold Ellen

59. The North Carolina NBC tournament program, 1956

60. *The Independent* of Fuquay Springs, "Sports Corner," Aug. 11, 1955

61. Salemmuseum.org, website of the Salem, Va. Museum, Internet

Chapter 14

62. *The Independent* of Fuquay Springs, "Sports Corner," June 14, 1956

63. Established in 1879 to prevent players from freely going from one team to the other, causing salaries to escalate dramatically, the reserve clause bound a player to one team for his entire career - unless the team decided to release him or to trade or sell his contract to another team. Professional baseball players worked under this type of contract until 1975.

64. *The Independent* of Fuquay Springs, "Sports Corner," Aug. 7, 1956

Chapter 15

65. Mike McCann's Minor League Baseball Page, Internet

66. Hobe Hays, *Take Two and Hit to Right*, (University of Nebraska Press), pp 183-184

67. nbcbaseball.com, the official website of the National Baseball Congress, Internet

68. NBC national tournament information, *The Wichita Eagle*, Aug. 17-22, 1956

69. *The Independent* of Fuquay Springs, "Sports Corner," Sept. 27, 1956

Chapter 16

70. Chris Holaday, *Professional Baseball in North Carolina,* (McFarland, 1998), p. 6

71. *The News & Observer* of Raleigh, "Semi-Pro Loop For Collegians Under Study," July 21, 1957

72.Campbell's basketball school was founded in 1954

73 *The Independent* of Fuquay Springs, "Sports Corner," July 11, 1957

Chapter 17

74 National Baseball Congress Official Baseball Annual, 1957

75 National Baseball Congress Official Baseball Annual, 1958; and from interviews with Harold Ellen and James Stevens

76 *The News & Observer* of Raleigh, "Pea Ridge Club In Dire Straits," Aug. 25, 1957

77. Ruth Summerlin Gregory, Ozella Barbour Adams, Earl Eugene Gray, Sr., Jean Adams Lee, Linwood Alford Matthews, Peggy Barnes Partin, *More Voices of Yesteryear* (Twyford Printing Company, 1993), p. 344

78. *The Wichita Eagle*, Aug. 9, 1957

79. *The Wichita Eagle*, "Bombers Leave 15 Base-runners; Pearidge Pulls Tourney Upset," Aug. 28, 1957

80. *The Wichita Eagle*, "Tourney Topics," Aug. 31, 1957

81. *The News & Observer* of Raleigh, "Pea Ridge: 'Just Country Team'," Sept. 1, 1957

82. *The Wichita Eagle*, "Ft. Wayne Nips Pea Ridge 4-3; Fields Hits Solo In 10th to Clinch," Sept. 1, 1957

Chapter 18

83. A *News & Observer* story on July 20, 1957, had stated that an organizational meeting for an eastern N.C. college league would be held on Sept. 30. It apparently never took place.

84. Based on interviews with Ben Price, Frank Gardner and Harold Ellen. No "official" salary range was related.

85. *The News & Observer* of Raleigh, "Tommy Byrne To Pitch; Signs With Angier Club," May 16, 1958

86. *The News & Observer* of Raleigh, "You Can't Top A 0.00 Earned Run Average," May 26, 1957

87. The *Raleigh News & Observer*, "Perry May Be In Line Shortly," May 25, 1958

88. Chris Holaday, *Baseball in The Carolinas*, (McFarland, 2000), p. 33

Chapter 19

89. Fayetteville announced in the Aug. 1 edition of *The News & Observer* that it was forfeiting the remainder of its league season. Dunn-Erwin's decision apparently arrived at the same time; there were no further newspaper references to the team after that time.

Chapter 20

90. The Fuquay team was sometimes referred to as Fuquay-Varina and nicknamed the Twins because of the close association. The towns would officially merge in 1963 to become Fuquay-Varina.

Chapter 21

91. *The News & Observer* of Raleigh, "Attendance Off In Carolina Loop," June 5, 1960

92. *The News & Observer* of Raleigh, "Pitching Is Busy Sideline For Mangum Now," July 26, 1960

Bibliography

Newspapers

(Raleigh, N.C.) News & Observer
1920: July 21
1932: May 30, 31; June 4, 10, 26, 28; July 7, 8
1933: May 3, 5, 7, 8, 9, 10, 11, 13, 14, 16, 18, 20, 21, 24, 25, 27, 28, 29;
June 2, 3, 4, 11, 13, 17, 24, 26; July 5, 15, 23, 25, 26, 27, 28, 29, 30, 31;
Aug. 1, 4, 6, 11, 12, 21
1934: May 28, 31; June 1, 6, 9, 10, 11, 24; July 8, 17, 22, 24; Aug. 1, 2,
5, 6, 13, 19, 20, 25, 26; Sept. 7, 8, 10, 11
1935: May 8, 12, 13, 17, 25, 26, 27, 29; June 4, 6; July 3, 4, 5, 6, 8, 11,
12, 13, 17, 18, 20, 21, 26, 27, 31; Aug 22, 25; Sept. 3, 5, 12, 15, 16
1936: May 14, 16, 17, 19, 23, 24, 25; June 2, 3, 4, 8, 15, 21; July 13, 20;
Sept. 6
1937: May 29; June 5, 6, 11, 12, 13, 14, 20, 25; July 2, 3, 4, 10, 16; Sept.
5, 6, 7, 8, 10, 11, 12, 13
1938: June 2, 3, 5, 7, 10, 11, 12, 13, 17, 18, 19, 23, 27; July 2, 4, 5, 10,
11, 16, 18, 22, 29; Aug. 5, 7, 11, 15, 22, 23, 24, 25, 27, 28, 29, 30, 31;
Sept. 2, 3, 4, 6, 7, 9, 10

1939: May 1, 2, 5, 6, 7, 8, 10, 28; June 4, 7, 8, 9, 10, 13, 14, 20, 24, 26; July 12, 13, 15, 29, 30; Aug. 1, 3, 4, 5, 7, 8, 11, 12, 13, 18, 20, 21, 23, 24, 28

1940: June 2, 3, 6, 9, 13, 19, 20, 21, 27; July 4, 6, 7, 9, 10, 24; Aug. 6, 12

1941: June 2, 4, 12, 17, 22; July 3, 7, 10, 11, 14, 20, 21, 27; Aug. 5, 6, 7, 11, 13, 18, 22, 23, 26, 31

1942: June 2, 5, 8, 14; July 5, 9, 11; Aug. 1, 2, 10

1943: May 29; June 8, 16; July 3, 5, 8, 9, 12, 15, 18, 22; Aug. 7, 22

1946: May 5, 12; June 4, 5, 6, 9, 10, 15, 21, 26, 28; July 1, 3, 5, 6, 7, 12, 14, 19, 26; Sept. 5, 6, 7, 8, 9, 10, 11, 14, 15, 16, 17, 18, 22, 23

1947: May 1, 4, 8, 9, 10, 11, 17; June 14, 15, 17, 30; July 6, 7, 13, 14, 18; Aug. 7, 8, 20, 21; Sept . 3, 18

1948: June 6, 7, 10, 13, 15, 16, 19, 20, 21; July 4, 5, 11; Aug. 2, 7, 29, 31; Sept. 3, 5, 9, 10, 12

1949: May 17, 25; June 6, 12, 19, 20; July 3, 4, 11, 18, 21, 25; Aug. 23, 25, 26

1950: May 24, 27, 28; June 17, 18, 19, 24; July 3, 7, 16, 24

1951: June 10, 11, 14, 15, 16, 17; Aug. 1, 5, 19, 26, 29; Sept. 2

1952: May 30; June 1, 2, 6, 8, 15, 22, 23, 28, 29; July 12, 13, 19, 26, 27; Aug. 4, 11, 17, 24, 25; Sept. 7

1953: April 16; June 1, 4, 10, 14, 15, 21, 28, 29; July 13, 20, 26; Aug. 2, 3, 7, 16, 20, 23, 24, 30; Sept. 6, 7, 13, 14

1954: May 2, 3, 9, 24; June 1, 3, 6, 7, 11, 12, 13, 14, 15, 17, 19, 20, 21, 22, 28; July 11, 25, 31; Aug. 8, 15, 16, 23, 30, 31; Sept. 4, 10, 12, 13, 21

1955: June 4, 5, 7, 12, 14, 16, 19, 26, 27; July 4, 7, 10, 17; Aug. 2, 5, 6, 8, 14, 22, 24, 29; Sept. 18, 25; Oct. 10

1956: May 7, 14, 20, 25, 27, 28; June 10, 11, 17, 29; July 2, 23; Aug. 4, 11, 14, 23, 26, 27; Sept. 24

1957: May 15, 26; June 3, 5, 24, 25; July 16, 18, 20, 21, 23, 27, 28; Aug. 9, 11, 15, 24, 25, 27, 28, 31; Sept. 1, 2, 9, 15, 22, 30

1958: May 16, 20, 23, 25, 26, 30; June 25, 28; July 5, 14, 16, 19, 21, 26,

28, 29, 31; Aug. 2, 3, 8, 10, 11, 15, 19, 20, 21, 22, 23, 27, 28, 29, 30, 31; Sept. 1, 3
1959: May 31; June 2, 7, 11,12, 29, 30; July 1, 2, 24, 25; Aug. 2, 3, 6, 7, 8, 9, 11, 12, 21, 22, 23, 24, 28, 29; Sept. 3, 4, 5, 10, 11, 13, 14, 15
1960: May 31; June 1, 2, 3, 5, 8, 9, 11, 12, 16, 17, 18, 22, 23, 24, 28; July 4, 6, 7, 8, 12, 13, 17, 21, 22, 27; Aug. 8, 28; Sept. 7
1961: June 2; July 3, 4, 6, 16, 21, 31; Aug. 5, 6, 7
1971: Oct. 24

Durham Morning Herald
Sept. 20, 25, 1954

Fayetteville Observer
1935: April 5, 6
1938: Aug. 3, 8, 10
1957: Aug. 12, 20,

The Independent (Fuquay Springs)
1937: May 21
1939: July 27
1950: June 22
1952: Sept. 11
1953: May 28; June 4
1954: May 20; June 17, 24; July 11; Aug. 12; Sept. 2
1955: May 19, 26; June 2, 9, 16; July 7, 23; Aug. 11, 25
1956: May 10, 31; June 14, 21; July 5, 19, 26; Aug. 2, 7, 16, 23, 30; Sept. 27
1957: May 30; June 6, 13, 20, 27; July 4, 11, 18, 25; Aug. 1, 8, 15; Sept. 12

1958: Aug 7

Roxboro Courier-Times
1955: July 11, 14, 21, 27; Aug. 3
1956: July 18, 21, 28; Aug. 5, 9, 10, 11; Sept. 4
1957: Aug. 1, 5, 12

Wichita (Kan.) Eagle
1956: Aug. 17, 18, 19, 20, 21, 22, 23, 24, 25; Sept. 4
1957: Aug. 9, 14, 16, 20, 22, 23, 24, 25, 28, 30, 31; Sept. 1, 3

Wichita (Kan.) Beacon
Aug. 21, 1956

Books

Adams, Ozella Barbour, Ruth Summerlin Gregory, Earl Eugene Gray, Sr., Jean Adams Lee, Linwood Alford Matthews, Peggy Barnes Partin, *More Voices of Yesteryear*, Dunn, N.C.; Twyford Printing Company, 1993

Gaunt, Robert, *We Would Have Played Forever - The Story of The Coastal Plain Baseball League*, Durham N.C.; Baseball America, 1997

Hays, Hobe, *Take Two and Hit to Right - Golden Days on the Semi-pro Diamond*, Lincoln, Neb., University of Nebraska Press, 1999

Holaday, J. Chris, *Professional Baseball in North Carolina*, Jefferson, N.C.; McFarland & Company, Inc., 1998

Holaday, Chris, ed., *Baseball in the Carolinas*, Jefferson, N.C.; McFarland & Company, Inc., 2002

Utley, R.G. (Hank) and Scott Verner, *The Independent Carolina Baseball League, 1936-1938*; Jefferson, N.C.; McFarland & Company, Inc., 1999

Periodicals

National Baseball Congress Official Baseball Annual, 1957, 1958

National Baseball Congress North Carolina Tournament Program, 1955, 1956

Other Sources

Mike McCann's Minor League Baseball Page, Internet

Baseballlibrary.com, Internet

HistoricBaseball.com, Internet

Baseball-reference.com, Internet

Professional Baseball Player Database Version 5.0, Old Time Data, Inc., 1995-2003

About The Author

Webster Lupton

Webster Lupton is a writer and editor who worked in newspapers in North Carolina for twenty-five years. As a sportswriter and sports editor he covered baseball on all levels in the state. When his family moved to Angier in 1965, he began hearing stories of town baseball in "the old days." After retiring from his post as Copy Desk Chief of the Fayetteville Observer in 2001, Lupton began research into those stories. This book is the result of that research.

Lupton is fifty-six and currently resides in Fayetteville.

Printed in the United States
95202LV00001B/79-549/A